# Differentiation
## THROUGH
# Personality
# Types

# Differentiation

## THROUGH

# Personality
# Types

## A Framework for Instruction, Assessment, and Classroom Management

Jane A. G. Kise

**CORWIN PRESS**
A SAGE Publications Company
Thousand Oaks, CA 91320

KH

*For information:*

Corwin Press
A Sage Publications Company
2455 Teller Road
Thousand Oaks, California 91320
www.corwinpress.com

Sage Publications Ltd.
1 Oliver's Yard
55 City Road
London EC1Y 1SP
United Kingdom

Sage Publications India Pvt. Ltd.
B-42, Panchsheel Enclave
Post Box 4109
New Delhi 110 017  India

Printed in the United States of America.

*Library of Congress Cataloging-in-Publication Data*

Kise, Jane A. G.
Differentiation through personality types : a framework for instruction, assessment, and classroom management / Jane A. G. Kise.
     p. cm.
Includes bibliographical references and index.
ISBN 1-4129-1770-0 or 978-1-4129-1770-4 (cloth)
ISBN 1-4129-1771-9 or 978-1-4129-1771-1 (pbk.)
   1. Individualized instruction. 2. Typology (Psychology) I. Title.
LB1031.K415 2007
371.39′4—dc22

                                        2006019603

This book is printed on acid-free paper.

06  07  08  09  10   10  9  8  7  6  5  4  3  2  1

| | |
|---|---|
| *Acquisitions Editor:* | Rachel Livsey |
| *Editorial Assistant:* | Phyllis Cappello |
| *Production Editor:* | Jenn Reese |
| *Copy Editor:* | Barbara Ray |
| *Typesetter:* | C&M Digitals (P) Ltd. |
| *Proofreader:* | Ellen Brink |
| *Indexer:* | Judy Hunt |
| *Cover Designer:* | Rose Storey |
| *Graphic Artist:* | Lisa Riley |

1/28/08

# Contents

# Acknowledgments

The ideas *Differentiation Through Personality Types* contains have been developed over several decades by teachers, principals, professors, psychologists, consultants, and others who, as they learned about personality type, began making sense of their own school experiences and envisioned how the concepts could help schools truly leave no child behind. I am especially indebted to the work of Elizabeth Murphy, Gordon Lawrence, and Len Tallevi, all of whom willingly shared ideas and provided feedback on my work with students.

Also, thank you to all of the teachers at Lake Harriet Community School in Minneapolis who wrestled with draft versions of various chapters in their professional learning communities and provided excellent feedback I used in shaping the final book.

Perhaps more important to classroom teachers reading these pages are the contributions of teachers who partnered with me in creating differentiated lessons and trying classroom strategies that honored the needs of all students. Their enthusiasm for more ideas, and quickly increasing confidence in their ability to differentiate, increased my confidence in the power of personality type as a tool for differentiation. Thanks to all of you!

The contributions of the following reviewers are gratefully acknowledged:

Lori L. Grossman
Instructional Coordinator
Professional Development Services
Houston Independent School District
Houston, TX

Kathy Grover
Assistant Superintendent for Curriculum and Instruction
Clever R-V School District
Clever, MO

Sharon L. Jeffery
National Board Certified Teacher
Plymouth Middle School
Plymouth, MA

# About the Author

**Jane A. G. Kise, EdD,** is an educational consultant specializing in teambuilding, coaching, and school staff development. She is also the coauthor of nearly 20 books, including *Differentiated Coaching: A Framework for Helping Teachers Change, Introduction to Type and Coaching, Using the MBTI Tool in Organizations, LifeKeys,* and *Work it Out.* She holds an MBA in finance from the Carlson School of Management and a doctorate in Educational Leadership from the University of St. Thomas.

Kise has worked with diverse organizations, including Minneapolis Public Schools and various public and private schools, The Bush Foundation, Twin Cities Public Television, and numerous other institutions. She is a frequent workshop speaker and has presented at NSDC, World Futures, and APT International conferences. She has taught writing at the university level. She is a faculty member of the Center for Applications of Psychological Type and an executive board member of the Association for Psychological Type. In 2005, she won the Isabel Briggs Myers Award for Outstanding Research in the Field of Psychological Type.

Workshop descriptions, speaking schedule, and contact information are available at www.edcoaching.com, or e-mail Dr. Kise directly at jane@edcoaching.com.

*For Dr. Bruce Kramer, who made me think*

# Introduction

*Before you read on . . .*

- How do you define differentiation?
- What makes differentiation difficult?

Bring to mind the names of two or three students that you think would benefit from differentiated instruction.

Ask teachers to define differentiation and you'll get a wide variety of answers. For a moment, let's look at a definition:

Differentiation: tailoring instruction to meet individual learners' needs, styles, and interests.

That's the problem right there. In one sentence, teachers are being asked to differentiate for student needs, multiple intelligences, learning styles, interests, cultural background, abilities, and more. You can read books and attend workshops on how to differentiate for each one of these factors.

It's overwhelming, isn't it?

But what if you had one framework that helped you organize all of these facets of differentiation into one model for planning lessons? What if it gave all students access to rigorous thinking tasks? What if that same model helped you understand your own strengths as a teacher and those of your colleagues as well?

## WHY READ THIS BOOK?

That's what this book is about, helping you organize all the above ways to look at students through *one* framework so that you can

- Recognize genuine differences in what individual students need to both *love* school and *learn*
- Develop and use differentiation strategies that are manageable and effective
- Put into practice concrete ideas that have been tested in diverse schools.

That framework is personality type.

## WHAT IS PERSONALITY TYPE?

Type isn't a panacea, but a rich theory. Think of it as a toolkit that helps you organize, and therefore access, the tools you need to reach the wide variety of students who enter your classroom each day. Personality type explains *normal* differences in

- How people take in information. When students read, or listen to directions, or take a field trip, or think quietly, there are distinct patterns in the information they attend to. They do not notice the same things, nor do they process perceptions in the same way.
- How people make decisions. Every day, students need to decide what is important, what to do with the information they have, what it means for their lives, or how to organize it. They come to these judgments in intensely different ways.

Taking in information and making decisions. These are two profoundly important elements in education. Our personality type preferences affect how we teach and how we learn—to a significant extent. The theory is fully explained in Chapter 2, but consider this: **Woven throughout the practical strategies and lesson planning techniques in *Differentiation Through Personality Types* are the results of type research studies that demonstrate how our schools are actually biased toward some personalities, leading to higher grades, test scores, and scholarships for students whose natural personality fits best with our notions of academics.** Type is that important to conversations about teaching and learning.

If you've taken the Myers-Briggs Type Indicator, then you've learned something about type. However, if a workshop leader handed you your results and said, "That's who you are. That's how you act," he or she not only used the instrument unethically but denied you the chance to experience and discover how the theory behind the instrument—the heart of type—makes sense of the interests, needs, and behaviors of people around you and the students you teach. Type is so much more than a four letter code; as one teaching team put it, "Can we sit in our type groups at this meeting so that we can remember the different 'foreign languages' we're speaking?"

## HOW TO USE THESE PAGES

The purpose of *Differentiation Through Personality Types* is to help you learn the "language" of type so you can better meet the needs of students. When I'm working directly with teachers, I find that it often takes several weeks for them to understand how personality type and differentiation apply to their own teaching and learning style. Usually, they prefer working with me to develop their first differentiated lesson plan. I tried to fill these pages with ideas and tools that would provide readers with that kind of support.

You can read cover to cover, but that might not be the most useful strategy. Differentiation is a huge topic, and to read quickly may make it seem even more overwhelming. One of the biggest barriers to success that teachers acknowledge is the trap of trying to do it all at once and becoming overwhelmed with trying to meet the needs of every student. Instead, try the following strategy.

*Work with someone else.* You can read this book on your own. However, if you can meet with at least one other educator to discuss its contents, chances are you'll gain more insights into students who will benefit most from these strategies. In professional learning communities in which teachers have developed trust, discussing your varying reactions to different ideas, tools, and strategies makes the theory of type come alive. Together, you will *see* the very real differences in how you take in information and make decisions. And, most teachers discover new benefits from collaborating.

Embedded in each chapter are reflection and study questions. Record your own responses and compare them with those of other teachers.

- Work together to analyze a lesson plan, using the concepts discussed in Chapter 5. You might start with one designed by a teacher not *in* your group, because teachers often hesitate to critique each other's ideas.
- Try an idea from *Differentiation Through Personality Types,* perhaps a classroom management strategy from Chapter 6. Discuss your experiences. Were they influenced by your own personality preferences? How did different students react?
- Finally, plan a lesson together. What new insights do you gain from other teachers, now that you have a common language for discussing differences in teaching and learning styles?

*Differentiate for your interests.* Read the opening chapters and then move on to the sections that will be of most benefit to you.

- Read Chapter 2, "Who You Are Is How You Teach," to understand your own personality type.
- Bring to mind one or two students you have struggled to reach. Read Chapter 3, "What Type Looks Like in Students," to explore whether type differences explain some of your difficulties.
- Read Chapter 4 to grasp the basic differentiation model.
- Revisit the table of contents. Which topic might most clearly address your biggest needs right now? Classroom management? Multiculturalism? Mathematics? Read that chapter next. Try a few concrete strategies—perhaps a suggestion for helping students develop better study habits from Chapter 6 or a reading activity from Chapter 7.
- Then, pull out a lesson that *almost* worked. Revisit Chapter 4 to discover ways you might improve it.
- Think about introducing type concepts to students, as described in Chapter 11. Skim the lesson ideas. Might teaching about one of the preference pairs improve your ability to talk with students about their potential as learners?

*Think process, not pages.* Too often, professional learning communities set goals such as finishing a book before the end of a semester, or reading a chapter a month. With *Differentiation Through Personality Types,* a better idea is weaving reading goals with application goals. *Try* the concepts before moving on. You can use many of the strategies and techniques described in this book long before you finish it.

- Use your prep periods to observe other teachers in your study group as they try new strategies. Were some of the ideas easier for them to implement? How might you adapt one to your own style? Focus later discussions on student learning. What happened?
- Take time to examine student work together and look for patterns. Is there evidence that students with certain personality types are more engaged than others? How might the assignment or instruction be tweaked or changed?
- Finally, get student feedback. Did your differentiation strategies meet their needs? Did they learn? Seek their thoughts, opinions, and suggestions.

May this book provide strategies that will simplify and enrich your life as a teacher, helping you move forward in the tremendous task of educating the incredibly diverse students who enter your classroom.

# 1

# Why Use Type for Differentiation?

*Before you read on . . .*

Think of a student you've struggled to reach academically.

- Why do you think that student struggles?
- What academic strengths does the student have?

About two weeks into the school year, a middle-school math teacher asked me to observe a class of students whose test scores the previous year were low. "I'm trying out a new number sense activity," she said. "I'd like your opinion."

I sat on the back ledge of the classroom, watching the 17 students estimate, measure, and take notes. Within two minutes I knew one boy's name. "Alex,[1] where's your notebook?" "Alex, please write this down." "Alex, head off the desk." "Alex, put that away!"

Later, the teacher commented, "I've tried moving Alex close to me, pairing him with my best student, calling his home, but he won't work on the basic skills he needs to progress."

Next door in Language Arts, another boy named Carl stared into space, completing only two of a dozen worksheet questions on a story the teacher had read aloud. "He has to be ADD," the teacher whispered. "Unless I'm on him every second, Carl does nothing."

For the final project on that story, I helped the Language Arts teacher plan several options from which the students could choose. Alex and Carl decided to work together on a picture book. They made up an entirely new adventure tale about the story's characters. They turned it in on the due date. Their drawings were detailed and humorous. They even spent a precious lunch period adding color with the teacher's art supplies. We took pictures of the two boys, grinning broadly, their book open to their favorite illustration.

---

[1]Throughout these pages, names and details have been changed to protect both teachers and students.

What happened? As the teachers and students on that team learned about themselves and their learning styles, the teachers discovered that Alex and Carl's learning styles were opposite their own. Alex spoke English as a second language, and the teachers hadn't noticed how creative he yearned to be. And Carl was so quiet that he never shared any of his imaginative thoughts.

## DIFFERENTIATION: HELPING STUDENTS FIND FLOW

Like Alex and Carl, *all* of us seek activities that are interesting enough to engage us. Csikszentmihalyi (1997) found that flow experiences occur when activities

- Allow for focus on clear goals
- Provide immediate feedback
- Are neither too hard nor too easy—they engage a person's abilities
- Present an interesting task.

For schoolwork, one might use the following equation to designate how student can attain flow:

$$Ability + Interest = Flow$$

The art of differentiation is creating this equation. Listen to comments from students who were considered at-risk for academic achievement:

I tried out for a higher-level humanities class instead of regular language arts, but I didn't make it because of a test score. Those kids get to keep learning new things, while we get stuck with same old.

[My teacher] thinks I should be in a low one . . . I told her, "I can do the green packet." And she's like "No, you can't" and I'm like "Don't tell me what I can't do . . ." That's nothin' to be tellin' us.

I don't like my reading class. We do this easy work. Cat, mat, sat, fat. What is that? [laughter from other students] And then we got these big old books and you gotta do these little listening journal things and you need to put this cat, rat up on the things . . . Oh yeah, if I see a real good book, I'd be like I wish I was in that book, I wish I could meet those characters, I wish I was flying with them and all that.

How can we differentiate the instruction students receive, on the basis of their needs, while keeping students engaged?

"We aren't here to entertain them," teachers rightly protest. Fortunately, flow isn't about being entertained but being engaged. Csikszentmihalyi (1997) reports that flow most often occurs during studying and active leisure time and at work.

Very rarely do people report flow in passive leisure activities, such as watching television or relaxing. But because almost any activity can produce flow provided the relevant elements are present, it is possible to improve the quality of life by making sure that clear goals, immediate feedback, skills balanced to action opportunities, and the remaining conditions of flow are as much as possible a constant part of everyday life. (p. 34)

Tomlinson et al. (2002) point out that when students work on tasks just slightly above their ability, but are provided with scaffolding, coaching, or other support, their ability to work independently expands. They need harder tasks. They call "that escalating match between the learner and curriculum 'ascending intellectual demand'" (p. 13). The more we can create flow, engaging student interest while stretching their abilities, the more we can accelerate the ascending intellectual demands for all students.

## ABILITY VERSUS FLOW

For the middle-school students I've worked with, the ones who most need to practice basic skills are least likely to engage at a sufficient level to achieve anything close to flow—if they choose to complete the activity at all.

Important as foundational skills are, two things keep ability levels from being a wise focus for differentiation. First, Mueller (2001) notes that in the vast majority of reading programs, when skills are emphasized, keyed to hierarchical scope-and-sequence charts, authentic reading activities that allow students to make meaning are lost. Students lose the point of why anyone would read. The tasks aren't engaging, and the students soon give up.

Second, in many classrooms, students' basic skills proficiency determines their access to higher level thinking opportunities. For example, several teachers I've worked with read aloud to students who are poor readers and then have them either discuss or complete worksheets to clarify the facts of the story. "Knowledge is the first level of Bloom's Taxonomy. We need to start them there," they say.

Do we? Do students really struggle with facts? Test them. Show a feature movie and ask the same kinds of questions. "Describe . . . who . . . where . . ." Stop the film and ask them to make predictions or discuss a theme, questions from the second level of Bloom. They can do it, can't they? They can probably also judge, compare, summarize, conclude—in other words, they can "evaluate," the top level of Bloom's Taxonomy. They struggle with *reading*, and it keeps them from practicing the other skills.

## A FRAMEWORK GROUNDED IN RESEARCH

This theory of how people take in information and make decisions has been the subject of research for over eight decades. Used widely for teambuilding, career development, and other applications, the evidence of its implications for education is growing. In other words, type differences are real. Further, analyzing data through the lens of type reveals invisible biases in how we measure intelligence, creativity, and academic achievement.

- Type demonstrates a measurable bias in standardized tests. For example, 82 percent of the National Merit Scholarships go to students with one particular personality preference (Intuition), even though they make up only 30–35 percent[2] of the population (Myers, 1993). A 140-point "Intuitive gap" exists on the PSAT, with a 250-point gap between the top three personality types in score and the bottom three types. The test favors their innate style of guessing (Wilkes, 2004)!

- Tests of giftedness and creativity identify certain personality preferences over others and ignore other ways of being creative (Robinson, 1994). Certain personality types are overrepresented in our gifted and talented programs.
- Teachers create assessments that favor students whose learning styles match that of the teacher (Murphy, 1992).
- A compendium of research on type in education (Hammer, 1996) concludes that teacher beliefs about how students learn correlate with their own personality preferences.
- Teacher subject area and instructional practices vary according to their type preferences (Hammer, 1996). Therefore, the preferred methods in many disciplines are biased against students with other learning styles. This includes mathematics, writing, reading, science, and many other disciplines.

In other words, who you are is how you teach. Type helps you understand and meet the needs of students whose informational needs are opposite to your own.

- Teachers are more likely to discipline students who do not share their type preferences (O'Neil, 1986).
- Multiple studies, confirmed in my own work at many schools, show that students with certain personality types are vastly overrepresented in alternative schools and other programs for at-risk students. Further, these same types are vastly *under*represented among teachers.
- Students with certain personality preferences drop out of school at a much higher rate than students with other preferences—and are least likely to become teachers (Giger, 1996; Hammer, 1996). This means that their knowledge of how students learn is largely absent from the educational debates, perpetuating the problem.

To summarize, type is an essential tool for examining our current educational system, revealing disturbing patterns in how we measure intelligence, creativity, and even behavior. How do schools favor certain students? How can we better differentiate to meet the needs of *all* learners if it is true that our current practices put students with normal, positive personality preferences at a disadvantage, let alone students whose home situations put them at risk academically or who are learning English as a second language?

## WHY PERSONALITY TYPE?

Why not other models? For a framework for teaching and learning to be truly effective, it needs to meet several criteria. In fact, most schools end up using multiple frameworks because they haven't chosen one that

---

[2]All of the information on percentages of people with different type preferences comes from the data bank of the Center for Applications of Psychological Type, Gainesville, Florida.

- Describes teaching and learning in nonjudgmental ways. No one should feel labeled. *All* personality preferences are normal, good ways to be.
- Is strengths-based, emphasizing how each person teaches and learns rather than limiting what they can do. Type research shows that students with all preferences can master reading, writing, math, and higher level thinking if teaching practices meet their early needs and help them build academic confidence.
- Describes which students a practice will reach, so that discussions focus on student learning. So many educational battles have been either/or when the truth is both/and (whole language versus phonics is one example). Type moves the discussion away from right and wrong to who and how.
- Applies across cultures and to both adults and students. Chapter 10 discusses the cross-cultural uses of type.
- Provides bridges among varying staff development efforts. Type gives you one toolkit for finding and implementing research-based strategies for
  - Classroom management
  - Differentiation
  - Student work habits and study skills
  - Basic skills remediation
  - Working with difficult students
  - Collaboration with colleagues
  - Building relationships with students
  - Motivating students for academic achievement
  - Enriching and accelerating learning for all students.

## CONCLUSION

Personality type meets these criteria. It isn't a panacea, but a framework that helps tie together what teachers see in their classrooms, learn about in staff development, discuss with colleagues, and experience in their own ongoing professional learning.

Further, differentiating using type lets you start with your own strengths and style. You can use some concepts right away even as you continue to learn the theory. You'll find that it makes sense of what has worked—and didn't work—in your classroom in the past. You might feel less guilty about some of your struggles, perhaps even discovering natural pathways to avoid burning out in this demanding profession.

Is type really that useful? To find out, the first step is understanding yourself and how you teach, the subject of Chapter 2.

# Who You Are Is How You Teach

***Before you read on . . .***

Quickly journal your responses to the following prompts.

- List a few school projects or kinds of assignments you enjoyed as a student
- What are your favorite classroom activities as a teacher?
- How would you complete, "If only more teachers would _____, more students would succeed"?

Essay test or multiple choice?
Hands-on projects or library research?
Independent study or group work?
Whole language or phonics?

Chances are, you have a clear preference for many of the above choices. Do you have a clear idea, though, where your preferences came from? What drives those particular choices around teaching and learning?

- Do they match with your own learning style? The successful experiences you had as a student?
- Are they particularly easy for you to manage in your classroom?
- Are they tied to how you were taught to teach?
- Are they school expectations?

Educators deeply disagree over many essential beliefs in education. Conflicts erupt over homework policies, rigor of assignments, whether to provide students with choices, classic literature versus relevant literature, forms of assessment, the amount of time designated for physical education and recess . . . the list is endless. However, our *educational beliefs* arise in great part from our own *experiences*, as teachers and as learners. You probably have fond memories of learning experiences similar to ones you favor as a teacher. Further, teachers seldom see what works in other classrooms because of the way they are naturally isolated by school schedules, norms, and ever-increasing demands of the job. We receive little input that would cause us to question our beliefs. Who you are is how you teach. In fact, beliefs can be so ingrained that we might not even know we hold a particular belief until someone tells us to change it!

The first step in differentiation is examining whether our core beliefs leave out any students in our classroom. We want to ask the following questions—and more—to distinguish between style differences and actual learning problems.

- That student who makes multiple mistakes on practice problems: Is she lazy? Missing basic skills? Or, is she bored by assignments that require little imagination?
- The student who constantly asks, "Is this right?" or "Can I see an example?" Is he unwilling to think through problem-solving? Or, does he need different scaffolding to feel confident?
- What about the students who don't share in discussions? Are they shy, or apathetic, or in need of different ground rules to join in?

Sometimes the above situations reflect developmental issues, lack of motivation, or resistance to authority, but sometimes the issues arise because of differences in the *natural, normal personality preferences* of the teacher and the student.

Let's think for a moment about that word "preference." Pick up a pen or pencil with your *nonpreferred* hand, the one you don't usually write with, and sign your name in the blank below:

_____

Most people say that writing with their nonpreferred hand is awkward, difficult, messy. They have to think to complete the task correctly. Now, switch hands and sign again below:

_____

Most people say that writing with their *preferred* hand is easy, natural, flowing. They can do it without thinking. It's part of who they are. And, it's a relief to again write with one's preferred hand after using the other.

We have a *physical* preference for left- or right-handedness. Parents often watch their toddlers to discover which hand they prefer. Neither hand is right or wrong. Further, for many tasks we can practice and become skilled with both hands—think of shooting hoops or fencing or running hurdles.

Type theory holds that we have similar *personality* preferences for how we

- Gain energy
- Take in information
- Make decisions
- Approach life.

In educational circles, considering these preferences involves asking, do all students have the energy they need for learning? Are they getting the information they need to make sense of new ideas and tasks? Are they learning to make informed decisions in ways that make sense to them? Are we giving them ways to approach assignments and tasks that honor their natural approach to life? If not, they may struggle to learn.

As we work through this chapter, you'll see that many teacher strengths are tied to personality types; because of our preferences, certain classroom tasks, learning activities, and procedures come more naturally than others. That makes it hard to distinguish between "truths" and "beliefs." However, a tension arises between our strengths as educators and the needs of students:

- We need to use our strengths in the classroom to avoid burnout.
- We also need to meet the needs of all the learners in our classrooms, ensuring that some students aren't always being asked to "write with their nonpreferred hand."

Clearly, it isn't desirable for children to always be taught in their own styles—effective learning, as we will see, requires some skill with *all* of the preferences. But, imagine if you always had to write with your nonpreferred hand and didn't understand why! The power of understanding "Who You Are Is How You Teach" is that you can consciously plan for avoiding burnout while not leaving out any students.

So, let's look at the preferences, what they mean for teachers, and which ones best describe you.

---

*Before you read on . . .*

For a moment, consider an ideal classroom for how you learn best. Draw a floor plan. How many students are there? Where do you sit to read, write, and work in groups? Describe the noise level. What other spaces are there? Compare your drawing with those of other teachers. What is similar? What is different?

---

## THE FIRST PREFERENCE PAIR: EXTRAVERSION AND INTROVERSION

### Energy for Learning

The first preference pair concerns how you are *energized*. Think about the kinds of environments that put you at your best—your most motivated and effective self. The two preferences are

Extraversion (**E**)   Gaining energy through action and interaction, the outside world

Introversion (**I**)   Gaining energy through reflection and solitude, the inner world

This preference pair is *not* about sociability. Note that in type language, Extr*a*version is even spelled differently. Introverts can be very social, but group gatherings can be draining even if they enjoy them.

It's not about shyness. Extraverts can be very shy around strangers, yet need contact with friends and the outside world to be energized.

It's not about being the life of the party. Introverts can be very entertaining; many actors, musicians, and sports figures are Introverts.

It also isn't about excellence at being reflective. Instead, ponder whether action and interaction energize you or drain you. Do quiet spaces and places for reflection jazz you up or make you nervous? Remember, this is a *natural* preference.

Yes, Extraverts can be quiet, but Extraverted teachers often long for chances during the day to have adult interaction to process what is happening in their classrooms.

Yes, Introverts can interact and collaborate. However, too much noise or required conversation leaves the Introverts drained of energy for teaching.

We all have an Extraverted side and an Introverted side—we need time with people and time for reflection. The question is, how much of each? How many people? How long for reflection before we're ready to talk?

Which best describes your *natural* style?

| *Extraverts prefer:* | *Introverts prefer:* |
| --- | --- |
| ☐ Talking things out | ☐ Thinking things through |
| ☐ Variety and action | ☐ Concentration and reflection |
| ☐ Forming thoughts through discussion | ☐ Waiting to share until thoughts are formed |
| ☐ Focusing on the outer world | ☐ Focusing on the inner world |
| ☐ Activity before reflection | ☐ Reflection before activity |

To consider your own style, think of times that you needed help with a problem, or hoped to try something new in your classroom. Do you like to first talk it through with a trusted colleague or first think about your own solutions and ideas?

Back in the classroom, let's look at Extraverted and Introverted environments. When I have adults *or* students draw their ideal classrooms, as in "Before you read on. . ." on page 11, these are some common features for each preference. How do these compare with your drawing?

The ideal classroom for . . .

| *Extraverts:* | *Introverts:* |
| --- | --- |
| ☐ Space for movement, doors to the outside | ☐ Space for individual work—laptop stations, beanbag chairs |
| ☐ Exercise mats and dance floors (students have added basketball courts and hot tubs) | ☐ Books, windows to the outside, and flowers and other visual aids for reflection |
| ☐ Many students (>15) | ☐ Few students (1–12) |
| ☐ Activities for five to six students to work on together | ☐ Activities for two students to work on together |
| ☐ Moveable furniture, chairs on wheels, etc. | ☐ Study carrels or individual desks (or their own room at home with online capabilities) |

Most Extraverted teachers run classrooms that have Extraverted characteristics. Introverted teachers run more Introverted classrooms. That shouldn't be surprising—the teacher needs to gain energy for teaching! However, without understanding we can look with disapproval on the rooms of teachers who don't share our preferences. One Introverted teacher said, "When students come from *her* room, it takes me 10 minutes to settle them down!" whereas her Extraverted colleague said, "When students come from *his* room, it takes me 10 minutes to get them going!" Who we are influences how we teach.

Without an understanding of how our own preference for gaining energy influences our teaching style, we can easily fall into traps. Chances are, you've learned to avoid some of those given below for your preference. If so, consider how you became aware of the needs of students who aren't like you, perhaps through experience, mentoring, or a class you took.

| *Common traps for Extraverted teachers* | *Common traps for Introverted teachers* |
| --- | --- |
| ☐ Look for outward enthusiasm as a sign of student engagement. | ☐ Mistake the Extraverted need to share thoughts as rude blurting-out. |
| ☐ Not give enough wait time for Introverted students to process their thoughts. Some Introverted students describe it this way: "By the time I'm ready, all the good stuff has been said." | ☐ Require too much quiet, causing Extraverts to lose focus. All students need quiet for difficult tasks such as test-taking, but Extraverts often need more breaks in that quiet. |
| ☐ Give second and third prompts when a student delays in responding, thinking the student needs more information. This actually interrupts the Introverted process and causes a longer delay. | ☐ Overestimate how long Extraverted students can read or write quietly without sharing their thoughts. |
| ☐ When trying to elicit enthusiasm from Introverted students, for whom just being in school all day is difficult, instead overwhelm and tire them out. | ☐ Delay hands-on learning too long while providing background information or explanations. |

Which preference seems most like you?

Extraversion (**E**) _____ or Introversion (**I**) _____

Sometimes people get the misunderstanding that they should be striving for balance. They want to be "ambiverts." Actually, mature people do know which preference to use in various situations, but we still *have* a natural preference. Several topographical brain-mapping studies, measuring brain activity while subjects performed different tasks, show that there are clear differences in brain electrical activity patterns for people who prefer Extraversion and Introversion (Myers, McCaulley, Quenk, & Hammer, 1998). Frame

> **TRY THIS!**
>
> Use the "Red Card/Green Card" exercise (page 79) with students in your classroom.
> Compare notes. Did students show preferences for Extraversion and Introversion?

this exercise as figuring out your preference so that you can better understand what energizes you.

*Before you read on . . .*

Put yourself back in sixth grade. If you had a choice of the following two unit project assignments for Greek mythology, which one would you choose and why? What might you do?

A. Choose from the following topics:
   • Ceremonies for worship of Greek gods
   • Compare and contrast two Greek temples built for different gods
   • The importance of the gods in Athens vs. Sparta

   Your report should be 3 pages long, double-spaced, 1" margins, 12 pt. font. 4 bibliographical references, at least one drawing, chart, or other illustration. Related oral report to be 5 minutes long and include at least 1 visual aid. Aids may be pictures, a model you construct, or a video clip (less than 1 minute).

B. To conclude this unit, design your own project to demonstrate your knowledge of the gods of ancient Greece. Your project may take any form but must include a class presentation.

# THE SECOND PREFERENCE PAIR: SENSING AND INTUITION

## Getting the *Information* You Need to Learn

This second preference pair describes two normal processes for gathering information. Your choice in the above assignments might hint at your preference for

Sensing **(S)**      *First* paying attention to *what is*, to information you can gather through your five senses—the facts

INtuition **(N)*\***      *First* paying attention to what *could be*, to hunches, connections or imagination—a sixth sense

As with Extraversion and Introversion, this isn't an either/or. Instead, Sensing and Intuition describe a person's *preferred* starting place for gathering information. Sensing types start with the facts, defining what is. They usually pick Choice A above, saying, "Plunging in without being sure of the requirements can lead to a lot of wasted time if you guess wrong." Getting the details right seems sensible.

Intuitives start with their hunch, or a connection or insight. They usually pick Choice B (unless they struggle with or dislike the subject area). As soon as they read the assignment, they get an idea for a myth to write or a game to construct, saying "I've got great ideas and I can't wait to start!"

---

*Note that the *I* was used for Introversion, so the *N* stands for INtuition.

Learning takes both Sensing and Intuition—think of using facts to support big ideas or conclusions. However, it's easy for educators to favor classroom activities that emphasize their own preference.

Which best describes your natural style?

| *Sensing types prefer:* | *Intuitive types prefer:* |
| --- | --- |
| ☐ Accuracy | ☐ Insights |
| ☐ Using experience as a guide | ☐ Using imagination as a guide |
| ☐ Following the steps (orderly directions and information) | ☐ Plunging in (using hunches to fill in missing steps or information) |
| ☐ Paying attention to reality | ☐ Paying attention to possibilities |
| ☐ Working with proven methods and curriculum | ☐ Working with innovative methods and ideas |

Teachers sometimes discover their own style by thinking about curriculum. Sensing teachers, especially in their first few years in the classroom, often view curriculum as their lesson plans. They may work straight from it, perhaps not feeling comfortable skipping over sections for fear of leaving out an important concept. In contrast, Intuitive teachers often view curriculum as a platform for brainstorming. Their actual lesson may or may not bear much resemblance to the original materials.

There are advantages and pitfalls to both approaches to curriculum. For Sensing teachers, the danger is failing to make curriculum relevant to particular students, or thinking that what has worked in the past will always work. For Intuitive teachers, the danger is failing to cover certain standards, or overlapping with assignments students will receive in other grades. They may also rush to try new ideas rather than perfect lessons they've tried.

Our preference for Sensing and Intuition, then, influences the kinds of assignments we're most comfortable with, the information we need to proceed with them, and the content of lessons we enjoy the most.

| *Sensing types like assignments where:* | *Intuitive types like assignments where:* |
| --- | --- |
| ☐ Facts and details are valued | ☐ General concepts launch opportunities for imaginative or critical thinking |
| ☐ Expectations are clear | ☐ Expectations are to dream big |
| ☐ Motivation comes from safety in specificity | ☐ Motivation comes from room for individuality |
| ☐ Set materials are covered | ☐ Themes are tapped and opened |
| ☐ Connections are made to real life | ☐ Knowledge is interesting even if it isn't useful |

Think about it: Do you tend to give choices (Intuition) or structured tasks (Sensing)? Do you give clear directions (Sensing) or are students always asking for clarification (Intuition)? One Intuitive teacher said, "By my last hour class, I finally know how to explain assignments because students have pointed out everything I omitted!"

Below are a few common traps teachers often fall into without an understanding of this preference pair. If you've learned how to avoid some of these traps, think about the strategies you use. How do you meet the needs of students who aren't like you?

| Sensing teachers might: | Intuitive teachers might: |
| --- | --- |
| ☐ Think that Intuitive students are sloppy or heedless of directions | ☐ See a student's need for clarity as a lack of creativity |
| ☐ Overstructure assignments, believing that practice and procedures will help students discover underlying concepts | ☐ Understructure assignments, not wanting to stifle the imagination or individuality of students |
| ☐ Emphasize factual learning or basic skills so that students have the foundation for higher level thinking | ☐ Emphasize themes and projects or drama more than teaching or reinforcing fundamental skills |
| ☐ Grow almost too comfortable with lessons, strategies, and techniques they've developed over time. | ☐ Embrace almost any change, jettisoning techniques or curriculum that should be kept |

Another way to put the trap each side might fall into is that when things aren't going well, Sensing teachers tend to do more and more of the same, hoping that by repetition it will finally work, whereas Intuitive teachers tend to try something new, then something else, then something else, searching for anything that might help. In truth, a middle ground of keeping what is working and replacing what isn't, through reflective practice on what is really going on, is the best approach.

> **TRY THIS!**
>
> Use the "Object Lesson" (p. 171) exercise with your students. Can you see the differences between Sensing and Intuitive students? Share examples of student work with your colleagues.

The differences between Sensing and Intuition are key to differentiation, as explained more fully in Chapter 4. What *information* do students need to learn? We need to build a bridge, step by step, for Sensing students, until they grasp the big concepts being taught. Intuitive students often grasp the big idea, but need to learn to build arguments and use details to support reasoning.

Which describes you best?

**S**ensing (S) _____ or I**N**tuition (N) _____

*Before you read on . . .*

What are your rules when students don't finish assignments or fail to turn in homework on time?

# THE THIRD PREFERENCE PAIR: THINKING AND FEELING

### How We Make *Decisions*

This third preference pair describes two normal, rational approaches to making decisions:

Thinking **(T)**     Making decisions through objective, logical principles

Feeling **(F)**     Making decisions by considering the impact of each alternative on the people involved

Thinkers have feelings; Feelers can think. Remember, this pair is about how we decide what we believe, choose courses of action, form guiding rules, or determine likes and dislikes. Sometimes comparing the ideal world for each preference pair helps clarify the difference:

*In an ideal world for Thinking types,* one set of rules, principles, and truths would work for everyone. No exceptions would be necessary.

*In an ideal world for Feeling types,* there would be different sets of rules, standards, and values for each person, depending on individual needs and circumstances.

Neither ideal world can truly exist, can it? Most situations call for balance. If homework rules are too lax, some students declare, "You're not being fair!" If homework rules are too rigid, some students give up trying. We need balance, the wisdom of both preferences, to make good decisions.

Which best describes your natural style?

| *Thinking types prefer:* | *Feeling types prefer:* |
| --- | --- |
| ☐ Objectivity, logic | ☐ Subjectivity, values |
| ☐ First seeing what's wrong | ☐ First seeing what's right |
| ☐ Striving for competency | ☐ Striving for harmony |
| ☐ Analyzing | ☐ Sympathizing |
| ☐ Sticking to rules | ☐ Making room for exceptions |

Teachers often recognize whether Thinking or Feeling describes them best by considering how conflict affects them. How do you react to a phone call from an angry parent? Most Thinking types report that they calmly work through a standard protocol for shifting the conversation back to facts without placing blame. After the call ends, they think through needed follow-up and then move on.

Most teachers with a preference for Feeling work through a similar protocol, but after the call their calm often dissolves into a jumble of emotion. Did they handle things right? Is it their fault that the parent is upset? Could they have avoided the problem? Conflict stays with them for awhile before they can move on.

Thinking and Feeling in the classroom involve rules, the subjects we enjoy most, our level of need for praise and feedback, and much more. In the classroom, clues to preferences include

| *Thinking types prefer:* | *Feeling types prefer:* |
| --- | --- |
| ☐ Understanding why | ☐ Understanding people |
| ☐ Math and science | ☐ Stories and culture |
| ☐ Fairness | ☐ Caring |
| ☐ Debate and competition | ☐ Consensus and cooperation |
| ☐ Being in charge | ☐ Being liked |

When I interview Thinking and Feeling teachers about their ideal classroom, Thinking teachers often say something like, "The bottom line is learning. Life is about meeting expectations. These should be clear so students know where they stand. I shouldn't be making things easier for them when the real world won't." Feeling teachers might say, "I'd do away with grades, both A, B, C, and grade levels. Students should each be allowed to learn at their own natural pace and evaluated on the basis of progress from where they were, not someone else's standard."

Below are common traps that Thinking and Feeling teachers naturally fall into, although you may have developed strategies to avoid them:

| *Thinking teachers might:* | *Feeling teachers might:* |
| --- | --- |
| ☐ Underestimate the impact of put-downs and sarcasm on learning for Feeling students | ☐ Get drawn into unproductive arguments, trying to reason with a Thinking student who just enjoys verbal sparring |
| ☐ View the Feeling need for positive reinforcement as ploys for attention | ☐ Offer too much nonspecific praise |
| ☐ Fail to bend rules when exceptions would help motivate students or when rules actually affect different students in different ways because of their varying needs or reactions | ☐ Not hold fast enough on rules, which can undermine authority |
| ☐ Strive for rigor over building relationships, when both are essential | ☐ Strive for building relationships over providing rigor, when both are essential |

Which seems more like you?

Thinking **(T)** _____ or Feeling **(F)** _____

Thinking and Feeling are key to communication and motivation, as well as to developing a productive classroom culture. A few implications for education:

- Although 78 percent of principals have a preference for Thinking, 68 percent of elementary and 60 percent of middle-school teachers have a preference for Feeling.[1]
- 71 percent of art, drama, and music teachers have a preference for Feeling, whereas 70 percent of industrial arts teachers have a preference for Thinking.
- Math teachers are almost evenly split between Thinking and Feeling. However, "math anxiety" may be found most often in Feeling students (Huelsman, 2002).

> **TRY THIS!**
>
> Have students write a response to one of the following "Dear Abby"-style letters:
>
> I don't think my sports coach likes me. What should I do?
>
> Or,
>
> My mom says I'm too sensitive. What should I do?
>
> In your study group, compare student work. Can you see differences in Thinking and Feeling?

---

**Before you read on . . .**

Picture yourself as a student. You've got a big project to complete, due three weeks from now. Which statement is most true for you? Why? Give an example.

- I'd choose a topic and get started right away. If I'm behind, I struggle to enjoy other activities. Besides, if I finish early, I have time to check my work. I like that.
- I'd start thinking about the project right away, but I wouldn't want to lock into a topic too quickly. Something more interesting might come up! Besides, I can't really start early. It's the pressure of a looming deadline that spurs me on to do my best work.

---

# THE FOURTH PREFERENCE PAIR: JUDGING AND PERCEIVING

## Our Approach to Work, School, and Life in General

The final preference pair describes our natural approach to life, through

Judging (**J**)      A preference for planning their work and working their plan

Perceiving (**P**)      A preference for staying open to the moment

Judging types are *not* judgmental. Instead, they like to come to closure (judgments). Perceiving types are *not* more perceptive. Instead, they like to remain open to new information (perceptions). The preferences often approach tasks entirely differently.

Judging types are often adept at estimating how long things take, sequencing tasks, planning their approach, and sticking to that plan as they work at a steady pace to wrap things up.

Perceiving types search out options, continually gather information, and digress from their initial plans—if they thought it was necessary to make any. Their plans often emerge as they work from ideas, in bursts of energy.

---

[1]Occupational data are from the Center for Applications of Psychological Type database.

| *Judging types prefer to:* | *Perceiving types prefer to:* |
|---|---|
| ☐ Plan your work and work your plan | ☐ Stay open to options |
| ☐ Enjoy finishing | ☐ Enjoy starting |
| ☐ Work before they play | ☐ Let work and play coexist |
| ☐ Have things settled | ☐ Search for more information |
| ☐ Know what will be happening | ☐ Experience surprises and variety |

Which preference pair describes you best?

Judging teachers often find lesson planning a natural process. In contrast, a Perceiving teacher said, "Why plan when classroom activities never take the amount of time you think they will?" For Judging types, a curriculum map is a way to avoid problems: supplies can be ordered on time, the computer lab reserved. For Perceiving types, a curriculum map can be a straightjacket. What if the new Newberry winner is from your town or a news event piques student interest? All that planning, wasted!

In classrooms,

| *Judging types prefer:* | *Perceiving types prefer:* |
|---|---|
| ☐ Clear deadlines and goals—no surprises because they start working right away | ☐ Flexibility and surprises—they process longer before moving to production |
| ☐ A workload that allows for steady effort | ☐ A workload with high and low activity levels |
| ☐ Clear expectations so they know when they're done | ☐ Flexible timelines so they can stick with something that interests them |
| ☐ Produce product quickly (perhaps rushing the process) | ☐ Enjoy the process, forgetting to move on to producing something |
| ☐ Knowing what is coming so they can plan ahead | ☐ Concentrating on what they need to do now |

At all levels of education, nearly 70 percent of teachers have a preference for Judging; for principals, it's 85 percent! In school, deadlines and timeliness matter.

Below are common traps that Judging and Perceiving teachers might fall into.

| *Judging teachers might:* | *Perceiving teachers might:* |
|---|---|
| ☐ "Rush" Perceiving students toward completion | ☐ Change deadlines and plans, frustrating Judging students |
| ☐ Stick to schedules, cutting short exploratory time | ☐ Under- or overestimate how long activities might take |
| ☐ Lock into a lesson idea too soon, not seeking other possibilities | ☐ Not give parameters; students don't know when they're done |
| ☐ See Perceiving students as unmotivated or one step from irresponsible | ☐ See Judging students as too rigid or complaining |

Consider where you naturally fall on the continuum below for when you might begin a project (if you feel stuck in the middle, go back to your college mindset when you first called your own shots).

| J | I | I | I | I | I | P |
|---|---|---|---|---|---|---|
| Start project right away, finish ASAP | Start early, work steadily | Goal: Halfway at halfway point | | Think all along, start producing when deadline adds pressure | | Put things off until last-minute adrenaline inspires |

Judging and Perceiving are key to understanding how to ensure work quality and work completion for all students, as Chapter 6 explains in detail. Also, teachers often find it easier to collaborate with colleagues when everyone understands that people actually do their best work when they approach tasks in ways that honor their natural preference.

Which seems more like you?

Judging (J) _____ or Perceiving (P) _____

Take a moment to record your four preference letters below. If you're still unsure on one of the pairs, read through the next chapter, "What Type Looks Like in Students." Often, adults verify their preferences by recognizing patterns from their own childhood. The more you know about your own style, the more you'll recognize when you need to adjust so that students who are very different from you can develop academic confidence.

| _____ | _____ | _____ | _____ |
|---|---|---|---|
| Extraversion or Introversion | Sensing or Intuition | Thinking or Feeling | Judging or Perceiving |

## Population Patterns for the Preferences

In the United States, numerous studies have shown the following distributions of type preferences in the general population (Myers, McCaulley, Quenk, & Hammer 1998):

- Extraversion and Introversion: just about equal
- Sensing and Intuition: 65–70 percent Sensing
- Thinking and Feeling: just about equal, but about 60 percent of men prefer Thinking and 60 percent of women prefer Feeling
- Judging and Perceiving: 60–65 percent prefer Judging

Which preferences work best in teaching? In truth, every preference is an asset when we teach from the strengths of our personality, but can adjust when either the task or the students' needs require us to use the other preferences. However, historically, there are patterns in the preferences of people who choose teaching as a career, as shown in Table 2.1, below, which summarizes numerous studies on thousands of teachers.

Because the preferences aren't equally distributed in the population (remember that 65–70 percent prefer Sensing, for example), more important than the absolute percentage of teachers of any type is that percentage in relationship to the general population. Shaded are the personality types that are underrepresented in teaching, using this measure.

**Table 2.1**    Percentage of Elementary Teachers of Each Personality Type

| **ISTJ** 10.7 % Gen pop. 11.6 % | **ISFJ** 17.9% Gen. pop. 13.8% | **INFJ** 5.1% Gen. pop. 1.5% | **INTJ** 2.1% Gen pop. 1.9% |
|---|---|---|---|
| **ISTP** 1.7% Gen pop. 5.4% | **ISFP** 4.7% Gen pop. 8.8% | **INFP** 4.6% Gen pop. 4.4% | **INTP** 1.5% Gen pop. 3.3% |
| **ESTP** 0.9% Gen pop. 4.3% | **ESFP** 5.7% Gen pop. 8.5% | **ENFP** 10.2% Gen. pop. 8.1% | **ENTP** 1.5% Gen pop. 3.2% |
| **ESTJ** 8.5% Gen pop. 8.7% | **ESFJ** 12.4% Gen pop. 12.3% | **ENFJ** 7.2% Gen pop. 2.5% | **ENTJ** 5.2% Gen pop. 1.8% |

SOURCE: Elementary school teachers type table data in *Psychological Type in Education* by Mary H. McCaulley, 1993. Used with permission of the Center for Applications of Psychological Type, Inc.

At higher levels of education, there are more Thinking and Intuitive types. The four SP types (on the left-hand side of the table) remain underrepresented at every level. As we move on to Chapter 3, "What Type Looks Like in Students," you might begin to see some reasons why these people may not be attracted to traditional school environments.

## CONCLUSION

Look back to the list of activities you journaled about at the start of the chapter. How are these tied to your personality type? Can you see that how you teach in many ways reflects who you are? As we move to "What Type Looks Like in Students," we'll see that who they are is how they learn. Although teachers cannot (and should not) meet the needs of all children at all times, type becomes a tool for examining our practices, not in terms of right and wrong, but in terms of "What children will this reach?"

# 3

# What Type Looks Like in Students

*Before you read on . . .*

Think of a time when school really clicked for you—you learned easily or connected well with a teacher. What was happening? What factors created this environment for you?

Then, think of a poor school experience—where you felt unable to grasp concepts or connect with a teacher. What factors created this environment for you?

Leon was failing most of his classes. The teachers brought up his name during a meeting on behavior problems. "He won't even lift a pencil. Instead, he's disruptive. If we don't send him out, he keeps the rest of the students from working." They discussed whether Leon had been properly evaluated for special services.

Later that week, the teachers had all students complete an exercise that helps students understand the difference between Sensing and Intuition. Students are given the instructions, "Write about a snowman. No questions. You will have five minutes." (This is a variation of the Object Lesson Exercise on page 171). Sensing students (and adults) tend to write detailed descriptions, directions on how to build a snowman, or information about an actual snowman they built. The Intuitive students either name their snowmen and write a fictional story or describe a one-of-a-kind snowman that they built.

Leon wrote about a snowman who forgot to wear a scarf and got so sick that he coughed up snowflakes. Yes, a Sensing student might come up with a similar response if asked to write a fictional story about something that might happen to a living snowman, but as the teachers pondered whether Leon might be an Intuitive, one commented, "We've been giving him rote work because we thought that lack of ability was driving his behavior. What if instead he's totally bored with the work?"

Try as we might to treat all students fairly, most teachers can recall a few children over the years who knew just how to push their particular button. Which students are hardest for you?

Maybe it's the apathetic student who refuses to engage, no matter how creative your activities.

Maybe it's the student who loses assignments and comes without paper and pencil, no matter what you do to help.

Maybe it's the student who constantly peppers you with questions, not able to wait until you've finished giving directions.

Maybe it's the student who declares, "That's bogus" or "That's not fair" to your every idea.

Is it true that that student just, well, isn't like you? Doesn't seem to fit into the way you best run your classroom? When teachers develop an understanding of personality type, they can look at the above behaviors without saying, "What's wrong with that child?" Instead they ask, "How is that child different from me?"

In this chapter we'll look at each preference and behavior clues that might help you identify a child's type. Then we'll examine portraits of different types of students. What do they look like when school is working? Or, as with Leon, when it isn't working?

Finally, we'll explore how to use this information to shift discussions from "What's wrong with this child?" to "Could type strategies help this child learn?"

## TYPE PREFERENCES: WHAT YOU MIGHT SEE IN STUDENTS

Sometimes it's easier to see the preferences in children because they haven't matured enough to adjust behavior to match situations. Chapter 11 lays out the ethics of using type with children and adolescents; in this chapter, the purpose is viewing student behaviors through the lens of type to identify different learning or motivational strategies.

Before you read through Chart 3.1, bring to mind a particular student that puzzles you in some way. Does the checklist help you identify any of his or her type preferences? What insights might that knowledge provide?

You might use the following observations to hypothesize about a student's preferences.

*Extraversion and Introversion.* Watch how students act during silent seatwork. Extraverted students usually fidget more, tap pencils, sharpen pencils, or otherwise find ways to get out of their seats, even if they are following directions.

Introverts aren't necessarily always quiet. They can give speeches, speak up, and work in groups, but they might want more time to think and to prepare. If they're bored or sitting with friends, they may get in as much trouble for talking out of turn as the Extraverts.

*Sensing and Intuition.* Concentrate on the kinds of questions students have and the ideas they share. Sensing students often ask for examples and clarification of directions until a sturdy "bridge" is in place from what they know to new learning.

Intuitive students often ask questions that go beyond your directions or the topic at hand. Either they want to be unique or they're making connections that can seem

**Chart 3.1**     Behavior Clues and Type Preferences

| *Extraversion and Introversion: How do students get the energy to learn?* | |
|---|---|
| **Extraversion** | **Introversion** |
| • May talk louder, move more than Introverted students | • May be slow to respond in class discussions, unless they knew the topic in advance |
| • May forget answers in between raising their hand and being called on—they need to talk to think | • May prefer reading and writing over discussions |
| • May work more efficiently when quiet chatting or group work is allowed | • May prefer to work alone or with partner of choice |
| • May prefer activities to reading in their spare time | • May pause before responding even in one-on-one conversations |
| • May say what they're thinking—reactions, feelings, thoughts | • May keep reactions, thoughts, feelings to themselves unless asked |
| • May prefer to try, then read about what should happen | • May prefer to read what should happen, then try |
| • Not bothered by interruptions | • Annoyed by interruptions |
| *Sensing and Intuition: What information do students first attend to?* | |
| **Sensing** | **Intuition** |
| • May interrupt as you give directions, asking about things you'd be telling them in a few moments if they'd wait | • May not read directions; may start working before you've finished giving oral directions |
| • May struggle to come up with ideas for projects | • May come up with project ideas that are too big for them to carry out |
| • May ask for extra examples, disliking unclear expectations | • May make many careless mistakes |
| • May seem to learn better from hands-on learning than from books | • May ask if they can alter assignments |
| • May ask, "Did that really happen?" | • May enjoy "unrealistic," imaginative tangents |

*(Continued)*

**Chart 3.1** (Continued)

| Thinking and Feeling: How do students make decisions? | |
| --- | --- |
| **Thinking** | **Feeling** |
| • May like to critique things, find the flaw | • May be visibly upset by sad stories or disrespect in the classroom |
| • May need to be in charge of things | • May look out for the underdog |
| • May shut down if they don't think they can successfully do something (need to feel competent before taking risks) | • May shut down if they decide a teacher doesn't like them |
| • Seem to need to have the last word—debate even those in authority | • May seek feedback, encouragement— "Teacher, did I do this one right?" |
| • May seem competitive—will not lose face | • May learn better when assignments relate to needs of people |
| • May be uncomfortable with affection | • May view any critique as evidence that someone dislikes them |

| Judging and Perceiving: How do students approach life? | |
| --- | --- |
| **Judging** | **Perceiving** |
| • May rush through work in order to be done, resisting revision | • May work without really getting anything done, e.g., reading without taking notes for reports, brainstorm without coming to conclusions |
| • May resist exploring new sources of information or paths for investigation | • May underestimate or overestimate how long something will take |
| • May be upset by surprises or changes in agenda or scheduled activities | • May enjoy surprises and changes in class schedules |
| • May lock into formats or ideas too quickly | • May delay choosing topics, projects, or strategies—still searching |
| • May seem to hold selves to schedules, goals, checklists (may be mental, not written) | • May still be working at the last minute or ask for extensions—surprised at how time has flown |
| • May show increasing anxiety by continuing to work until overly exhausted, bent on finishing work before play | • May surprise parents with project needs at last minute—poster board, diorama boxes, etc.—even though the assignment was given days before |
| • May dislike unclear expectations | • Too many expectations seem like barriers |

unrelated. They may do their poorest work on easy tasks, such as practice problems in mathematics or fill-in-the-blank worksheets.

*Thinking and Feeling.* Consider the student's interactions with you. Some Thinking students, especially if they are Extraverted, have no hesitation telling a teacher what they're doing wrong. A sixth grader informed his science teacher, "I think you're giving too many points for the oral portion of the science fair project. Our displays should have the heavier weighting."

Feeling students may struggle with gentle critiques. For example, a parent requested a meeting with the school principal because her daughter, who had gotten A's in seventh-grade English and liked to write, was barely doing C work in eighth-grade English. The girl had said, "The teacher doesn't like me, so I'm not going to do the work." In talking to the girl, the principal discovered that she had a preference for Feeling. The teacher had critiqued the girl's writing without giving any specific praise, assuming that the student would interpret her comments as advice for making her excellent writing even better. When the principal reinterpreted the situation in terms of Thinking and Feeling, it gave the teacher and student a fresh start together.

*Judging and Perceiving.* Imagine taking a class of students to the library to gather information for country reports. All students are to answer the same questions for their country, perhaps filling out a graphic organizer. The Judging types grab books and look for answers to a specific question. They quickly move to filling in blanks (although not necessarily in order). The Perceiving types also grab books. They start to page through. A picture captures their interest and they begin to read that page. Then they might skip to another spot, reading the text under an attention-grabbing headline. Twenty minutes later, the Judging students are halfway done. It may appear as if the Perceiving students have done nothing when in fact they may have skimmed half the book, yet not written anything down. That's what product versus process looks like!

Remember, neither preference is right or wrong. The Judging students may focus so intently on the task that they miss the richness of a more exploratory path. And the Perceiving students may not cut off their search in time and thus fail to finish.

## TYPE AND LEARNING DISABILITIES

One of the main goals of observing type differences in students is exploring whether a student's learning style needs are being met before wondering whether the student has learning disabilities. Consider the following facts:

- In many studies of at-risk students, a high percentage have a preference for Perceiving—82 percent at one school I worked with.
- A perusal of indicators of ADHD shows that many also describe the Perceiving function. This is *not* to say that more Perceiving students have ADHD or that ADHD isn't real, but that what looks like ADHD may be a normal preference for Perceiving. Below is a common checklist for ADD (Centers for Disease Control and Prevention, 2005) and how students with these symptoms might be perceived through the lens of type:

| ADD Checklist | How type preferences might explain the same behaviors |
| --- | --- |
| Often does not give close attention to details or makes careless mistakes in schoolwork, work, or other activities | Students with a preference for Intuition often rush through rote work, making careless mistakes. They are less interested in accuracy than in ideas. |
| Often has trouble keeping attention on tasks or play activities | Extraverted students are drawn to external stimuli. Sounds, smells, and other distractions will pull their attention from the task at hand. |
| Often does not follow instructions and fails to finish schoolwork, chores, or duties in the workplace (not due to oppositional behavior or failure to understand instructions) | Many Intuitive students do not read directions, but instead assume they know what to do. Perceiving students may not have a good sense of how time is passing. |
| Often has trouble organizing activities | Perceiving students often lack skills in sequencing and chunking tasks. These skills seem to come more naturally for Judging students. |
| Often avoids, dislikes, or doesn't want to do things that take a lot of mental effort for a long period of time (such as schoolwork or homework) | Introverted students often have a narrow range of self-chosen interests. Extraverted students need chances to move. Intuitive students often want a say in activities and may not put in effort on things that don't interest them. |
| Often loses things needed for tasks and activities (e.g., toys, school assignments, pencils, books, or tools) | Intuitive students, because their minds are in the future, not the present moment, are often unaware of what they brought with them or where they set it down. |
| Is often easily distracted | Extraverted students are easily distracted by things going on in the outside world. |
| Is often forgetful in daily activities | Intuitive students are pulled by ideas and possibilities, not reality. |

There *is* a very real disorder known as ADD. However, before jumping to conclusions, we can look at the type clues and try teaching the student strategies and skills. Armstrong (1995) found that one of the biggest sources of misdiagnosis of ADD was a mismatch of teaching and learning styles. Jensen (1998) recommends that teachers and students first exhaust nonprescriptive options to determine whether crowded classrooms, teachers who demand too much classroom attention, or lack of self-discipline skills are contributing factors. In other words, view the child through the lens of type before assuming that a deeper problem exists.

# EIGHT KINDS OF STUDENTS

The preference pairs are useful in identifying student types, but to concentrate on *motivating* students, we're going to look at the eight **dominant** functions. All of us have one function that drives us: Sensing, Intuition, Thinking, or Feeling.[1] The *dominant* function is like a megaphone—it is the one you began using earliest in life. Think back to childhood.

- Dominant Sensing types often agree that they were known as sensible or matter-of-fact children.
- Dominant Intuitives were often viewed as imaginative children (or as daydreamers).
- Dominant Thinking children were often known for asking questions, wanting to know, "Why?"
- Dominant Feelers were known as empathetic children, aware of the feelings of others and concerned that everyone be included.

The theory of type dynamics describes how people develop their dominant, auxiliary, and other functions, but knowing that we each have dominant functions will allow you to dive into the information in this chapter and concentrate on how it might help you build better relationships with students.

*Rather than reading straight through the eight descriptions, consider:*

1. Read your own description first, using the adjacent box to determine your type's dominant preference.

2. Read the description for the type opposite your own. For example, a teacher whose dominant function is Introverted Sensing would read Extraverted Intuition. Ask yourself how you would fare in their preferred learning environment. Note that what motivates you might actually demotivate these students.

> **The Eight Functions**
>
> 1. Extraverted Sensing (ESTP, ESFP)
> 2. Introverted Sensing (ISTJ, ISFJ)
> 3. Extraverted Intuition (ENFP, ENTP)
> 4. Introverted Intuition (INFJ, INTJ)
> 5. Extraverted Thinking (ESTJ, ENTJ)
> 6. Introverted Thinking (ISTP, INTP)
> 7. Extraverted Feeling (ESFJ, ENFJ)
> 8. Introverted Feeling (ISFP, INFP)

3. Skip to page 38 and read a case study that illustrates how you might use this information with students.

4. Bring to mind a student that you've struggled to reach and work through the process described on page 41. Consider collaborating with other teachers for insights and ideas.

---

[1]What happened to Extraversion, Introversion, Judging, and Perceiving? Note that Extraverts use their dominant function in the extraverted world, whereas Introverts use their dominant function in the introverted world. And Sensing and Intuition are the *Perceiving* functions, whereas Thinking and Feeling are the *Judging* functions. Thus, all eight preferences are covered when we talk about the eight functions.

## Extraversion and Sensing

Types: ESTP, ESFP

At their best: Bringing energy, fun, and excitement to learning

### What you see when school is working . . .

Evan just about bounces into the classroom with a bright smile each day, full of energy and conversation. He knows how easily he can be distracted, so he prefers sitting close to the teacher and away from his friends unless they're working in groups. He once got a somewhat sarcastic award from a teacher for asking the most questions in class, but brushed it off, saying, "I can't concentrate on what's being said unless I get answers when the question pops into my brain!"

Evan claims to dislike reading, saying it's too much sitting still. However, true or realistic stories about sports or other interests hold his attention, especially when silent reading is followed by discussions in small groups (*not* large ones where he has to wait too long for another turn to talk). Evan really excels, though, when schoolwork lets him *do* something—measure the classroom and make an accurate scale model, conduct a science experiment, give a demonstration speech, or even get out of his seat to work a problem on the board. Teachers are often impressed by his impromptu ideas.

> **Examples in Literature:**
>
> Ron Weasley in *Harry Potter* (Rowling)
>
> Stargirl (Spinelli)
>
> Sodapop Curtis in *The Outsiders* (Hinton)
>
> Sammy in *Dicey's Song* (Voigt)

### What helps Extraverted Sensing types learn

- Chances to be active
- Content connected with real life
- Opportunities to work in groups
- Hands-on projects
- Lack of external distractions when listening is required
- Clear directions and expectations with explicit examples
- "Learning is fun" atmosphere

### What you might see if school isn't working

- Frequent blurting, off-task remarks
- Schoolwork ignored because "This stuff isn't real," "Schoolwork is dumb," "The teacher isn't fair," or "The teacher doesn't like me"
- Constantly unprepared for class

*Often*, nonengaging learning experiences turn into opportunities for Extraverted Sensing types to act out, resulting in behavior problems.

## Introversion and Sensing

Types: ISTJ, ISFJ

At their best: Working steadily, staying organized, following directions

### What you see when school is working . . .

Shandra keeps the neatest desk and notebooks in class. Her handwriting is usually quite legible, and she is very conscientious about following directions. You can count on her to be quiet during quiet time!

Usually, Shandra carefully copies down examples and uses them to complete her work. She asks questions that often help teachers clarify their instructions. She might check back with the teacher if the work differs from examples—Shandra wants to make sure she's on the right track before putting in too much effort.

Shandra digs into factual assignments—math problems, documenting science labs, writing reports, or work that requires memorization. She often seeks more feedback on open-ended projects such as creative writing assignments and science or invention fair projects, or when the work requires synthesis of multiple ideas.

> **Examples in Literature:**
>
> Nate the Great (Sharmat)
>
> Diana in *Anne of Green Gables* (Montgomery)
>
> Armpit in *Small Steps* (Sacher)
>
> Momma in *The Watsons Go to Birmingham—1963* (Curtis)

### What helps Introverted Sensing types learn

- Clear directions
- Prompt responses to questions about assignments
- Examples and feedback for assignments that go beyond factual knowledge
- Step-by-step learning
- Time to think before having to respond
- Orderly and predictable class time
- Opportunities to practice using new concepts

### What you might see if school isn't working

- Quick displays of helplessness if the child feels uncertain about how to proceed
- Lack of confidence with questions that have no right answers, such as making inferences, evaluations, or connections
- High test anxiety

*Usually,* instead of acting out, these students withdraw and may be labeled apathetic.

## Extraversion and Intuition

Types: ENFP, ENTP

At their best: Highly creative classroom leaders

### What you see when school is working . . .

Maggie always seems to be the center of a hub of activity. She's friendly, funny, and full of ideas for playground games and projects. Sometimes she even suggests classroom activities.

> **Examples in Literature:**
>
> Anne of Green Gables
>
> Pippi Longstocking
>
> The Cat in *The Cat in the Hat*
>
> Calvin of *Calvin and Hobbes*

The bigger the endeavor, the more engaged Maggie becomes. She enjoys writing and performing plays, classroom simulations, and big projects such as science fairs. Once, she designed a computer game to help other students learn the names of all the Greek gods. In sixth grade, she formed a volunteer group for tutoring first graders, lined up teachers to provide training, and worked out a schedule with a nearby elementary school.

Maggie can be a bit disorganized, but if deadlines are clear she usually pulls off good work. She admits, "I kinda wait until the last minute, or until I'm so excited by an idea that I can't wait to start!"

### What helps Extraverted Intuitives learn

- Assignments that let them work on their own ideas
- Chances to be entertaining
- Room for the imagination, flexibility in assignments
- Big projects
- Leadership opportunities, including teaching others
- Clarity around assignment requirements while having as few requirements as possible
- Big ideas

### What you might see if school isn't working

- Disorganization, rushed or sloppy work that doesn't reflect their abilities
- Great ideas that are never completed
- Disruptions, acting out

*Often*, if Extraverted Intuitives have no positive leadership opportunities, they are capable of leading the whole class in a negative direction.

## Introversion and Intuition

Types: INFJ, INTJ

At their best: Creative, self-motivated students

### What you see when school is working . . .

For the most part, Tom loves to learn. When a subject excites him, he often goes beyond the assignment. Reading is his favorite activity. In fact, sometimes teachers have to ask him to put away a book and join in what the class is doing.

Tom often asks to do assignments differently, such as writing a story instead of a report or reading a different book because he's often read the ones that are assigned. For Tom, groups work best when members divide up the tasks and work alone. He often puts together the final product because then he knows it'll be done right and on time.

If Tom is ready for class discussions, he'll be as vocal as anyone else. Otherwise, he's quiet when brainstorming how to add his own creative touch to assignments and rather chatty when schoolwork doesn't capture his attention.

> **Examples in Literature:**
>
> Hermione Granger in *Harry Potter*
>
> Charlotte in *Charlotte's Web*
>
> Claudia in *From the Mixed-Up Files of Mrs. Basil E. Frankweiler*
>
> Mrs. Piggle Wiggle

### What helps Introverted Intuitives learn

- Chances for creativity
- Independent study, minimal group work
- Opportunities to go deeply into subjects that interest them
- Theoretical or conceptual subjects for study
- Open-ended assignments that allow for individuality
- Independent reading and writing
- When teachers recognize and encourage their unique approaches

### What you might see if school isn't working

- Sloppy, rushed work, especially on structured or rote assignments
- Off-task behavior such as reading or chatting with friends
- Concentrated effort only on areas that interest them and ignoring directions

*Sometimes*, Introverted Intuitives can be disruptive, but they usually disengage by pursuing their own interests.

## Extraversion and Thinking

Types: ESTJ and ENTJ

At their best: Planful and organized, leading themselves and others

### What you see when school is working . . .

Teachers usually learn Andrea's name quickly, for she is lively, outgoing, and quite opinionated. In grade school, sometimes friends didn't react well to her blunt statements of truth, but Andrea soon learned to adjust her style and get along. She's often willing to help teachers and other students because it provides chances to talk and move about. Although Andrea enjoys reading and writing, she thrives on opportunities to engage in problem solving and group efforts, often demonstrating good leadership.

**Examples in Literature:**

Wallace in *No More Dead Dogs* (Korman)

Mary Poppins

Tom Sawyer

Stuart Little

Andrea admits that she studies harder when her abilities put her toward the top of the class because competition spurs her on. In contrast, she struggles not to give up if classmates are too far ahead of her or the material challenges her to the point where she doubts her abilities. She may then claim that an assignment is stupid. Teachers who know Andrea well, though, understand how to find logical reasons for her to do her best, setting reachable yet challenging goals for her.

### What helps Extraverted Thinking types learn

- Chances to be in charge
- Room for discussion, debate, and competition
- Clear, logical rules with consistent rewards and consequences
- Developing competency before being asked to demonstrate skills
- Logical presentation of materials and assignments
- Goals that stretch them to do their best
- Environments in which their opinions are valued

### What you might see if school isn't working

- Argumentativeness, insisting on the last word
- Abrasiveness toward teacher and other students
- Shutdown if they sense they might not do well on activities or assignments

*Usually*, Extraverted Thinking types will comply with logical rules, but above all they want to be competent and in charge. If teachers threaten these values, Extraverted Thinkers just might display leadership and competence in *mis*behavior—or drop out and start a business of their own.

## Introversion and Thinking

Types: ISTP, INTP

At their best: Observing and analyzing people and systems, applying logic to solving problems

### What you see when school is working . . .

Jared's habits of staying one step to the side, watching, listening, and wanting to think through ideas before acting made many teachers wonder if he had ADD. However, when asked, Jared's responses showed that he'd been carefully evaluating information and exploring possibilities. Ask the *right* question and you'll get a wealth of information.

Jared tends to cultivate just a few friendships at a time, partly because he's perfectly content to work or play by himself. He especially enjoys independent or computerized learning and once told a teacher, "I'd do just fine taking all online classes and never coming to school."

However, Jared also likes hands-on problem-solving opportunities. Although he often avoids group work, he will listen quietly and then add just what the group needs. He's at his best when teachers allow him to delve deeply into one of his own interests and wrestle with it until he comes up with new solutions or insights.

> **Examples in Literature:**
>
> Max in *Freak the Mighty*
>
> Spock in the original *Star Trek* series
>
> Bean in *Ender's Game*
>
> Charles Wallace in *A Wrinkle in Time*

### What helps Introverted Thinking types learn

- Independent study, minimal group work
- Chances for problem solving or synthesis of ideas
- Opportunities for reflection before ideas are shared
- Validation of their reasoning
- Ability to choose topics of study that let them develop expertise
- Emphasis on logic, objectivity
- Minimal requirements or rote assignments that they view as pointless

### What you might see if school isn't working

- Withdrawal, perhaps with harsh but thoughtful criticism of assignments they choose not to do
- Refusal to work for teachers they view as incompetent or hypocritical
- Brilliant work that defies the rules or requirements set by the teacher

*Usually*, disengaged Introverted Thinkers sit back, causing teachers to assume they don't care. In truth, once an Introverted Thinker passes judgment, persuading him or her otherwise can take significant data, logic, and reasoning.

## Extraversion and Feeling

Types: ESFJ, ENFJ

At their best: Organized, helpful, friendly, and cooperative

### What you see when school is working . . .

Jasmine loves school because it's a chance to be with friends all day long. She's a conscientious student, too, keeping on top of assignments and turning in neat homework. Science and math aren't nearly as interesting to her as classes that are about people, but she does well as long as her teachers are friendly and encouraging. Some teachers think Jasmine asks for too much feedback, but especially in elementary school, she thrived when teachers acknowledged that she was on the right track.

Jasmine enjoys working in groups. She listens well to others and then often steps in with suggestions for planning and organizing the best way to proceed. Her materials are organized and she's even volunteered to help teachers file or otherwise handle supplies. Clear schedules, goals, and expectations let her know she's on track.

> **Examples in Literature:**
>
> Meg in *Little Women*
>
> Doc in *Holes*
>
> Lucy in *The Lion, the Witch, and the Wardrobe*
>
> Caddie Woodlawn

### What helps Extraverted Feeling types learn

- Friendly, cooperative atmosphere
- Emphasis on how knowledge will prepare them to help others
- Clear expectations and goals so they can plan their work and please teachers
- Opportunities to talk and work with friends
- Chances to help others
- Positive feedback, assurances of being accepted
- Use of organizational and leadership skills

### What you might see if school isn't working

- Talking, note-passing, and otherwise concentrating on the social side of school
- Stating, "I'm dumb," "I can't do this," or "This is boring."
- High test anxiety, especially in math

*Usually*, Extraverted Feeling types whisper and pass notes rather than being openly disruptive—they disengage in a friendly manner.

## Introversion and Feeling

Types: ISFP, INFP

At their best: Thoughtful, friendly students who quietly hold firm to values

### What you see when school is working . . .

Matt once joked with his parents, "A good year is when no teacher knows your name." In truth, although Matt hates being called on in class or otherwise being in the limelight, his best years in school were when a teacher learned of Matt's unique interests and then used that information to motivate him.

Matt dislikes group work unless he has a say in forming his group. He tends to have just a handful of close friendships and either hangs with them or is content to work by himself.

Teachers often struggle to read Matt because he seldom speaks up about what is bothering him—or exciting him. However, when the subject is something he cares about, teachers who take time to listen may catch a glimpse of an entirely different child and learn to encourage that part of Matt. He does better when school work allows him to draw on his quirky sense of humor or stay true to his values.

> **Examples in Literature:**
>
> Johnny in *The Outsiders*
>
> Ferdinand the Bull
>
> Beth in *Little Women*
>
> Mary Ingalls in *Little House on the Prairie*

### What helps Introverted Feeling types learn

- Assignments and subjects that mesh with their values
- Harmonious atmosphere
- Positive feedback that recognizes their individuality
- Chances to observe and reflect before participating
- Time for individual work
- Learning that relates to real life or personal goals
- Choices in reading materials and projects

### What you might see if school isn't working

- Disengagement, appearance of being bored or apathetic
- Daydreaming, leading teachers to question whether they have a learning disability
- More than other types, tendency to slide toward clinical depression when school is frustrating for them

*Usually,* Introverted Feeling types withdraw, but they can also erupt in a storm of righteous indignation if a teacher either hurts another student or sets a requirement that would cause the Introverted Feeling student to violate a value.

# CASE STUDIES—USING TYPE FOR STUDENT DEVELOPMENT

The following case studies are designed to provide practice in distinguishing between normal type differences in students and other kinds of problems. Might type information provide new strategies a teacher could use before turning to behavior interventions or evaluation for learning disabilities?

Conjectures about a student's type, though, remain conjectures; the student has a right to confirm his or her own preferences, as is described on page 164. However, teachers can use type information to develop intervention strategies, just as they use a variety of other books and resources.

As you read through each brief description, look for clues to distinguish the child's type preferences. The information is designed to provide information on the preferences as opposed to comprehensive descriptions. You may not be able to distinguish all four preferences, but enough information is given to determine the dominant function, as discussed in this chapter. Examine the behavior clues (pages 25–26) and the information on the preceding eight pages for ideas.

Then look at the information on learning styles for students with that dominant function. Suggest a couple of ways a teacher might meet the student's needs. Consider, too, how closely the student's preferences match your own. How does this influence your ability to come up with new strategies to use with the student?

Note, too, that *all* of the case studies are examples of when school goes wrong, not typical behavior. In each case, though, teachers assumed a behavioral problem or learning disability until they rethought behavior in terms of type.

1. Jonathon moved here a few years ago from another school and has made a few close friends. He still talks about how small the classes were and how they could call teachers by their first names. Teachers here often get frustrated because Jonathon doesn't always pay attention—he seems lost in his own thoughts. Often, he procrastinates before starting, asking questions about what to do only if a teacher seeks him out. He seldom has time to finish up and do his best work.

---

Jonathon seems to prefer Introversion. He chose a few close friends, likes small classes, and seems to daydream, lost in his own thoughts. One might also guess that he prefers Feeling, given that he liked having close relationships with the teachers at his old school. The procrastination indicates a preference for Perceiving, although he may just be disengaged, still longing for his old school.

From these clues, Jonathon may be an Introverted Feeler. Reviewing the information on page 37, the description of John matches the description of "What you might see if school isn't working." A teacher might try the following:

- Find out Jonathon's interests and hobbies and then try to connect these with a school assignment. Although most teachers attempt to get to know their students in this way, Jonathon may not have been very forthcoming. The teacher still might need to open the subject after being very observant—noting the books he chooses to read or talking with other teachers about whether he's shown interest in other assignments.

- Assign Jonathon to work with one of his friends in most group efforts. Many Feeling students say, "My friends won't make fun of me."
- Smile, especially if the teacher prefers Thinking. Feeling students are very sensitive to how others perceive them.
- Make sure that Jonathon has plenty of reflective time before he needs to respond to questions or participate in discussions. Some Introverts need 5–10 seconds to form an answer; teachers often rephrase or give more information after just 2–3 seconds.

2. Tasha pays more attention to her friends than her schoolwork and often talks when she should be listening. She seems genuinely contrite when teachers correct her, but she can't seem to sit quietly and do her work. She does a bit better with writing assignments than with math. Teachers worry that she isn't taking school seriously enough, but they can't seem to move her away from friends because she is friends with everyone. When working with a group on presentations or other assignments, she often comes up with really good ideas that the group willingly adopts.

Tasha is most likely an Extravert, given the number of friends that she has. Also, she works well in groups, indicating that she thinks out loud. She may also prefer Feeling; she puts friendships first and seems to want to please the teacher. The description doesn't give much information regarding Judging or Perceiving, but because she doesn't seem to "sit quietly and do her work," she may prefer Perceiving. She doesn't seem to be looking for extra directions to get started, and enjoys the creative process of writing more than math, so one might assume Extraverted Intuition. Looking at page 32, a teacher might try the following:

- Examine how many opportunities Tasha has for creative work. Is she socializing because she is bored?
- Consider how Tasha might take on a leadership role, perhaps tutoring a younger student or serving as a mentor to students new to the building.
- Provide more opportunities for Tasha to work with one friend, rather than asking her to work alone.
- Help Tasha set goals for completing work. What will she accomplish during class? For big projects, what steps will she complete each day? Help her take responsibility for her own learning.

3. Ramesh is conscientious and hard working, taking assignments seriously. He's quiet and rather remote, seldom asking questions in class. When he doesn't understand something, he seems to concentrate on unimportant details, like numbering problems correctly, instead of asking for help. At times his work is totally off-target, even though he completes his assignments. Teachers are worried because so much of his work is unacceptable.

Ramesh seems to be Introverted, given his quiet and remote demeanor. His attention to detail indicates Sensing. Although many Sensing students will ask questions rather than proceed incorrectly, Ramesh seems to believe that he could figure it out if he worked harder. Sensing students can assume that the fault lies with them. "If I'd listened better, I'd know what to do." Given that he completes work on time, Judging is a good conjecture. He seems to be an Introverted Sensing type. Looking at the information on page 31, a teacher might try the following:

- Ask specific questions to ensure that Ramesh understands instructions.
- Provide more examples of acceptable work. Sensing students often need examples to know that they are on the right track.
- Use the red card/green card technique described on page 79 with all students, having them turn red side up when they've finished the first part of an assignment. That way, the teacher could check whether Ramesh is on track.
- Check the clarity of instructions, especially if the teacher is an Intuitive.

4. Teachers find it hard to like Ella. She asks questions that seem to challenge them on their teaching methods or the assignments themselves. Sometimes she does excellent work, but seems to shut down when the assignment is a bit harder than usual. Some teachers think she is lazy. In group work, she tends to get bossy. She also gets upset when assignments are changed or deadlines are altered.

Ella's questioning, challenging style indicates a preference for Thinking. Thinking students are also wary of assignments where they might not be as competent. The "bossiness" is often seen in younger Extraverted Thinking students who are simply expressing objective opinions and don't realize how frankness might affect their peers. Her discomfort with altered deadlines or directions suggests that she prefers Judging— she had planned for the original arrangements. This would make Ella an Extraverted Thinker. Looking at the information on page 34, a teacher might try the following:

- Find a leadership role for Ella. Extraverted Thinkers thrive on being in charge, whether it's organizing the classroom library, running errands, or taking care of recycling.
- Pose struggles as problems to be solved. If Ella offends other students, wait until things have calmed down and then ask, "What's your plan? How will you keep it from happening again?"
- Make sure that Ella can practice new skills or learning with a sense of safety. Some students laugh easily at their own mistakes; Extraverted Thinkers do not! Provide logical reasons for trying, be specific about strengths and skills they possess that will help them succeed, and don't give fuzzy praise.
- If Ella questions an assignment, talk with her about it in private. Ask her not to challenge you in front of the class, but let her know that you will take her critique into consideration—at least for the next time—if she writes it down and supports her reasons.

## USING TYPE TO DISCOVER NEW STRATEGIES FOR HELPING STRUGGLING STUDENTS

Think of a few students that are struggling in your classroom, either academically or behaviorally. To avoid using type as a label, or inferring limits on what a child can do, focus on finding strategies that will help the child perform better academically. "What will help this child learn? How can I help this child engage in school?"

- Use the "Behavior Clues" (pages 25–26) to form a hypothesis about their personality preferences. Remember that you see them only in the classroom. There are many other aspects to their lives, so your hypothesis may not be correct. Still, understanding one or more preferences may lend new understandings.
- Read the information for their dominant function (pages 30–37). By comparing these pages, you might also be able to improve your hypothesis about their preferences.
- Use the information about their dominant function to come up with new strategies for helping them succeed in school.
- Wherever possible, involve the student in choosing which strategies to try. For example, a teacher might say to Jonathon, "For this project, do you want to work in a group with three other students or with your friend? If just the two of you work together, there will be more work for each of you."
- Look for new ways to motivate the student. In general, the following considerations work to motivate students with different preferences:
  - Sensing—experiences that are physically real, useful, and practical
  - Intuition—experiences that hold fascinating possibilities, engage the imagination, or allow for independent exploration
  - Thinking—experiences that allow for control and competency, logical orderliness, things making sense
  - Feeling—experiences that build harmonious relationships in one's life or offer chances to help others
- As you try new strategies, evaluate the results. Do they affirm your hypothesis as to the child's preferences?

Remember:

- Each person, including a child, has the right to determine his or her own "best fit" type. Your hypotheses are conjectures that a child can reject if he or she learns more about type.
- Working through this process collaboratively with other teachers who know the child can help you avoid misinterpreting the actions or styles of children who hold preferences opposite to your own.

## CONCLUSION

The goal of using type is to look at the *whole* child: learning style, energy needs, relational needs, motivations, and so on. Type is a framework for this multidimensional approach. It will not solve all problems, but can help teachers view children in new ways and therefore identify new strategies that their own educational strengths and beliefs might not unearth.

# 4

# Type as a Framework for Differentiation

---

*Before you read on . . .*

Using two different highlighters, mark on the Chart 4.1 (page 43) the statements about assignments that you *easily* incorporate into your classrooms and the ones that are *difficult* for you. Then think about the following:

- Why some of them are hard
- Fears you have about adopting some of them in your classroom
- Students you think would be helped if you adopted new ones and why
- Which ones you hope to become more skilled at

## LEARNING STYLES AND DIFFERENTIATION

Most teachers who complete the above exercise agree that they *easily* incorporate the statements from two of the quadrants, perhaps even three, but that the fourth calls to mind some areas that they've had little success with or that don't fit with how they want to run their classrooms. Almost always, it's the one opposite to their own learning style.

In this chapter, we will examine using the learning styles model for planning lessons, based on the *quadrants* of the type table. The statements in Chart 4.1 are grouped by the quadrants. Using the quadrants to differentiate helps us make sure of the following:

- All students have the *energy* they need for learning.
  - With too much quiet or inactivity, the Extraverted students start using all their energy to sit still. They're out of energy for learning.
  - With too much noise or movement, the Introverted students start feeling drained and lose their concentration.
- All students have the *information* they need for learning.
  - Sensing students' academic confidence increases through beginning with the details or step-by-step processes, then working toward the big picture.
  - Intuitive students' academic confidence increases when they begin with the big picture, work with their hunches, and then gather supporting details.

**Chart 4.1**    The Four Learning Styles

| **Introversion and Sensing:**<br>*Let me know what to do* | **Introversion and Intuition:**<br>*Let me follow my own lead* |
|---|---|
| • Set clear expectations and goals | • Let me delve deep into things that interest me |
| • Show me examples | • Avoid repetition and routine |
| • Provide the steps in writing | • Let me figure out for myself how to do things |
| • Answer my questions as I have them | • Give me choices |
| • Give me time to think | • Listen to my ideas |
| • Let me work with and memorize facts | • Let me learn independently |
| • Avoid too many surprises | • Let me start with my imagination |
| • Build on what I know | • Help me bring what I envision into reality |
| • Let me know along the way if I'm doing things right | • Give free rein to my creativity and curiosity |
| • Connect content with past efforts and experiences | • Provide references for me to build my own knowledge base |
| **Extraversion and Sensing:**<br>*Let me do something* | **Extraversion and Intuition:**<br>*Let me lead as I learn* |
| • Start with hands-on activities | • Start with the big picture, not the details |
| • Give me steps to follow | • Let me dream big without penalties |
| • Build on what I already know | • Let me find a new way to do it |
| • Tell me why I'm learning something | • Let me experiment |
| • Give me chances to talk, move, and work in groups | • Give me choices |
| • Set a realistic deadline | • Keep changing what we do |
| • Give me examples | • Let me teach or tell someone what I've learned |
| • Provide clear expectations | • Let me be in charge of something |
| • Go light on theory | • Let me talk or work in groups |
| • Let me apply it immediately. | • Let me come up with my own ideas |

SOURCE: Adapted from "I am likely to do my best work when . . . ," chart, pages 54–55, *People Types and Tiger Stripes, 3rd Ed.*, 1993, by Gordon D. Lawrence. Used with permission of the Center for Applications of Psychological Type, Inc.

The other preference pairs are important. Thinking and Feeling are essential to providing student feedback, forming relationships, and setting classroom ground rules. Judging and Perceiving play roles in classroom pacing and work completion. But, this basic four-quadrant framework provides a manageable and effective starting place. Chart 4.2 compares this model with other differentiation methods.

Why *isn't* this model overwhelming when teachers start using it? Because you can begin with three basic steps:

1. Start with your own style. Your strengths as a teacher flow from your personality and create the core of who you are as a teacher.

2. Adjust to meet the needs of your opposite. Think about it in type terms. If I as an INFJ adjust my lesson for ESTPs, I just met the needs of all eight personality preferences.

3. Remind yourself that you do not need to meet the needs of *all* students *all the time*. You can't; you'd burn out. Further, students need to learn in different ways to master different content and skills.

You can start differentiating with type, basing lessons on the examples provided in these pages, even as you're learning about the model.

Before we begin, there are two overarching principles to remember:

---

- Students do not benefit academically by being constantly matched with teachers of their own style, nor from learning only in their own style. Some students, though, may be more comfortable in classrooms of teachers with styles similar to their own.
- Students also do not benefit by being grouped exclusively with students who share their learning style, although this may be helpful for certain tasks and for short periods (Hammer, 1996).

---

## HOW TO DIFFERENTIATE WITHOUT BEING OVERWHELMED

*Not every part of every lesson—or even every unit—needs to be differentiated.* Remember, and remind students, that sometimes we learn the most when we are outside of our own learning style because it isn't so routine—we often pay more attention. Trying new activities can be fun. And sometimes there's a special feeling of triumph when we succeed at something we know is difficult for us.

*In other words, teachers do not need to meet the needs of every student at every moment. In fact, certain content is best delivered in certain styles.* Consider three examples: Students perfect lab techniques by doing lab work (Extraversion and Sensing), not by reading procedures. To develop reading skills (Introversion and Intuition), students need to read text to themselves, not be read to. Math becomes easier when students commit certain facts to memory (Introversion and Sensing). All of these appeal more to one learning style than the others, but all students need to be able to adjust—to learn in different ways—when the content requires it.

**Chart 4.2** Differentiation Models

| Source | Differentiation for: | Key concepts | Planning model |
|---|---|---|---|
| Gregory & Chapman (2002) | Learning styles (choice of several models) Multiple intelligences Personal interests | Assessment for student readiness, progress, and mastery Use multiple instructional strategies | **B**uilding safe environments **R**ecognizing and honoring diversity **A**ssessment **I**nstructional strategies **N**umerous curriculum approaches |
| Heacox (2002) | Ability, using Bloom's Taxonomy Multiple intelligences | Flexible grouping Tiered assignments Choices | Matrix using Bloom's Taxonomy and Multiple Intelligences |
| McCarthy & McCarthy (2006) | Learning styles | Creating lessons that move students through each stage of the 4MAT® cycle | Eight-step lessons: Connect, Attend, Imagine, Inform, Practice, Extend, Refine, Perform |
| Smutny & Fremd (2004) | Abilities Cultural traditions and strengths Learning preferences Special challenges | Considering: Child Content Process Product | Setting goals for each student, designing instruction to meet their needs, identifying evidence of success, and planning assessment strategies |
| Sprenger (2003) | Sensory pathways, Bloom's Taxonomy | Differentiated instructional strategies for students with strong visual, auditory, and kinesthetic memory | Planning for all three pathways, using activities at all levels of Bloom's Taxonomy for each pathway |
| Tomlinson (1999) | Readiness Interest Learning profile | Modify content, process or product based on readiness, interest, and/or learning profile | Differentiate What (content, process, product, learning environment) Differentiate How (instructional strategies for student readiness, interest or learning profile) Differentiate Why (student access, motivation or efficiency for learning) |
| Personality type | Personality type preferences as an organizing theory for numerous learning styles, interests, multicultural considerations, classroom management, study habits, thinking and rigor | Students have natural psychological preferences for how they are energized, take in information, make decisions, and approach life | Plan for four learning styles: Extraversion and Sensing, Introversion and Sensing, Extraversion and Intuition, Introversion and Intuition |

If you're teaching a skill (report writing, research, giving speeches, etc.), consider whether students can choose content. If you're teaching new content, can you give students choices in how they show what they've learned?

If content fits one learning style best, are there ways to adjust activities to keep all students motivated?

How well was the previous lesson differentiated? How can you ensure that the same students aren't at a disadvantage again?

The answers to these questions determine which of the following basic differentiation strategies you might use:

- Plan a lesson or unit that honors all four styles.
- Develop learning stations based on the quadrants. Examples in this chapter and in Chapter 5 will show a variety of ways to use stations other than creating ability-based activities. Sometimes, students spend time at every station, with each station covering a different concept. At other times, students might choose among a greater number of stations.
- Vary activities during the lesson period or over the course of a unit—a hands-on problem, a short reading, a demonstration or step-by-step explanation, a group project, etc.
- Give choices. This strategy is effective in differentiating for interests, learning styles, ability, and culture, provided the choices are real. Often, teachers give choices that favor their own learning style.

Let's look at one lesson, following the thoughts of a teacher named Kay as she created it. Here is the lesson:

---

### Kay's Differentiated Lesson

**Goal**: Good group discussions about how things are the same and different now as in Roman times.

**Lesson Summary**: Students will examine models of artifacts of ancient Rome and, as a group, hypothesize what they might have been used for.

IN activities (*Kay's style*): **Brainstorm** uses for different artifacts. Write out their **speculation**, with justification. **Compare** it to modern tools.

ES activities (*Kay's opposite*): Make **hands-on** artifacts. Students can **touch, examine,** and **discuss** them.

IS activities: Students **complete** a graphic organizer to help them **identify** the object. They **answer** specific questions such as "How might it have been used in a kitchen? Bedroom? Outside? How might a child have used it? An adult?"

EN activities: Groups **discuss and debate** the most probable use for the object, **synthesizing** ideas. They **collaborate,** choosing one group answer, and then **evaluate** their answers by comparing them to other groups.

---

## Step 1: Examining Lesson Content and Goals

Kay wanted students to (a) analyze how their lives were the same and different as those of people who lived in Rome and (b) have good group discussions. This activity would be new to Kay's students, 20 percent of whom were English language learners or received special education services, so she needed to provide scaffolding.

Tomlinson (1999) points out how clear goals are essential to differentiation.

A fuzzy sense of the essentials results in fuzzy activities, which, in turn, results in fuzzy student understanding . . . This kind of situation also works against differentiated instruction. With many differentiated lessons, all students need to understand the same essential principles and even use the same key skills. Yet because of variance in student readiness, interest, or learning profile, children must "come at" the ideas and use the skills in different ways. If a teacher isn't clear about what all students should understand and be able to do when the learning experience ends, he or she lacks the vital organizer around which to develop a powerful lesson. (p. 37)

## Step Two: Start as Usual

Although Kay could have delivered the content for discussion through movies, lecture, Web searches, or reading, her first inclination was to have students evaluate "mystery artifacts."

Chart 4.3 is a blackline master for planning lessons. It lists brainstorming, speculating, and comparing as words that motivate Introverted Intuitives. This chart quickly allowed Kay to identify that her idea fit her own learning style—which is fine. The best place to start planning is with what you do best.

Often, teachers keep the blackline master taped on their desk so they can substitute "Motivating Words" to quickly differentiate simple assignments. Think about this concept. Would you rather

- Create or build?
- Identify or discover?
- Reflect or figure out?
- List or generate?

Note how Kay expanded the activity to include motivating words from each quadrant.

In examining the chart, Kay saw that the discussions and debates would engage students who preferred Extraversion and Intuition. However, without some scaffolding and structure, these students could easily dominate the discussion. Therefore, she looked at the quadrant opposite her own to begin differentiating.

## Step 3: Adjust for Your Opposite

Note that when Kay plans for her own style (IN), then adjusts for her opposite (ES), she reaches all four styles—Introversion and Extraversion, Sensing and Intuition. Your own style already reaches one of the preferences for the students whose learning styles are adjacent to you in the chart. Adding some elements for your opposite, then, is the crucial step.

**Chart 4.3**   Lesson Planning Grid

| **Introversion and Sensing** | **Introversion and Intuition** |
|---|---|
| *Motivating Activities*<br>• Labs<br>• Demonstrations<br>• Read and think<br>• Time lines<br>• Hands-on manipulatives<br>• Programmed learning<br>• Computer-assisted learning<br>• Direct instruction<br>• Clear writing assignments | *Motivating Activities*<br>• Reading<br>• Research<br>• Imaginative or open-ended writing assignments<br>• Self-paced tutorials<br>• Brain twisters<br>• Independent study<br>• Independent projects |
| *Motivating Words:* Read, identify, list, label, name, notice, observe, apply, analyze, graph, examine, work, prepare, do, organize, complete, answer, listen | *Motivating Words:* Read, think, consider, design, evaluate, clarify, speculate, dream, envision, paraphrase, brainstorm, create, elaborate, illustrate, write, reflect, chew on, make connections, compare, contrast, compose |
| **Extraversion and Sensing** | **Extraversion and Intuition** |
| *Motivating Activities*<br>• Videos<br>• Group projects<br>• Contests<br>• Games<br>• Skits<br>• Songs<br>• Physical activities<br>• Class reports<br>• Hands-on manipulatives | *Motivating Activities*<br>• Problem-solving<br>• Improvisations, drama, role play<br>• Discussions and debates<br>• Experimenting<br>• Group projects<br>• Work with ideas<br>• Field trips<br>• Self-instruction<br>• Developing models |
| *Motivating Words:* Build, show, assemble, tell, discover, make, perform, demonstrate, figure out, touch, design, suggest, solve, choose, construct, examine, explore, discuss | *Motivating Words:* Create, discover, pretend, design, develop, discuss, collaborate, find a new . . . , generate, visualize, evaluate, synthesize, problem-solve, experiment, invent, hypothesize |

However, the initial lesson lacked appeal for Sensing types, so she added the idea of hands-on models of the artifacts.

Kay realized that many Sensing students and English language learners would feel more comfortable speculating about the objects if they had some examples and specific procedures to use. She structured a graphic organizer for individual work, the realm of Introversion and Sensing. Kay wanted to have students brainstorm uses for the objects individually before working in groups, so she adjusted for all Introverted students. The organizer also provided Extraverts with a place to hold their thoughts as they waited for the group discussion to begin.

In this lesson, all students engaged in every learning style within a short period of time. The resulting discussions were so on task and at such a high level of thinking that Kay extended the unit by a day to allow more time for the discussions. She said,

> Without using the planning template, I may have thought to make the hands-on artifacts, but I doubt I would have structured the "thinking worksheet" that helped the students brainstorm independently. With that worksheet, *every* student came up with ideas rather than waiting for the "smart" kids to tell them the answers. And, the discussions were rich. The added structure prompted their thinking.

In other words, by differentiating for the four learning styles, this teacher also provided scaffolding for students at different ability levels. The individual time also let students from different cultures draw on their own experiences.

Let's look at another example, for a lesson in which the content was best learned through engaging specific learning styles.

## DIFFERENTIATING A LESSON, MATCHING CONTENT, GOALS, AND LEARNING STYLES

### Step 1: Examining Lesson Content and Goals

Several teachers I worked with were struggling to structure (without overstructuring) experiments designed to teach theoretical concepts. One problem asked students to drop a ball from different heights, investigating the relationship between the "drop" height and how high the ball bounced. The goal was to introduce linear algebraic relationships, but students executed the experiment so poorly that their graphs often failed to show the linear pattern that would lead them to the right mathematical thinking.

Because it is a **hands-on** experiment, done with **physical activities** in **groups,** the overall lesson meets the needs of Extraversion and Sensing. However, for students to grasp the underlying math concepts, both accurate procedures and individual processing time are needed, more the realm of Introversion and Sensing.

### Step 2: Start as Usual

I worked with Donna, whose preferences were for Introversion and Sensing, to structure the experiment. Her first inclination was to provide detailed instructions for conducting the experiment—her own learning style.

## Step 3: Adjust for Your Opposite

As Donna looked at the activities for the style opposite to hers, Extraversion and Intuition, she decided to let the students try to **problem-solve,** instead of providing the procedures herself.

Here is her lesson plan, which requires the use of all learning styles by all students at some point in the lesson. Her two goals were helping students obtain good results and ensuring that all students engaged in the process. The bold words are "Motivating Words" from Chart 4.3 (page 48) for the learning style named for each step.

1. **(EN)** Group **discussion** of experiment
   - All-class: **Visualize** measurement problems, **problem-solve** ideas to avoid them

2. **(IN)** Independent speculation
   - **Individually,** make **predictions** about the patterns you might see as you drop the ball from different heights. Will those patterns change if you use a super-ball, a kickball, or a baseball?

3. **(EN)** Small groups
   - **Collaborate** and determine what each group member will do

4. **(IS)** Setting up accurate measurement procedures (variables brainstormed in EN activity)
   - **Practice** taking an accurate measurement by **observing** as the ball is dropped from the same height several times
   - **Identify** the various heights from which the ball will be dropped
   - Prepare a table for **listing** the measurement data

5. **(ES)** Use of hands-on manipulatives
   - Bounce the ball from several different heights

6. **(IS)** Data stage
   - **Graph** your results
   - **Analyze** your results. Do the data show any patterns?

7. **(EN)** Data comparison
   - **Compare** results with another group
   - **Evaluate** what variables might have produced different results

8. **(IN)** Extensions
   - Assign problems that ask students to make other **predictions** about bouncing balls

Note that in this example, different parts of the experiment called on different learning styles if students were to produce satisfactory results.

# DIFFERENTIATION TO HELP STUDENTS BECOME COMFORTABLE WITH EACH LEARNING STYLE

This poetry lesson was created for a middle-school team to provide a common experience for collaborative discussions. In this lesson, every student participated in four separate activities, each one of which met the needs of a different learning style. Why do a lesson this way?

- Because some content is best delivered through a specific learning style, *all* students need to be able to use all four styles well.
- Concrete experiences with each of the learning styles helps students recognize them. They might then advocate for their own needs or consciously draw on skills they've developed in using the other styles.
- These lessons help students learn that not every classmate enjoys the same activities. And, using different styles is fair if the needs of all students are to be met.

All students completed the four activities, designed as stations, each of which taught a different aspect of poetry. The teachers worked with me to finalize the stations, thinking through our own preferences to try and make each station as attractive to all students as possible. We also developed instructions to help the students work as independently as possible.

As you read through the lesson, think about which station you would enjoy the most. Which are like the majority of activities in your classroom? What concerns would you have about teaching any of the stations?

## Station-Based Poetry Unit

**Lesson Goals:**

To introduce different forms of poetry
To let the students use different learning styles
To make poetry fun!

| Introversion and Sensing | Introversion and Intuition |
|---|---|
| **Haiku**<br>Individual work<br><br>• **Analyze** sample poems silently<br>• **Write** own poem following same rules<br>• Paint with watercolor to illustrate poem | **"Choice" station**<br>Individual work<br><br>**Possible activity** *choices*<br>• **Write** and **illustrate** a poem<br>• **Read** various poems<br>• **Design** own project<br>• **Reflect** on and memorize a poem<br>• **Evaluate and consider** a poem's meaning, using a worksheet<br><br>Note that the last choice was a more structured activity, yet still a choice, for Sensing students who wanted more structure. |

*(Continued)*

(Continued)

| Extraversion and Sensing | Extraversion and Intuition |
|---|---|
| **Story poems**<br>Group work | **Parodies**<br>Group work |
| • Read poem aloud<br>• **Discuss** rhythm scheme, agree on cadence and clapping pattern<br>• Plan how to **perform** it for the class (one individual or as a group) | • Read parody examples aloud<br>• **Discuss** the examples for patterns and ideas<br>• **Collaborate** on writing another poem using the same patterns<br>• **Perform** the new poem for the class |

Compare how teachers with different preferences react to the poetry stations. Their comments reflect their prejudices even though they knew that these were designed as *pure* examples of each style. Note, though, that their comments also reflect how easy it would be to tweak each station so that it would appeal to more learning styles:

| *Haiku* | |
|---|---|
| **Sensing teacher:** | **Intuitive teacher:** |
| I like this kind of assignment because I can follow the steps and end up with a successful poem. | When too much information is provided, does imagination suffer? What if a student wanted to write a Haiku-like poem about death? |

| *Story poem performance* | |
|---|---|
| **Introverted teacher:** | **Extraverted teacher:** |
| This is my worst nightmare, performing with a group! Too much togetherness! | This gives opportunity for those kids that need to be heard. Sounds like fun! Easy, with a variety of activities. |

Because of our strong reactions to learning activities that are out of our own styles, teachers often benefit by collaborating with teachers with other styles to practice designing activities that both are engaging *and* meet the needs of each style.

## DIFFERENTIATION TO PROVIDE GENUINE CHOICES

Another strategy, especially for reports or unit projects, is to allow students to select from a variety of choices, with several given for each learning style. Note that these also allow for differentiation in ability. The following choices were developed for a chess class taught as a middle-school elective. In this case, the teacher preferred Extraversion and Sensing. His goals were to have students learn the basic rules of chess, but also to have options for students who were intermediate or advanced players.

**TRY THIS!**

Evaluate an assignment in which you gave choices. Did your choices cover every learning style?

This teacher knew that the first few activities he came up with all met his own style, so he used Chart 4.3 (page 48) to design at least two choices for each of the quadrants, as shown below:

**Chart 4.4**    Chess Class Choice Assignments

All students will complete *at least one* of the following projects. You are expected to show quality work for each project you select. If you want to get an "A," complete three projects. For a "B," complete two projects. For a "C," complete one project.

| Introversion and Sensing | Introversion and Intuition |
|---|---|
| **Book Report.** Select a book on chess. Write a three-paragraph report: an introduction, a main topic paragraph with supporting information, and a conclusion. Topics you might cover include: Who would benefit from reading the book? What you learned. What sections of the book you liked best and why? What didn't you like about the book? Who might wish to read the book? | **Make a Game.** Design a game that would help someone learn the rules for chess or learn new strategies. It can be a card game, a game that uses chess pieces, or something of your own design. Remember to give it a name. Test it by playing it with three others to make sure the rules work. Their signatures are required. |
| **Make a Quick Reference Sheet.** Design a reference sheet (1 page) that a chess player could use as a quick reference guide (rules, strategies, etc.). Work to create a good layout of the information. | **Web Site Review.** Choose two Web sites that give information about chess. Write a review of each site. For each one:<br><br>• Name and describe what's on the site: the facts about it<br>• Tell about your favorite feature on the site.<br>• Critique the site: What is good/bad about it? What level of player might like it most—beginner, intermediate, or advanced—and why? |
| **Extraversion and Sensing** | **Extraversion and Intuition** |
| **Learn to play *two* other chess games.** Pick two of the following games. Turn in a report that identifies: (1) what games were played, (2) the names of the players, (3) the date the games were played, and (4) who won/lost. Choose two:<br><br>• Queen vs. Pawns<br>• Pawns vs. Pawns<br>• Take Me<br>• Double Chess | **Mentor a Classmate.** Spend two class periods mentoring another student. Make arrangements with your teacher before starting. Record on a piece of paper the top three things the student most wants to learn. Be specific; examples include good opening moves, basic rules, etc. Then, at the end of the two mentoring sessions, submit a written report summarizing your activities and what your classmate learned. Both students must sign the report. |
| **Game Notation.** Record all the moves for two different games—your moves and your opponent's moves. You can notate your own games or someone else's games. Make sure your notation sheet is signed by all players and dated. | **Teach Chess to Someone at Home.** Teach a brother, sister, parent, or anyone else at home how to play chess. (Then you'll always have an an opponent available.) Document the following information in your report:<br><br>• Record how many hours you spent doing this (2 is the minimum).<br>• List three things that you did that most helped the person learn the rules.<br><br>Have a parent/guardian sign it to verify your effort. |

Another teacher wanted some quick ideas for helping students learn the names of states. Her preferences were for Introversion and Sensing, and she had been relying on worksheets and spelling drills. Using the planning grid, she devised the following alternatives to appeal to the different quadrants.

> **TRY THIS!**
>
> Pull out a lesson that you like but you think could be modified to engage more students. Sit down with other teachers and brainstorm ideas for each other's lessons.

When teachers first begin using this differentiation process, I emphasize these first steps: Determine how much differentiation is needed, start with your own style, and adjust for your opposite. They report a marked increase in student engagement and work quality. Once they feel confident in planning lessons that meet the needs of the quadrants, we add one more step—examining Thinking and Feeling needs.

**Chart 4.5**    50 Great States

As we've learned about each region of the United States, you've spent some time studying the states. Probably, you can name almost half of them by now if given a blank map! To learn the others, choose from the following activities. Which ones will help you learn best? Which ones sound most fun to you? You can repeat an activity more than once. Your goal: be ready for the practice test on _____.

| **Introversion and Sensing** | **Introversion and Intuition** |
|---|---|
| Name-the-state worksheet | Write stories or poems about the states |
| Add-a-state cut-out map, tracing states | Invent a mnemonic—a gimmick to remember states |
| Practice tests | Take a "beat-the-clock" test, competing with yourself |
| **Extraversion and Sensing** | **Extraversion and Intuition** |
| Learn a song that has the names of the 50 states | Create a game that will help you and others learn the states |
| To your state map, add real-life connections (trips, events, historical figures) | Play name-the-state games and contests |
| Use flash cards with a friend, testing each other | Practice naming the states with one or two of your classmates |

## ONE LAST STEP: USING THINKING AND FEELING TO MOTIVATE ALL STUDENTS

To finalize their lessons, in all of the above examples, the teachers completed the extra step of considering the needs of Thinking and Feeling students.

For her "Roman archaeological artifacts" unit, Kay wanted students to cooperate in group discussions. Kay felt that because the group debate process emphasized cooperation, both Thinking and Feeling students would enjoy the lesson. Further, the Thinking students would enjoy the problem-solving aspects, whereas the Feeling students would be comfortable because the artifacts had been used by real people and the lesson emphasized understanding their everyday lives.

Here are some basic rules for meeting the needs of Thinking and Feeling students:

| *Thinking students flourish when:* | *Feeling students flourish when:* |
| --- | --- |
| ☐ They're in charge. The teacher allows to them debate, ask "Why?", and occasionally have the last word. | ☐ They know a teacher likes them. *If they experience criticism without being sure they're liked, they may shut down.* |
| ☐ They can demonstrate competency. They thrive on competition and performance goals. *If they aren't sure they can succeed, they may avoid trying.* | ☐ The teacher values their work. Feeling types often need praise along the way as they work on assignments so they know they're headed in the right direction and doing good work. |
| ☐ The subject or assignment is logical, objective. Thinking students may not take kindly to "mushy" stories or descriptive writing. They prefer logical, factual reading and writing. | ☐ The subject is about people or can be applied to helping others. The teacher may need to add either a people-oriented hook to science or mathematics material *or* incorporate cooperative learning into subjects requiring logic to help Feeling students stay motivated. |
| ☐ The teacher is fair. Although fairness is an important concept for all children, Thinkers may discount a teacher's expertise if he or she doesn't seem to uniformly enforce stated rules or seems to play favorites. | ☐ Atmospheres are harmonious. Whether put-downs come from the teacher or students, or are directed at the Feeling student or others in the classroom, disharmony can take their attention and energy away from academics. |

Motivating and building relationships with Thinking and Feeling students happens along very different pathways. Sometimes the pathways are directly contradictory. Think of how some educational circles recommend avoiding competition for fear of hurting children's self-esteem. A total lack of competition harms many Thinking students by taking away a key motivation. Or, consider how unmotivated some Feeling students are by computerized instruction, where teacher-student contact is minimized.

## CONCLUSION

So, what happens if we *don't* meet the needs of every learner? If we don't teach to every style? Let's peruse the quadrants one more time, reviewing how they learn, what they can't stand, and how they might react to not having their needs met:

**Chart 4.6**     Meeting the Needs of Each Quadrant

| Introversion and Sensing | Introversion and Intuition |
|---|---|
| Prefer structured, safe, predictable learning<br><br>• Organized directions and examples<br>• Requires details and accuracy<br>• Time to think things through<br><br>**Pet Peeve: Lack of clarity on assignment goals or procedures**<br><br>*When school goes wrong:* They retreat into their own worlds and act apathetic because they lack the confidence that they can succeed. Or, they will refer to themselves as stupid. | Prefer creativity, depth in topics of interest<br><br>• Independent study<br>• Imaginative, creative<br>• Time for reflection and inspiration<br><br>**Pet Peeve: Lack of choice or room to roam within an assignment; tasks with one right answer**<br><br>*When school goes wrong:* They may<br><br>• Complete work that has nothing to do with directions<br>• Finish one or two fantastic projects and fail others<br>• Rush through rote work or not complete it, earning the label, "Not working up to potential . . ." |
| Extraversion and Sensing | Extraversion and Intuition |
| Prefer practical, real-life, hands-on learning<br><br>• Thinking out loud with others<br>• Working with concrete things<br>• Clear steps to work toward clear goals<br><br>**Pet Peeve: Lack of doing, too much sitting still to listen or complete seatwork**<br><br>*When school goes wrong:* Off-task, silly behavior or complaints such as, "Why do we have to learn this?" | Prefer ever-changing activities, being in charge<br><br>• Group work in solving problems<br>• Big picture efforts, not details<br>• Create new ways of doing things<br><br>**Pet Peeve: Sitting still and having to do what they're told**<br><br>*When school goes wrong:* Rebellion, perhaps leading others off task as well |

Study the information for the quadrant opposite your own. Is it easy for you to incorporate their preferred activities? Have you seen students act in the ways described? *Motivating* students through activities that naturally appeal to them is a big first step in differentiation, perhaps even more important than matching their ability level. Why? Because if students are interested, they tend to work a bit above their ability. One can nudge them toward more rigorous tasks. If they aren't interested, they may not bother completing a task that is a perfect match for their ability. Engagement is key to differentiation, whether for ability or interests or culture or learning styles or any other criteria.

# 5

# Key Differentiation Strategies

**Before you read on . . .**

How do you use Bloom's Taxonomy in lesson planning, differentiation, and assessment?

The following chart lists question cues from Bloom's Taxonomy and the motivating tasks or words for each of the learning styles:

IS: Introversion and Sensing
IN: Introversion and Intuition
ES: Extraversion and Sensing
EN: Extraversion and Intuition

Look at the pattern. Frequently, assignments designed for students working on basic skills address only the Sensing preference for taking in information, not the Intuitive style. This hurts both Sensing and Intuitive learners.

**Chart 5.1**    Learning Styles and Bloom's Taxonomy

| Bloom's level of abstraction of questions | Question cues |
|---|---|
| **Knowledge (first level)** | list (IS), define (IS), tell (ES), describe (ES, IS), label (IS), examine (IS, ES), tabulate (IS), quote (ES, IS), name (IS) |
| **Synthesis (sixth level)** | create (EN, IN), design (EN, IN), invent (IN), compose (EN, IN), generalize (EN, IN), hypothesize (EN), synthesize (EN), develop (EN) |

SOURCE: Bloom (1984).

- Intuitive learners are quickly bored because they can't connect the facts with a purpose. Murphy (1992) explains, "The problem is that most intuitives gather information to support an intuitive idea. Gathering information without an end as a guide means they have no filter to know which information is relevant and which is not. This creates confusion" (p. 40).
- Sensing learners miss out on opportunities to move toward higher level thinking as assignment after assignment emphasizes knowledge or word recognition.

Remember, Sensing and Intuition are about the *information* students need to learn. We *do* need to pay attention to the needs of "high, middle, and low" students, but "low" Sensing and Intuitive students have very different informational needs—and tests that identify which skills students are missing don't reveal these differences. They may be missing the same skill but for different reasons.

Ability + Interest = Flow. The following techniques help *all* students engage in higher level thinking while engaging them at their present skill level by examining the task in terms of the information students need (through Sensing or Intuition) to be successful.

- What scaffolding can I provide to Sensing students so they can complete this task? Clear steps, examples, prompts, graphic organizers, prior knowledge, group practice?
- What scaffolding can I provide to Intuitive students so that they can complete the task? Important details or structure in a concise way so they'll pay attention? Chances for humor or variety to hold their interest? Ways to help them justify their Intuitive hunches and connections?

The following tools are designed to help students think no matter their level of basic skills by ensuring that they have the information they need, through Sensing or Intuition. They also help students develop basic skills as they grapple with interesting tasks.

## SCAFFOLDING TOOLS: SUPPORTING THINKING

Although many of these ideas will be familiar, many teachers *over*-scaffold, providing so much structure or information that students can fill in blanks without thinking. Balancing Sensing and Intuitive needs can help avoid this trap.

### "Universal" Graphic Organizers

"Useless" graphic organizers only exchange filling in bubbles for filling in worksheet blanks or taking notes in a linear format. Useful graphic organizers require students to think as they work to complete them; they are unearthing relationships, organizing their thinking, or brainstorming new ideas.

Hyerle (2004) uses the term "Thinking Maps" for his set of eight such tools that assist students in carrying out such tasks as comparing/contrasting, ordering events, looking at cause-effect relationships, and developing logical reasoning. His eight maps, with student examples, can be viewed at http://www.thinkingmaps.com. Once students understand a tool such as a flow map for sequencing and ordering, they might use it in science to identify the necessary steps in an experiment and in social studies for a timeline of historical events. Similarly, a universal organizer for comparing and contrasting might be used in math to sort out differences between rectangles and other polygons and in language arts as a prewriting tool for a comparative essay.

Universal organizers can also be three-dimensional, such as the "Mobile Outlines" technique for writing stories (p. 114). Other lesson plans and activities that reference universal organizers include Big Notes (p. 82) and prior knowledge stations (below).

## Prior Knowledge Stations

You'd like students to read a novel about the Civil War or ancient Rome or the Great Depression, but they don't know enough about John Brown or centurions or macroeconomics to get through the first chapter. What *doesn't* work is lecturing or interrupting the flow of reading frequently to explain terms and events.

Instead, try frontloading prior knowledge through a series of stations. Students engage in reading and writing as they draw information from pictures, primary sources, nonfiction texts, maps, Web sites, and other sources. They enjoy the autonomy. In one group of over a hundred sixth-grade students I worked with, 73 percent ranked the activity as an 8, 9, or 10 out of 10 as a way to learn; 30 percent gave it a perfect 10.

The activity allows for differentiation in several ways. Stations are designed with different learning styles in mind. Students thus complete both comfortable and "stretch" activities. Students choose whether to work alone or with a partner, meeting the needs of Extraverted and Introverted students.

As for ability, a high percentage of students tackle the stations with little teacher assistance, leaving the teacher free to help students who need more directions or help. Sometimes, students who have completed a station can help others get started on it. And, with the logistics hints provided below, you can easily direct struggling students to a station they will be able to complete independently until you have time to help them with one they are stuck on. This strategy also allows for what Heacox (2002) recommends for making tiered assignments less visible to students and fair to all, by ensuring that they

- Are different work, not simply more or less work
- Are equally active
- Are equally interesting and engaging
- Are fair in terms of work expectations
- Require the use of key concepts, skills, or ideas (p. 99).

*Logistics.* If you are using prior knowledge stations for the first time, be ready to invest a week of class time in helping the students work independently in this manner—yes, they may not naturally use their time wisely in the beginning! It's well worth the investment; students will be developing the exact skills they need to conduct library research. Here's how to move from chaos to student-centered control as quickly as possible:

- "Rate" the stations on the basis of how long you anticipate it will take students to complete them. Mark them with colors or stars rather than minutes, so that you'd have one-, two-, and three-star stations. This helps students manage their time since they can grab a "quick" station toward the end of class rather than quit working because they aren't sure they have time for another.

- Provide a "Stations Guide" to students, with one page for each station. Depending on the kinds of activities you select, the station pages might include all the directions students need *or* blank pages that the students label, one for each station. Because the activities are so varied, students soon catch on that this isn't a typical worksheet packet.
- Have students set goals for how many stations they should complete, both overall and each day. Include a goals sheet in their packet. Remember, goal-setting is a requirement for flow.
  - Students enjoy "choosing their grade," such as completing all 20 stations satisfactorily to receive an A, 18 stations for a B, and so on.
  - Have them set a goal each day for the number of stations they will complete. In the last five minutes of station time, ask them to reflect on why they met or didn't meet their goal and what they could do differently to improve their performance.
  - Post a "Completed Stations" chart at the front of the room. The chart lists student names down the side and the stations across the top. When students complete a station, they check it off on the chart. *Many* students report that they sped up as they saw how many stations others were completing (many others were already working quickly). Further, at a glance you can see how to help an idle student get busy, perhaps even selecting a station you believe would engage them.

- Use the stations as a reflection tool for students to discover more about how they learn. Build in time for reflection on at least one of the following. Note that these can be done with or without the language of type.
  - Learning styles: Inform students that the stations are differentiated for learning styles; they will like some more than others, but each activity is the best way to convey the information they need from that station. At the end of the unit, students can reflect on learning style patterns in the stations they enjoyed the most.
  - Extraversion and Introversion: Designate "alone" and "with a partner" stations. Have students journal on "When I work alone . . ." "When I work with a partner . . ." Many students grasp which way helps them be most productive.
  - Judging and Perceiving: Judging students often complain about setting goals for the stations because they would have worked at a steady pace anyway. Perceiving students often discover ways to keep themselves on track through this unit. Have them reflect on how they paced themselves and what they will do next time.

*Examples.* The following are brief descriptions of stations.

For a short story, "The Dog of Pompeii," here are summary descriptions of some of the stations:

- Label map of Pompeii for places mentioned in the story (Sensing).
- Read Pliny the Younger's letter describing the eruption of Mt. Vesuvius and respond to questions about his experience (Sensing).
- Write step-by-step directions for how to make casts of the bodies found in Pompeii (Sensing).
- Examine pictures of different artifacts and speculate what they might have been used for (Intuition).

- Graph information on various volcanic eruptions (Sensing).
- Read about archaeological excavations of Pompeii and write about what future archaeologists might learn about your house or school if it were "preserved" by ash and lava (Intuition).
- After examining pictures of the plaster casts of people buried in the ash, write a last letter from one of the people (Intuition).

For *The River between Us* by Richard Peck, a Civil War–era book filled with words unfamiliar to twenty-first-century students, all students were expected to complete the following stations:

- From pictures, learn about the various modes of transportation used in the book—buckboards, traps, etc. (Sensing).
- From pictures, learn about the various items of women's clothing mentioned in the book—bloomers, crinolines, etc. (Sensing).
- Make a flow map of Civil War events important to the story (Sensing).
- Read first-hand accounts of a soldier's life in the camps and write a fictional letter home (Intuition).
- Read a newspaper article on a steamboat explosion (Sensing).
- Review recipes of New Orleans food. Taste pralines (Sensing).
- Learn about Civil War army surgeons in a picture-rich nonfiction book and write a paragraph on what surprised you the most (Intuition).
- Create a map of places mentioned in the story (Sensing).
- Watch a clip from Ken Burns' documentary *The Civil War* on getting soldiers to engage in battle. Write a short speech a commanding officer might give (Intuition).

## Provide Full Examples

Although most teachers show examples of large projects to their students—science fairs, models, narrative stories, report binders, or display boards—students also benefit from examples for basic tasks such as answering questions, working math problems, or journaling. Why? Sensing students thrive on clear expectations, especially when they lack academic confidence. Here are some ideas.

*Journal entries.* The examples given on page 84 show how we modeled short journal entries for middle-school students to improve the quality of their writing.

*Brainstorming.* In another class, the students were going to brainstorm at least four other courses of action a character in a story could have taken (*perceiving* more ideas) and then rank the choices to *judge* which one was best. This particular group of students tended to be disruptive unless they were involved in very clear assignments such as copying information, but the day's work would be open-ended, with no right or wrong answers. To ensure that they knew what to do, I created a sample chart (Chart 5.4) using *Green Eggs and Ham* (Seuss). What else could Sam-I-Am have done to get his friend to eat the green eggs and ham besides chase him onto trains and boats, with mice and goats?

*Procedures.* Another student struggled to understand how to complete a step sheet, which is a detailed list of the steps needed to complete a project. Step sheets are explained on page 154. We brainstormed together the first few steps. He then used those as an example to come up with the remaining steps, checking with me every third step for reassurance that he was on track.

**Chart 5.2**   Using Judging *and* Perceiving in Decisions

| Possibilities | Cost | Time | Inconvenience | Distaste | Total |
|---|---|---|---|---|---|
| **Sam-I-Am could bribe him to try the green eggs and ham** | 4 | 1 | 1 | 3 | 9 |
| **Make his favorite foods if he'll try the eggs** | 3 | 3 | 3 | 1 | 10 |
| **Have him watch trusted friends taste the eggs** | 2 | 4 | 4 | 2 | 12 |
| **Offer to eat something he doesn't like** | 1 | 2 | 2 | 4 | 9 |

## Two-Way Organizers

Sensing types naturally start with facts and work with them to discover the big picture. Intuitive types start with the big picture, or a hunch they have, or an idea of what they hope to write about, and then need to find details to support it. Two-way organizers allow students to proceed in the way that works best for them.

One example would be "character sheets," shown in Chart 5.3, that students can use to prepare to write character analyses or to compare two characters.

## Layered Curriculum

Nunley (2006) defines Layered Curriculum as "A teaching model that divides the learning process into three layers based on the complexity of the student's thought process."

Layered Curriculum asks students at each layer to

C Layer: Gather information.

B Layer: Apply or manipulate that information.

A Layer: Critically evaluate an issue (p. 28).

To implement this model, provide students with choices for how they gather C-level information, apply that knowledge, and use it for critical evaluation. A 100-point assignment might look like this.

C Layer: Basic Understanding (65 points maximum). This section might include eight to ten activity choices such as listening to lectures, reading a textbook, answering worksheet questions, or researching basic concepts, with points for each activity based on its complexity.

**Chart 5.3**     Character Sheet

Which method suits you best? Start with the questions on the left side of the sheet OR start by writing out the conclusions you've drawn about the character.

| *What Do I Know About This Character* | *What Conclusions Can I Draw About This Character?* |
|---|---|
| What significant things does the character do in this story? Why? | |
| What does ___ care about? How do you know? | |
| What problems does this character face? Why? | |
| What is admirable about this character? Give examples. | |
| What does this character learn? What events or quotes from the story show this? | |
| **Now, what conclusions can you draw about this character? Organize your facts around themes.** | **Now, find evidence from the story that supports the conclusions you've drawn.** |

B Layer: Applying the information to previous learning (15 points). Students choose one from three or four choices. These might include an experiment, analyzing a real-life application of the principles, or using the information to write a story, design a game, or create an art project.

A Layer: Evaluation (20 points). These involve students using what they have learned to investigate problems with no right or wrong answers, such as current events or leadership decisions.

Nunley summarizes, "Now a letter grade earned in my class had some consistent meaning: A student who earned an A was one who could gather information, manipulate that information, and critically evaluate the topic with some level of proficiency and accountability" (p. 28).

Note how this differs from many examples of tiered assignments: *All* students are asked to perform each level of the assignment. Level C provides scaffolding so that all students have the information they need to go on to levels B and A, and meets the needs of Sensing students for certainty. Intuitive students, though, can preview Level A and understand the purposes for which they are gathering information. Further, *all* students can see from the point distribution that a C is possible on the assignment even if they might struggle with the Level A portion of the assignment.

## DIFFERENTIATED CHOICES

Choice is perhaps the strongest motivation tool a teacher can employ.

*Daily choices.* Although choice isn't possible in every assignment (nor should it be; sometimes students benefit from carrying out a specific task), think about giving choices in the following small ways:

- Having students answer five of six questions on a worksheet.
- Allowing students to work alone or with a partner.
- Providing more than one journal prompt. By default, journaling is an Introverted activity. Think about choices that might motivate Sensing, Intuitive, Thinking, and Feeling students. The journal exercise on page 101 gives some examples.

*Speech options.* In one class, all students were to give presentations on the Civil War. The teacher added choices (Chart 5.4) to make the mandatory speeches more palatable to all students. She also differentiated for Extraversion and Introversion by providing practice time, allowing Introverted students to prepare written text to read if that made them more comfortable, and letting students indicate whether they wanted to be among the first presenters. Many Introverts prefer to go first to get it out of the way. She also talked with students about how these factors made it fair to require all students to give speeches.

*Lab choices.* Teachers can increase student comfort and motivation with experiments by keeping factors given in Chart 5.5 in mind.

Again, you don't need to meet the needs of all students at all times. However, an easy way to differentiate for lab work is to give students the choice of reading

**Chart 5.4**  Speech Options

| Introversion and Sensing | Introversion and Intuition |
|---|---|
| • Read a short biography on a prominent Civil War person and give a report to the class.<br><br>• Prepare and label a poster showing the uniform and equipment of a soldier of either the Union or Confederate army and present it to the class. | • Write a letter home from a famous Civil War person that conveys information about the events that person was involved in. Read it to the class.<br><br>• Design your own project on the Civil War that includes a class presentation. Get teacher approval before starting. |
| **Extraversion and Sensing** | **Extraversion and Intuition** |
| • Make a model of a Civil War battlefield and use it to explain the battle to the class.<br><br>• Give a report on the typical life of a Union or Confederate soldier. | • Dress up as a Civil War personality (costumes provided) and be interviewed by the class as if you were that person.<br><br>• Solve three problems brought to you by soldiers in the company of which you are the commander. Role-play as you explain your solutions to the class. |

**Chart 5.5**  Laboratory Choices

| Introversion and Sensing | Introversion and Intuition |
|---|---|
| • These students might prefer to read about what might happen and then try it. | • These students might want to read background material, make predictions about what will happen, and then try it. |
| **Extraversion and Sensing** | **Extraversion and Intuition** |
| • These students often like to try the experiment and then read about what happened. | • These students often like to design their own experiments to discover something. |

background information first or conducting the experiment first. Or, rotate among the four approaches over the course of many experiments.

# HETEROGENEOUS GROUPS

The following activities allow all students to engage in higher level thinking during group activities.

## Scaffolded Discussions

The Roman artifacts lesson on page 46 is an example of providing tools for thinking so that all students can participate in group discussions. In addition, giving individual think time before the group discussion gives everyone a chance to generate ideas.

## Pocket Problems

Often used for math review, this activity differentiates for Extraversion and Introversion by allowing student movement, individual thinking time, and group discussion. It also differentiates for Sensing and Intuition by providing structured tasks within a format that allows for variety and choice. The teacher prepares 26 problems and places two copies of each, labeled by letters A–Z, into a board outfitted with pockets labeled A–Z. Students work in groups of four, assuming one of the following roles:

- Messenger: Goes to the pocket problem board and selects the group's next problem.
- Reader: Reads the problem aloud, then places it where everyone can review it.
- Calculator: Operates the group's calculator. For language arts or social studies, the student might be in charge of a reference book or notes on specific subjects.
- Writer: Records the group's solution.

Once the Reader has read the problem, all students keep the red side of their card up (see page 79 for red card/green card explanation) while they think about the problem. When they are ready to talk, they turn their green card up and the group works together to solve the problem. The group can put the problem back if no one knows how to solve it. Once they agree on a solution, the Writer records it on the back. The Messenger then returns it to the Pocket Board, clipping it face down to the outside of the pocket. When two groups have completed a problem, the second Messenger checks to see if the answers agree. If not, the groups conference to determine who is right.

The teacher at the end checks the cards to see if the solutions are right. Sometimes, classes are motivated by setting goals for how many total problems will be solved correctly.

## Keeping Everyone Engaged

Techniques that help all group members participate include the following:

- Structuring discussions to allow for individual reflection, through techniques such as red card/green card or tools such as the graphic organizer used to jump-start thinking for the Roman artifact lesson on page 46.
- Having each student record group conclusions or talking points, using some sort of thinking tool so the teacher can see at a glance whether all students are listening and participating.
- Establishing procedures for getting help. For example, on the pocket problems, a teacher might require that groups check their notes and a math glossary before asking for help.

### Scaffolded Role Assignments

One of the best examples of this technique is literature circles, where students have clear responsibilities for group discussion time. This is described more thoroughly on page 107. In general, this works best if students organize who will take each role.

# HOMOGENEOUS GROUPS

Ability + Interest = Flow. Sometimes being paired with students above or below one's ability dampens interest. Unchallenged students get bored, and struggling students let others take over.

Fosnot and Dolk (2002) provide examples of math problems that allow students to grapple with the *same* math problem, but at their own level of mathematizing. One problem has the children work out a fair system for dividing sub sandwiches among groups of varying sizes that are going on field trips. Four students received three subs, five students received four subs, eight students received seven subs, and so on.

One group is able to move to the idea of unit fractions. Another group simply divides each sub by the number of children, so if there are five children and four subs, each child gets a fifth of each sub. In another group, students grasp for the first time that one-fifth is smaller than one-fourth as they try to determine fairness. Fosnot and Dolk comment, "Children are exploring ideas—fair sharing, equivalence, and common denominators; the connections between fractions, division, and multiplication; common fractions—in relation to their own level of cognitive development" (p. 15).

Literature circles can also be formed this way, with groups reading various books that touch on the same theme, as explained on page 108.

# NATURAL PATTERNS FOR EXTENSIONS

What do you do with students who are done? If only fun activities are provided, the students who don't work as fast will complain. If extra work is given, the students who finished first will complain. A better way is to use Sensing and Intuition as a framework for designing natural extensions that students find attractive. In general, one might use the following brief guide to extension:

Here are some examples.

- As elementary students finished *Stuart Little*, they had a choice of creating a story board for the novel (Sensing) or writing another chapter to continue the story, which ends with Stuart still on his search to find his friend Marigold the bird (Intuition).
- For the bouncing ball problem (page 49), students had choices of working on problems that had data similar to that of the bouncing ball problem (Sensing), conducting another experiment and graphing the results (Extraverted Sensing), or thinking in the abstract about possible results for an experiment involving weighted springs or designing and conducting their own experiment that they predicted would produce a linear relationship (Intuition).
- In a history class, students could ponder a "what if" question (Intuition) or construct a fact sheet or timeline that would help other students review (Sensing).

**Chart 5.6**    Natural Patterns for Extensions

| Introversion and Sensing | Introversion and Intuition |
|---|---|
| These students often want to practice what they have learned with more advanced problems. | These students are often motivated through extensions that allow them to use their imaginations. |
| **Extraversion and Sensing** | **Extraversion and Intuition** |
| These students may prefer extensions that somehow let them work with their hands or tell others what they have learned. | These students like to take a leadership role, teaching others what they have learned, designing something new for a future lesson, or perhaps creating a way for the class to review what they've learned. |

## WHAT ABOUT ASSESSMENTS?

In an exercise repeated over two dozen times, Murphy (1992) grouped teachers according to dominant function—Sensing, Intuition, Thinking, and Feeling. The groups were given the following assignment: "Your class has just completed an intensive course in drug prevention awareness. Design three test questions to assess their students' level of learning." Each group designed different questions (shown in Chart 5.7) and, in the discussions that followed about the questions, often stated that they would have a difficult time answering or grading the questions other groups developed.

Examining how we assess students, then, is essential for true differentiation. Here are a few strategies.

### Provide Choices in Test Questions

Find a balance between subjective and objective questions, using the examples in Chart 5.7 as a starting place. Then, consider how you might give students choices in which questions to answer. For example, students might need to complete the first 10 problems on a test and then choose one of the last three to answer.

### Use Checklist Rubrics

Checklist rubrics match assignment requirements with how they are weighted in grading. Students usually understand and put these to use better than descriptive rubrics, which, although helpful for teachers, aren't always explicit enough, especially for Sensing students. Everyone can use checklist rubrics. Sensing students use them to plan their work. Intuitive students use them when they're just about finished to see if they complied with the assignment.

Sensing teachers use rubrics as a guide for grading subjective assignments. Intuitive teachers use them as a guide for being consistent in grading, especially in

**Chart 5.7**    Sample Test Questions Created by Teachers with Different Dominant
Functions

**Sensing Preference**

1.  List 3 reasons why people try drugs:

    •

    •

    •

2.  Name and describe the major classifications of drugs and their effects on the human body.

3.  Give an example of how drugs may have had adverse effects on the life of someone famous.

**Intuitive Preference**

1.  Is the war on drugs succeeding? Why or why not?

2.  If you were the President of the United States, what would you do to help America's youth?

3.  In essay form, design three questions and explain why these would cover the material.

**Thinking Preference**

1.  Why say no to drugs?

2.  Should drugs be legalized? Why or why not? Be prepared to support your answer.

3.  How would you punish the drug pushers?

**Feeling Preference**

1.  How could you persuade your best friend to say no to drugs?

2.  What do you feel society should or could do to win the war against drugs?

3.  How does drug abuse affect the entire family?

SOURCE: Modified and reproduced by special permission of the Publisher, Davies-Black Publishing, Mountain View, CA 94043, from *The Developing Child* by Elizabeth Murphy. Copyright 1992 by Davies-Black Publishing. All rights reserved. Further reproduction is prohibited without the Publisher's written consent.

remembering where to give or subtract points. Some Intuitive teachers object to using these rubrics because they seem to restrict student imagination; however, many, many students report that the rubrics are helpful.

The rubric in Chart 5.8 was developed to assess sixth-grade reports on a country.

**Chart 5.8**    Research Paper Grading Rubric

---

> **Rough Draft is DUE BY Monday, May 24 in class**
> **Final Paper is DUE BY Tuesday, June 2**

---

**Planning**

☐ Parent signature                                   5 points
☐ One book source for information                    5 points
☐ One Internet source for information                5 points

**Rough Draft**

☐ Turn in a copy of your notes                      10 points
☐ Turn in a copy of your outline                    10 points
☐ Turn in your rough draft

    ☐ Quality of information                      10 points
    ☐ Amount of information                       10 points

**Final Paper**

☐ Did you have an adult read it over for you?
☐ Are you proud of your effort?
☐ Is your name on your work?

**Check your work. Can you receive maximum points?**

☐ Research paper in correct format                  10 points
    ☐ At least 2–3 pages if typed, 4–5 pages handwritten
    ☐ Double-space your pages
    ☐ Font: maximum of 16-pt Times
    ☐ Write on only one side of the paper
☐ Clear introduction and conclusion                  5 points
☐ Cultural universals paragraphs                    20 points
☐ Spelling and grammar                               5 points
☐ Bibliography in correct format                     5 points

**Total Points:**                                 **100 Points**

**Extra Credit: Any one of the following is worth 5 points; choose only one**

☐ Make a decorative report cover that shows a map or other illustration
☐ Find a current event article on the country and write a short paragraph
☐ Make a list of the top 10 reasons why someone should visit your country
☐ Make a list of why you would and wouldn't want to live in your country (at least five reasons why and five reasons why not)

**Turn in this sheet with your project!!!!!!**

## Give Choices

Provide choices for final projects that match the different learning styles. The following choices were developed for *The Outsiders* by S. E. Hinton:

**Chart 5.9**    Final Project Choices

### *The Outsiders*
### S. E. Hinton

#### Introversion and Sensing (IS)

- Provide the details:
  - o Describe the setting for *The Outsiders*. Where did it take place? When? How is the setting the same or different from where you live?
  - o Plot: What was this story about? Summarize the plot in approximately 100 words.
  - o Main characters: Describe at least four of the main characters. Besides physical appearance, list at least four adjectives that describe the character's personality and provide evidence from the book (quotes or examples) that support the adjectives you chose.
  - o Details: Choose five main events in the story and describe them. List them in chronological order. Your descriptions should include why the event is important to the story.

- Make a time line for *The Outsiders*. Include at least 15 important events. For each event, describe what happened in 2–3 sentences. In addition, describe why the event is important to the story.
- Be a critic. What did you like about *The Outsiders?* What was not so great? What didn't make sense to you? What comments would you like to make to the author? What do you think students would learn from reading this book? Include vivid examples to prove your points.

#### Extraversion and Sensing (ES)

- Develop a "Hall of Fame, Hall of Shame" poster for the main characters in *The Outsiders:* Ponyboy, Johnny, Soda, Darry, Dally, Cherry, Bob, Randy. For each, draw or find a magazine picture. Designate which "Hall" you would assign them to. Under each picture, write down your reasons, with evidence from the story, to support your placement.
- With a partner, develop a trivia contest game for the class based on *The Outsiders*. Have at least 15 questions that you think the class should remember the answers to (don't go for hidden facts like the name of Ponyboy's English teacher, but for facts that are important to the story).
- Pick two important scenes from *The Outsiders* to illustrate. Your drawings should accurately depict the scenes as described by the author. Use dialogue quoted directly from the book, using captions or thought bubbles. Write a few paragraphs describing why you picked each scene and why it is important to the plot/theme/character development.

#### Introversion and Intuition (IN)

- Write another scene that takes place after the end of *The Outsiders*. What might Ponyboy do next? How might his relationship with his brothers or the gang change? How might he relate differently to someone else in the story or to someone new that he meets?
- Write a letter to a character in the book. What would you like to communicate? What did you think of their actions or events in the story? What advice or criticism would you like to give? Have the character reply to your letter.

*(Continued)*

**Chart 5.9** (Continued)

- Put together a newspaper that reports on the final scenes in *The Outsiders.* Articles could include interviews with key characters or people on the streets who witnessed the events, editorials or letters to the editors on gangs or other social issues, political cartoons, "eyewitness" reports, crossword puzzles, and articles that report on the events of the story (such as the church fire). Note: these must accurately reflect the events of the story.

**Extraversion and Intuition (EN)**

- Design a project (poem, sculpture, short video, model, diorama, pop-up book, labeled diagram, etc.) that illustrates a theme of *The Outsiders.* Then choose three of the following questions to answer. Write a full paragraph to answer each one.
  - What lesson does the author want her readers to learn by the end of the story?
  - Is the message of the story clear and effective? Why or why not?
  - What were some of the key moments in the story relating to your theme?
  - What about the theme is most meaningful to you in your own life?
  - How does Ponyboy grow or change with respect to this theme?

- With a partner, act out a conversation between Ponyboy and another character in the book that takes place after the end of *The Outsiders.* In the conversation, show what Ponyboy or another character learned, related to one of the themes of the book. Hand in an outline of your script that describes the theme your conversation reflects, is detailed enough to show the main points you were trying to get across to the class, and lists scenes from the book that illustrate your points. Hint: to receive a good grade, most students find that they need to write out everything they want to say.
- Create a project of your choice. Check with the teacher before beginning; write out what you will do and obtain permission.

## Whole-Class Modifications

Nunley (2006) points to the advantages of offering modifications required by individualized education programs (IEPs) to the whole class. First, it avoids stigmatizing students. Second, it provides variety, choice, and new learning strategies to all students. Examples include the option of having an exam read aloud, presenting photocopies on paper of different colors, providing graphic organizers to anyone who wants them, and offering reductions in daily class work.

# CONCLUSION

Murphy (1992) emphasizes the importance of differentiated instruction and assessment by the phrase, "Make them reach while you teach, but test for the best." In other words, we *want* students to access different learning styles and gain skills with each one. However, only by differentiating assessment can we reach the point where students with different learning styles are honored where it counts—in how we measure academic success.

# 6

# Differentiated Classroom Management

**Before you read on . . .**

What is your biggest classroom management concern? Noise? Transitions? Keeping early-finishers engaged while other students work? Respect? Use of class time? Others?

In *Otis Spofford,* Beverly Cleary (1953) paints a picture of a disengaged student that still rings true today.

> Otis knew that when he wanted to be he was the smartest boy in arithmetic in Mrs. Gitler's room. This morning he decided he wanted to be. He worked his problems quickly, not because he cared about finishing first, but because he wanted Mrs. Gitler to scold him for not working. Then he planned to drop a sheet of perfect problems on her desk and wait for her look of amazement when she saw that he had not only completed his work but had not made a single mistake.
>
> As soon as Otis finished his problems he looked around for a good way to waste time. Maybe there was something interesting in his pockets . . . he tried to unsnarl the yo-yo string but soon lost interest. Wishing he could think of something more interesting, he tore off a corner of his arithmetic paper, put it in his mouth, and chewed it. Then he blew it out and watched it turn and twist as it floated through the air and landed on the back of Stewy's neck. (p. 41–42)

Otis probably has preferences for Extraversion, Sensing, Thinking, and Perceiving, ESTP. Look at the chart on page 22; that's the personality type least likely to go into teaching, perhaps leaving these children with few adults who understand why they act the way they do. As one ESTP teacher told me, "I *know* how students can get into trouble." Many ESTP children excel in school, but they may also, like Otis, be naturally tempted to have a bit of fun at their teachers' expense, especially if schoolwork doesn't engage them. Thus, classroom instruction and classroom management are integrally linked. In this chapter, we'll look at common classroom problems and solutions that involve both academic and classroom management ideas.

## DIFFERENTIATING THE LEARNING ENVIRONMENT

To clarify what classroom management has to do with differentiation, consider that often I'm asked to help teachers get particularly unruly classrooms under control. The teacher tells me, "They sit still only if they're copying notes from an overhead or doing seatwork. Their skills are too low to do the assignments I'm giving other classes." After observations, here are my usual first two suggestions:

- Change the desk arrangements to better meet the needs of these particular students.
- Begin class with a routine.

Both of these are classroom management suggestions, yet they change the learning in the room. One teacher quantified the result: time on task rose from around 70 percent to over 95 percent. Further, within two weeks, the students were tackling the same tasks as her other classes, including using learning stations and all-class debates. Classroom management *is* a differentiation strategy.

## SOURCES OF CLASSROOM MANAGEMENT PROBLEMS

Before looking at solutions, though, let's break classroom management into three categories.

- Some classroom management problems are directly attributable to skills and habits teachers need to develop—many of which tie directly to the teacher's own personality. The "Common Traps" charts for each of the preferences in Chapter 2 highlight some of these.
- Some classroom management problems are due to clashes between teachers and students who are direct opposites. Teachers are more likely to discipline students who do not share their type preferences (O'Neil, 1986).
- Some classroom management problems are directly attributable to the problems certain students bring to class with them. Behavior disorders, difficult home situations, and other personal difficulties are certainly real sources of classroom management problems. However, certain personality types are consistently overrepresented in various studies on at-risk students or dropouts. Those with a preference for Perceiving top the list. At one alternative high school, 90 percent of their students, "dropouts" from traditional programs, were Sensing-Perceiving (Giger, 1996)—just like Otis Spofford. The researcher characterized the students this way:

> While working with SP [Sensing-Perceiving] students in both school and treatment settings, they shared some fascinating and "true to type" information about "teacher testing." SP students enjoy the thrill of the

reaction from SJ [Sensing-Judging] teachers (*My job is to teach, your job is to learn*) and find it much less exciting to test NF [Intuition-Feeling] (*Let me know what I can do to help you*) and NT [Intuition-Thinking] (*I'm here when you're ready to learn*) limits. They report that SPs (*I expect you to participate and be a team player . . .* ), when they can find them, can be the most fun to engage in conflict. Many SP students, particularly Extraverted, report enjoying the adrenaline rush of confrontation and may create a situation, if necessary, to experience this feeling. (p. 388)

- Note that 70 percent of all elementary teachers have a preference for Judging; perhaps this starts many Sensing-Perceiving students off on the wrong foot?

Look back to Chart 3.1, "Behavior Clues," on pages 25–26. Do any "problem" students come to mind? Although type isn't a panacea for every classroom management problem, viewing your practices, rules, and procedures through the lens of type often solves a variety of learning style problems—and student/teacher conflicts—before they become bigger problems.

## WHY DO TEACHERS NEED TO ADJUST THEIR STYLES?

Teachers often raise four objections to adjusting their teaching styles to meet the needs of students with different preferences. I address these concerns below.

*Shouldn't students learn to follow each teacher's rules? Doesn't that mirror the real world?* Students aren't mature. They aren't yet skilled at using the preferences least natural for them. Whereas yes, students need to learn to adjust, the teacher needs to consider whose needs—emotional and academic—are greatest, the teacher's or the student's.

*Some of these suggestions are contrary to my natural style. I don't want to use them!* You always start with your own style and then adjust for your opposite. Which suggestions would be easiest for you? Which could you use at least once in awhile to meet the students' needs?

*If I'm meeting the needs of students with one preference, doesn't that mean that the needs of students with the opposite preference go unmet?* Many of the suggestions in this chapter bridge *between* the preferences. Others work when the *task* requires students to all use a certain preference. Remember, the goal isn't to meet the needs of all students at all times. The goal is to help them appreciate differences and know how to adjust when schoolwork or activities require it. For teachers, another goal is to ensure than no students are consistently expected to operate outside of their preferences.

*What about students with ADHD or ODD (oppositional defiance disorder) or other definite problems?* Whereas type is about normal differences among normal people, researchers are finding that many of these conditions represent *exaggerated* forms of the various personality preferences. Parallels between ADHD and Perceiving are discussed on page 28. Many of the strategies that research is showing are most successful in helping these students with academic achievement are similar to type-based strategies. Specific interventions or medications may still be needed, but using strategies grounded in type also helps these students achieve more academically.

## HOW TO USE THIS CHAPTER

Before reading, you might review the "common traps" for each of your preferences, listed in Chapter 2.

Then, instead of reading this chapter sequentially, look through the list of common difficulties below, arranged by the type preferences that can be used to explore new solutions. Which ones have you longed to solve? Read those suggestions first. Some will sound more plausible to you than others; remember, though, that you're most likely having problems with students who are very different from you and who therefore may respond to strategies that seem impractical or even implausible.

### Common Classroom Management Problems

#### Use the concepts of Extraversion and Introversion to

- *Control classroom noise and interruptions*
- *Balance student participation*
- *Allow students to think*

#### Common problems include

| | |
|---|---|
| If students are talking when they should be listening . . . | Page 77 |
| If students blurt out answers, questions or comments . . . | Page 78 |
| If students get out of their seats without permission . . . | Page 81 |
| If students participate unequally in class discussions . . . | Page 81 |
| If students struggle to work well in groups . . . | Page 82 |

#### Use the concepts of Sensing and Intuition to

- *Provide adequate directions and expectations*
- *Balance scaffolding with student higher-level thinking*

#### Common problems include

| | |
|---|---|
| If students ask questions that were just answered in oral directions or fail to follow directions . . . | Page 83 |
| If students ask teacher to check correctness of work too often . . . | Page 84 |

#### Use the concepts of Thinking and Feeling to

- *Build relationships*
- *Motivate students*
- *Deal with conflict*

*Common problems include*

*Use the concepts of Judging and Perceiving to*

- *Help students settle down for classwork*
- *Improve student use of class time*
- *Help more students complete work*
- *Balance process and product in learning*

*Common problems include*

NOTE: Many of these techniques work for grades K–12, and with adults as well. In the older grades, teachers might use some of the strategies a few times and then find that students automatically begin adjusting their behavior. Younger students might need to use the strategies all year.

# THE STRATEGIES: EXTRAVERSION AND INTROVERSION

### If Students Are Talking When They Should Be Listening . . .

In almost any adult workshop, if the instructor lectures for more than 15 minutes, the level of side conversations begins to rise, even when people are engaged. As people listen to new ideas, they want to process them—and Extraverts process by talking about them, whether they are seven years old or seventy.

- *Clear listening time boundaries.* Students can often muster better self-control if they know how long they need to be quiet. "Class, I'll be giving directions for about 10 minutes today. Then you'll be able to talk quietly with the other students at your table while you work on the assignment."
- Some teachers are far better at estimating listening times than others. Make sure you can see a clock. Students would rather hear, "Oops, I need three or four more minutes," than wonder whether you'll ever finish.
- *Red card/green card.* Laminate together two pieces of construction paper, one red and the other green. Find a way to display it prominently. One teacher punched holes in it and hung it from her overhead projector. You could also put a magnet strip on each side and post it on your whiteboard. When students need to listen, turn the card to the red side and announce, "Class, it's red card time. That means we're all listening. Find your Introverted side so that you can get the directions you need. In about 10 minutes it will be green card time again."

- *Teach fairness.* Remind students that whereas Extraverts need to talk to think, Introverts need quiet to think. It's only fair that class time meets the needs of both preferences.
- *Provide concrete tasks.* Many Extraverted students listen better if a task allows for processing what they are hearing. Nunley (2006) suggests giving students the perception of control by offering lecture options such as
  1. Listen to the lecture and take notes (with no other distractions). 25 points.
  2. Quietly listen to the lecture while completing [a] diagram. Label parts and color. List five key ideas from the lecture on the back. 25 points.
  3. Quietly complete the worksheet packet . . . Form it into a booklet and make a full-color cover. 25 points. (p. 45)
- *Build a habit.* The dynamics of some groups of students can be overwhelming! Perhaps there's a "ringleader" who riles up the others, or friends who can't seem to limit socializing, or a general atmosphere of disrespect. In these cases, use a short block of instructional time at the start of each day or class period to *teach* listening. Yes, instructional time is precious, but think of the time you will eventually gain if you solve the talking-out-of-turn problem. Here are some examples:
  o Read aloud from a story or novel related to concepts you are teaching. A science teacher might use *Hoot* by Carl Hiaassen to generate thinking about environmental issues. Social studies teachers can choose a theme-related historical or contemporary novel. Math teachers can draw on *Chasing Vermeer* by Blue Balliett or *The Devil's Arithmetic* by Jane Yolen. As you read, have students complete a simple task, such as filling in a picture-and-journal entry. See page 106 for an example.
  o Pose a puzzle. Find a book of brain teasers, two-minute mysteries, or math problems. Once students have listened (and taken notes), differentiate for ability by allowing students to work alone or in pairs to find a solution.
  o Develop a class code. Begin class by giving a sentence using the code. Add to the fun by coding jokes, silly sayings, or surprise announcements.
  o Use listening games. Books such as *Listen! Hear!* by Graeme Beals contain exercises in which students follow oral directions to fold paper, draw, or write. Collaborate with other teachers to find or create more.
  o Read "Strange News" aloud. Search the Web for "Strange News" sites—daily anecdotes about silly world records, crazy animal attacks, dumb things people try to do, 93-year-old skydivers, and so on. Think of quick ways students might journal about their reactions. What might they want to try before they're 93? What animal would they be most shocked to see in their basement? Would you try moose cheese? Why?

## If Students Blurt Answers, Questions, or Comments . . .

Although some of this behavior is outright rude, it can also reflect the inability of Extraverted students to hold their thoughts. Have you called on students wildly waving a hand to answer, only to have them say, "I forgot . . ." They're probably being truthful; Extraverts need to say it to really think it. Here are some strategies for helping Extraverts.

- *Write it down.* Teach your students about why Extraverts might blurt answers. Then emphasize how for fairness, they need to learn to hold their thoughts by writing them down. Students might jot down a word or a small picture symbol to help them remember a thought, or leave a column to the left of their notes and write questions and comments there.
- *"Little" red card/green card* (Murphy, 1992). Give each student a small card that is red on one side and green on the other. Laminate construction paper or have students color red and green circles on index cards. You can use the cards in several ways.
  - Have students turn their cards to the red side. Ask a question or pose a problem, asking them to stay silent, but turn their cards to the green side when they are ready to answer. In some instances you might wait for all students to turn to the green side. In other instances, you might see that some students need more information or help and gather them together while giving others a different assignment.
  - You might also ask students to complete a certain section of an assignment and then turn their red side up so that you can check their progress. Math teachers might check how students are setting up a story problem. Language arts teachers might check topic sentences or an outline of main ideas. With the cards as visual reminders, teachers find that students keep working independently and are more likely to wait quietly for help.
  - Some students prefer to sit and think and may not be ready to write immediately. Students use the green side to indicate they are fine, understand the assignment, and do not wish to be disturbed. Turning the red side up indicates that they need help *or* they would like the teacher to stop by so they can share what they are thinking.
- *Whiteboards.* Teachers can create wait time and quiet by having students write answers or responses on individual whiteboards. Using this larger surface also makes it easier for the teacher to quickly check for student understanding.
- *Active roles.* Some Extraverts can channel their energy through active roles. Consider having them record directions on the front board or a blank overhead, having them prompt you when a given amount of time has passed, or passing out folders or some other activity.
- *Response cards.* Chapman and King (2005) suggest response cards as formative assessment tools, allowing teachers to gauge students' knowledge, interest, and confidence. Note that the cards provide an Extraverted, hands-on activity for whole-class instruction.

    Prepare cards with the same response choices, duplicated in the same spots, front and back of the card. The teacher asks a question; students respond by pinching the card on their response and then holding up the card for the teacher to see. Figure 6.1 contains examples.

    Chapman and King suggest dozens of content area uses for these cards. Science teachers might test for student knowledge of rock or animal classifications. Math teachers might display word problems and have students point to "add, subtract, multiply, divide." All teachers might use "I understand," "I have a few questions," "I don't get it" as a way to assess understanding before moving on.

**Figure 6.1**   Sample Response Cards

| Card Front | Card Back |
|---|---|
| True | True |
| False | False |

| Card Front | Card Back |
|---|---|
| period | period |
| comma | comma |
| question mark | question mark |

- *Was that your final answer?* Extraverts may blurt things out unintentionally—including comments that definitely spur negative reactions in teachers. To avoid an escalation over comments that can't be ignored, ask, "Is that what you meant to say?" before assuming the worst. Often the student will retract the comment, realizing it was inappropriate. The teacher is viewed as reasonable and the student often begins to recognize a pattern in how such comments lead to trouble. If the student remains belligerent, the teacher can still take the next disciplinary step.

## If Students Get Out of Their Seats Without Permission . . .

The best way to keep students in their seats when you want them there is to plan in ways for them to be out of their seats. Here are some ideas:

- *Adding machine tape.* This office supply is inexpensive and versatile. Let students write (individually or in groups) on a length of tape and then post their answer. It can be used for math equations, brainstorming ideas, listing questions, prior knowledge, and many other ways. Because the strips are moveable, teachers (or students) can then sort the answers into categories.
- *Writing on windows.* Many erasable markers wipe off of windows as easily as off of whiteboards (test yours before handing them to students!!). Hold mini-contests and let students who come up with the right answer write it on a window. For example, in math class, students might need to write an equation with the answer "3" using only the digits 2 and 7 and three operational signs: $7^2 - 2 \times 22 - 2 = 3$. In language arts, students might work on "word continuums" like "good—better—best" or "nice—splendid—fabulous."
- *Pocket problems.* This strategy is fully explained on page 66, but in short, students are allowed out of their seats to collect problems to work on from a board filled with problems.
- *Multistation work.* Instead of handing students packets filled with worksheets or relying on textbook-based seatwork, students collect activities from 15–20 stations and then take it back to their desk to work on it. Prior knowledge stations, explained on page 59, are effective as a differentiation technique.

## If Students Participate Unequally in Class Discussions . . .

Many Introverted students, who prefer to reflect before speaking, tell me, "By the time I'm ready, all the good answers are taken." Teachers tell me, "It's so hard *not* to keep calling on the enthusiastic students whose hands shoot in the air. I feel like I have to drag comments out of the others."

A definitive study, using analysis of over 300 classroom tape recordings (Rowe, 1974a, 1974b), showed that teachers in early grades asked questions in rapid succession, waiting on average only one second for a child's answer before rephrasing the question or giving more information. When teachers were taught to wait three more seconds, the average number of words in a student's response and the frequency of inferences and speculation more than tripled. Teachers found that they were disciplining less. Students were more engaged. Further, the five students struggling most in the classes provided better answers; teachers realized that previously they consistently had been allowing more wait time for the five best students.

Remember that if quiet students are listening, they are participating. However, sometimes the teacher's goal is to have everyone speak. These strategies cover both situations.

- *All-share or choice* (Murphy, 1992). Let students know at the beginning of a discussion whether everyone is expected to contribute orally to the discussion or whether there are other ways they might participate. If it's an "all-share" event, many Introverted students speak early on to get it over with. Provide some reflection time before the discussion starts by using red card/green card; have students turn their card to the green side when they are ready to discuss. Begin the discussion when most or all students are "green side up."

  Tell students that they can summarize what others have said as part of their turn if they do not want to offer any new ideas. Sometimes, saying, "Share in the next few minutes or write down your thoughts" encourages more participation.

- *Call on teams for answers rather than individuals.* Tell students that they will agree on answers in teams of two or three. Have them record group answers on whiteboards to indicate when they are in agreement. This technique lets students hone their thoughts before risking answering before the larger group.

- *Measure participation by what they learn.* Measure discussion participation by asking everyone to write down two or three things they learned. If they can, they participated whether or not they raised their hand or spoke aloud.

## If Students Struggle to Work Well in Groups . . .

Both Extraverted and Introverted students can cite examples of groups gone awry. The following tips help get groups off to a good start.

- *Conversation sticks.* Have students form groups of five to seven. Ask each to use two pencils or game tokens as conversation sticks. Students place their sticks in the middle as "tickets" to talk. When their two sticks are spent, they remain silent until everyone in their group has used their two sticks. Then the group redistributes them and the process begins again. No teacher is needed to control the flow.

- *"Big notes" to check progress.* To monitor whether groups are on task without hovering over them, provide a specific method for recording work—and make it big enough for you to easily see their progress. Try poster paper, adding machine tape, whiteboards, or assigning each group a section of the class chalkboard or whiteboard. Require the groups to use similar note-taking formats, such as a graphic organizer for comparing and contrasting, a certain number of bullet points for supporting a position in a debate, or a KWL chart (What I *K*now/*W*ant-to-know/What I *L*earned; Ogle, 1986).

- *Explanation role.* For math and other problem-oriented group work, designate the student who will explain the group's answer to the class. Choosing a student who might struggle a bit with the concepts can help the whole group work together until everyone understands it.

- *Group grading.* Have groups evaluate themselves, using a rubric, on how well they worked together and the quality of their work. A top score would be for groups in which everyone participated, listened to one another, and used time productively (Parker, 1993). A well-written rubric reinforces what it means to work as a group, a process that requires new skills for most students.

- *Groups of one.* Some tasks can be accomplished equally well through individual or group work. Many Introverts respond better to mandatory group projects if they sometimes have the choice to work alone.

# SENSING AND INTUITION

## If Students Ask Questions That Were Just Answered in Oral Directions OR If Students Fail to Follow Directions . . .

Remember that Sensing and Intuition are about how we take in information—students in your classroom actually need different information to do an assignment well. Further, they differ in *when* they need that information. Here's an example of what goes on inside the heads of your students as you give directions for writing an essay on their summer vacation:

| Introverted Sensing: | Introverted Intuitive: |
|---|---|
| • *I'd better listen to find out just what I need to do. I don't want to write about everything if I only need to write about one thing I did.* | • *What did I do this summer that no one else did? I could write about my trip to Grandma's as if I were a news reporter. A "movie review" of camp? A poem like "Jabberwocky?" Twas summer and the household chores didst make me grumble in the shade . . .* |
| • Introverted Sensing students tend to listen carefully. | • Introverted Intuitive students often miss directions as they brainstorm unique ways to tackle the assignment. |
| **Extraverted Sensing:** | **Extraverted Intuitive:** |
| • *[out loud] "How long does it have to be? Do I tell about everything or just one thing I did this summer?"* | • *[out loud] "Let me tell you what I'm going to write about . . ."* |
| • Extraverted Sensing students want immediate answers to their questions. | • Extraverted Intuitive students want to process out loud their great ideas right away. |

In other words, students don't receive the same information in the same way, adding challenges to providing directions. Here are some ideas:

- *Answer person* (Murphy, 1992). Select an "answer person" to record and explain directions once you have finished explaining the assignment. Tell students that when they think they have enough information, they can begin the task. Give the directions and allow students to ask questions. After you've finished, students who discover that they need information direct their questions to the "answer person" rather than the teacher.

- *Checklist rubrics.* List requirements for an assignment and associated points (example given on page 70). Sensing students tend to use these to *plan* their work. Intuitive students tend to use these after they've started (or even after they've finished) to see if they've met the requirements. Other rubric formats may be more useful for grading, but checklists are a concise way of clarifying expectations, especially if details count.

- *Show examples.* No matter how old they are, many Intuitives often skip over reading directions, relying instead on looking at examples. Many Sensing types find that examples bolster their confidence.
  - When asking for short journal responses or answers to guided reading questions, show students examples of "good, better, best" answers. Here are examples for a journal entry where students were asked to provide an anecdote that showed their preference for Judging or Perceiving.
    - *Good: Incomplete, no story.* I put off my homework until later.
    - *Better: General example, no specific story.* I come home and play. Then when I've used up some energy I do my homework.
    - *Best: Complete, specific story example.* Once I had to make a game. I had all of winter vacation to do it, but didn't start until New Year's Day. Then we didn't have all the supplies, so I couldn't do what I planned.
  - When asking students to show their work in math, display an example in which you could spot a student's misunderstanding and help them not make the same mistake—evidence that showing work might be beneficial.
  - For reading circles, display comments about a text that you wrote on self-stick notes and then transferred to a notebook.

## If Students Waste Class Time They're Given for Structured Assignments . . .

Practice makes perfect . . . up to a point. Intuitive students may grow restless when faced with tasks with repetitive elements, no matter how valuable. To keep them motivated, try the following ideas.

- *Provide choices.* Instead of having all students do the same problems, assign the essential ones and give students the choice of which other ones they complete. For example, on a math assignment, all students might do the first six problems, but then choose among three story problems. Even if the assignment is to do nine out of ten problems, giving students the simple option of omitting one increases motivation. Let students choose between two writing prompts, working bottom up or top down on a worksheet, or sitting on a carpet square or at a desk while working.
- *Quiet chit-chat.* With the warning that excessive noise or lack of progress will end the privilege, allow students to chat quietly with students right next to them as they work. This may help Extraverted students stay on task longer because they aren't thinking about how long they need to stay quiet.
- *Engaging extensions.* This technique works especially well for math. Tell students that when they've gotten a certain number of problems right (post

answers so they can check their own work), they can move on to an applied problem or extension. For example, perhaps a worksheet has 20 problems. Students can do all 20, or if they finish 10 correctly and believe they understand the concepts, they can do 10 plus a problem that is worth 10 points. Often higher level students are asked to do the 20 problems *plus* an extension and view this as unfair. With this method, students who want to practice (often Sensing students) are given the opportunity while others can move on rather than becoming possible sources of disruption. Many math books have extra problems that are ideal for this purpose.

# THINKING AND FEELING

## If Students Are Insulting Each Other . . .

Both Thinking and Feeling students can engage in this kind of behavior. However, the academic performance of Feeling students is more affected by negative atmospheres, even if the insults aren't directed at them personally. Thinking students can also be affected, but they tend to enjoy arguments that Feeling students take personally, and may also recover more quickly from adverse situations.

- *Put a stop to put-downs.* Beers (2003) tells of a teacher who rang a loud bell every time her eleventh-grade students made a cutting remark. She offered incentives for the class to stop making what they began referring to as "ding-a-lings." It took over *three weeks* for students to go an entire class period without the bell, but over the month a positive atmosphere took root. Beers reports, "One student remarked, 'Ding-a-lings become so common that you don't even hear them. Now I hear them so much in my other classes that I'm amazed how awful they really are'" (p. 267).
- *Teach compassion.* Students can be taught to step into the shoes of another person to understand their needs. Here are ideas by grade level:
  - *K–2.* Enforce compassion. Make a team effort to supervise the classroom, hallways, playgrounds, and lunchrooms to ensure that all children are included and treated with compassion by their classmates. One first-grade teacher changed the dynamics of his room by separating—for seating, for group work, for lunch, and for recess—a clique of students who had excluded another boy from their lunch table. The class quickly learned to include everyone. Read aloud books such as *Best Friends for Frances* by Russell Hoban. Talk with your class about being friendly toward everyone.
  - *3–5.* Read aloud a novel about a child who is teased or bullied. Have students journal about questions such as, "How would you have felt?" "What could another student have done?" "If you were the adult, what would you do?" Hold discussions about classroom expectations. Possible novels include *Loser* by Jerry Spinelli, *The Girls* by Amy Goldman Koss, and *Freak the Mighty* by Rodman Philbrick.
  - *6–9.* Use literature circles, explained more fully on page 107, so that students have more choice in the novels they read. Consider *Petey* by Ben Mikaelsen,

*Inventing Elliot* by Graham Gardner, *Feather Boy* by Nicky Singer, *Milkweed* by Jerry Spinelli, *A Corner of the Universe* by Ann M. Martin, or *Pictures of Hollis Woods* by Patricia Reilly Giff. Concentrate journal entries or discussions on what these characters need and how others could show compassion.

- ○ *10–12.* Switch the focus to real-life events and the consequences of exclusionary or hurtful behaviors—bullying, hazing, or even information on school shootings. Social studies or language arts teachers could give students choices of projects based on *Queen Bees and Wannabes* by Rosalind Wiseman or some of the novels listed above. Or, use an article such as "The Great Game of High School" (Senge et al., 2000) to generate a discussion about cliques at your own school.

- *Intervene.* Advocate for staff development on how teachers can handle bullying and cliques without raining further harm on the victims. Now that we know about the lifelong impact of such behaviors—for the victims and the perpetrators—educators need to take a stand.

## If Students Question Assignment Design, Grading Rubrics, or the Value of an Activity . . .

Remember three things:

- Thinking students tend to see the flaws first—and are more likely to vocalize their critiques if they are also Extraverts. Feeling students might also point out flaws if they think that doing so will benefit other students.
- Thinking students may enjoy arguing for the sake of arguing. If you aren't going to change the assignment, say so and end the discussion.
- The student just might be right. If this is the case and the teacher doesn't entertain the ideas or suggestions, a Thinking student may permanently write off the teacher as incompetent, possibly leading to more discipline problems.

In other words, in an effort to remain in charge, teachers can inadvertently escalate Thinking-Feeling interactions that weren't necessarily disrespectful at the beginning. Consider which of the following suggestions might help you benefit from student insights without losing authority.

- *Structure in critique.* The adjacent chart lists several questions teachers might give students to evaluate an assignment. Some allow for critique of the assignment itself, whereas others ask students to reflect on their work habits and learning styles. Note that the questions call for specific, useful examples and suggestions. Teachers might help students improve their evaluation skills by requiring them to list both positive and negative aspects of the assignment.

### Assignment Evaluation Questions

- The thing I liked most about this assignment was . . .
- This assignment could be improved by . . .
- To do a better job on this assignment, I needed . . .
- On the next assignment like this, I will . . .
- Compared to other assignments, on a scale of 1 (worse) to 10 (better), I'd rate this assignment as ___
- I would have worked harder if . . .
- I would rather have demonstrated what I learned through . . .

- *Put it in writing.* If a student insists on arguing and you are open to altering the assignment, ask him or her to list specific reasons or suggestions for change. Point to the assignment goals and make clear that these must still be met.
- *Provide choices.* Most people, Thinking students especially, need to feel some control over their lives. Providing simple choices within required assignments, especially highly structured ones, can decrease their resistance.

## If Students Are Defiant . . .

Type doesn't explain everything. Anger, feelings of failure, lack of sleep, and mismatches between tasks and student ability can all lead to defiant behavior. Yet because differences in type preferences between teachers and students can lead to confrontations, teachers can use the concepts to review what happened and determine some alternatives. In addition to the "Was that your final answer?" strategy on page 81 the following techniques can lessen defiance.

- *Chances to be in charge.* Some students who struggle with authority thrive on chances to *have* some authority. Here are some methods that teachers have used:
  - *Hand them the marker.* Before unrest begins, ask the student to be a scribe, on either an overhead or a whiteboard. This privilege of leaving leave one's seat can be tied to cooperation.
  - *Ask a question.* Instead of saying "Stop that" or "Sit down," leave the child in charge by asking a question. Examples are "What are students supposed to be doing now?" "Where should you be?" "Are you making a good choice?" "How could you better use this time?"
  - *Give a firm alternative.* Make clear the choice that the student is making. "You can finish the work now or during lunch." "You can sit at your desk or right beside my desk." "You can start working now or when the rest of the class has free time."
- *Check for the obvious.* None of us act our best when we're tired. One assistant principal seats students referred for behavior issues in a soft chair and suggests that they put their heads back for a minute while he finishes handling a few papers. He reports that frequently, the students fall asleep.
- *Check the relationship.* Thinking students might discount teachers' authority if they view the teacher as incompetent. Feeling students might behave similarly if they don't think the teacher likes them. Review the advice for Thinking and Feeling teachers (page 55) for suggestions.
- *Discuss fair classrooms.* The language of Thinking and Feeling helps students think through and buy into rules. Choose an area where you find yourself constantly having to remind students of correct behavior or teacher expectations. Homework policy, group work norms, use of equipment, or class environment are all possibilities. Have students break into groups and come up with a rule to address the situation. Provide criteria:
  - The rule needs to be objective (Thinking). How will the class know if it's been violated or enforced?
  - The rule needs to take into account the needs of all students (Feeling). Is it fair in different circumstances?

Groups could work on the same rules or different ones. Have a group scribe record each suggestion and why the group did/didn't think it would work.

Give an example such as pointing out how unfair it would be if late homework assignments were *always* accepted (even if a student decided to go to the movies instead of doing it) or *never* accepted (even if a student's house burned down).

## JUDGING AND PERCEIVING

### If Students Take Too Long to Settle Down . . .

Often, Judging teachers find it easy to set up class routines. However, sometimes a Judging teacher's routine is so set that some students rebel out of boredom. Perceiving teachers may balk at the restrictive feel of routines. However, routines *can* contain variety. Students with both preferences often thrive with the clear expectations that routines provide.

In most cases, making the gathering time an Introverted activity helps students transition from hallway or bus or playground noise and prepare to learn. You can increase buy-in by providing choice where possible and giving points for completing the work (even for simple journal entries).

Here are some suggestions that balance routine and novelty:

- Have an activity ready to go as the bell rings, providing instructions in a consistent way. The activity might be written on the board or on an overhead. Or, students might always pick up the assignment from a basket near the door. Students might respond to a journal question, work a math problem, decipher a word puzzle, or ready supplies for the first lesson.
- Start each class with circle time, but draw the main activity from a hat to add an element of surprise.
- Begin with a daily problem, but rotate between handing out a worksheet and posting a problem on the overhead, having students work alone or with a partner, solving problems and writing their own story problems, or reviewing concepts and tackling logic puzzles.
- Display assignments and have students copy them down in their planners. This works best for grades six and up if a grade-level team implements using planners together. This ensures that all students have homework information and teaches many how useful planners can be.
- Start class with a five-minute review of work from the day before. Math teachers might ask students to work one problem. Language arts or science teachers might ask students to answer a question from material covered the day before. As you explain answers, increase engagement by having students record corrections in a different color of ink or pencil.
- Start class with a read-aloud, but change the follow-up journal entry format frequently. Include artwork, evaluating what they've heard, putting themselves into the shoes of the character, making predictions, comparing the passage to something else, etc. Post the instructions in the same spot each day.

## If Students Make Poor Use of Class Time . . .

The clearer your expectations of what students should be doing during class time, the more likely that they will complete the work. Strategies for improving use of class time include the following:

- *To-do lists.* In planners, or on separate sheets, have students make to-do lists and display them on their desks. Then have them check off items as they complete them.
- *Concrete product/process checks.* Let students record notes, ideas, or work in formats large enough that you can check progress with a glance. Show examples of the amount of text or level of detail you expect to see.
- *Verbal progress markers.* Comments like "Most students are on problem seven" or "You should be answering the questions now" can help students discern whether they're working fast enough. Judge when to make these comments by reviewing progress of students with different ability levels.
- *Quality or understanding checks.* Using the red card/green card technique (page 79), correct students' first few responses. Or, have them check their own answers. If their work is below the quality of the clear examples provided, or there are lots of careless mistakes, it is easier to convince students to redo a few problems and then continue at that quality level than it is to convince them to redo an assignment that they thought they had finished.

## If Students Rush through Work . . .

Judging *and* Perceiving students generally resist rewriting papers, rereading texts, revising science experiment procedures, and otherwise redoing work when they thought they were done! One way to improve work quality and student buy-in to revisions is ensuring that first drafts don't look like final products. Here are some methods:

- Insist that students use separate note cards, self-stick notes, or sheets of paper for each paragraph of a report or essay. This gives them more room for editing as they go and, because the paragraphs are now "moveable," encourages students to rethink overall organization. See page 114 for an example.
- The old standby—students prepare rough drafts by hand before they are typed or copied in pen. Have students write on every other line so there is room for correction. Otherwise, students hesitate to fit in even small corrections.
- Demonstrate revision. Write a short paragraph and display it on an overhead. Then, show where it could be improved and display the "final" version.
- Insist that at least one paper during the course of the year be revised for an A. Students aren't done if they receive only a C or a B; they receive an "incomplete." Students protest, and teachers face extra work in providing comments. However, real writing *is* revision, not a five-paragraph essay cranked out in a set amount of time.
- Create mini-deadlines for first drafts. Have students staple the drafts, which count toward their grade, to their final papers so that you can see that they followed suggestions for changes.

## If Students Transition Poorly From One Activity to the Next . . .

Judging teachers often enjoy planning how to help students refocus after recess or put away art supplies before beginning a math activity. Perceiving teachers often think of clever ways to transition as the day unfolds.

*General agendas. Judging* students find it easier to approach the day when they understand what they'll be doing. For them, a schedule provides certainty and safety. *Perceiving* students benefit from the warning agendas provide for inevitable interruptions in activities they're engaged in.

Judging teachers often naturally find a method for recording the day's schedule. Perceiving teachers may hesitate to post an agenda because they frequently change their plans for the day as they observe student needs (remember, these are tendencies, not predictions). Here are some tips for using agendas without feeling constricted:

- Make it general, not specific. Although many teachers can predict from experience how long an activity will take, they can't always plan around fire drills, a behavior problem, or an important discussion tangent. Post nonnegotiable times, such as lunch or specialist time, but simply list other items.
- Use hand signals instead of specific time frames. If a student asks, "How long until we're done with this?" measure with your hands (as if you were showing the size of a fish you caught) how much longer you plan to spend on the current activity. Range from a couple of inches if your estimate is five minutes to hands far apart if you're just beginning.
- Draw an "if there's time" line. Especially when working with new materials, draw a line after the agenda items you are confident you will cover. This is especially helpful for teachers who tend to overschedule and are tired of students complaining, "But we didn't get to _____!"
- Use movable strips of paper or other material that you can reorder so that all students understand that sometimes agendas need to change. Give as much warning as possible when you do need to change items around.
- Talk out loud about schedule changes with younger students. "From the number of hands in the air with questions, I can tell you right now that math will take longer than usual. Don't worry, we'll still get to the gym on time by a little change in how I planned to do science." Judging students will fare better with this warning than if they *know* math is taking longer and they no longer know the plan.

Elementary school: Posting agendas on moveable strips with hook-and-loop fasteners or magnets works well. If your students are just learning to read, use pictures with the words written below.

Secondary school: If you teach more than one subject or grade level, consider having a poster-size whiteboard for each class so that you can write down all of the agendas first thing in the morning. Many home improvement stores will cut these for free for you when you buy the material. Consider having two columns, the second being items students should copy into their own planners—homework, deadlines, a Web site reference they'll need, etc. In other words, get all the important information in one place first.

*Change warnings.* Make announcements such as, "We'll put this activity away in two minutes." "In five minutes, be ready to _____." *Judging* students, who tend to want to tie up loose ends and feel that they are finished, appreciate the warning so they can speed up if necessary. *Perceiving* students, if they are enjoying what they are doing, need five minutes to get used to the idea that they need to move on. They may also need this warning to get down on paper all of the ideas or conclusions they've been gathering in their heads, i.e., move from process to product. Some Perceiving teachers struggle with remembering to give the warning; they might ask a student to watch the clock for them.

*Gradual transition.* Consider in what instances students might transition at their own pace as long as they aren't disturbing others. For example, one first-grade teacher announces read-aloud time. Most students quickly sit down on the soft carpet where the teacher is waiting. The teacher begins reading. After a minute or two, the stragglers, busy with their own book or puzzle, notice the transition and join their classmates. No time is lost on confrontations.

*Routine practice.* Have students actually practice procedures for transitions. One teacher times his students on how fast they can reconfigure their desks for group work and back to straight rows for individual work. The classes race against their personal best, learning to cooperate in the process. Other teachers assign tasks—putting back supplies, handing in work, posting information, sharpening pencils, etc.

## If Students Struggle to Complete Work . . .

*Setting goals.* Marzano, Pickering, and Pollack (2001) list setting goals and objectives as one of nine instructional strategies that significantly increase student achievement. To be most effective, students need to have a hand in personalizing goals set by the teacher. In fact, if a teacher sets goals that are too narrow in scope, students might actually learn *less.* For example, if a teacher hands out a guide that lists the exact content students are responsible for in an ecology unit, how many students will investigate anything that isn't on the list? Or if a teacher says, "Be sure to complete at least one station today," how many students will slow down and complete only one? Having students add to or enhance the goals helps to avoid this problem.

Some ways to set meaningful, individualized goals include the following:

- When providing choices in math problems, journal prompts, or other assignments, have students write down their choice as one of their goals.
- For units that will last more than a day or two, have the class create a KWL chart (page 101). Then let each student choose an item from the Learn column that they want to answer and share with the class before the end of the unit.
- Students can set goals through contracts. These are especially effective for independent study, but can also be used to help students develop better habits for regular class work.

Elementary school: Payne (1996) recommends using visual representations of goals for young elementary students. For an assignment involving five math problems, students make five circles on a piece of scrap paper and check one off for each problem they solve.

Secondary school: Students might write goals in their planners. Some teachers include a place for setting goals in instruction packets for major assignments. If students have class time to work on projects, they can write goals on self-stick notes and place them on their desk where the teacher can glance at them.

## CONCLUSION

Note that these strategies deal with differentiating the *process* of learning—getting students ready to learn. Often, implementing these decreases how much we need to differentiate the *content, products, or assessments* of learning. The latter will still be necessary, but a differentiated approach to classroom management often helps more students thrive academically.

# 7

# Differentiated Reading Instruction

*Before you read on . . .*

How do you rate yourself as a reader? Check one:

☐ I seldom read for pleasure because reading takes too much effort.
☐ I seldom read for pleasure because reading is boring.
☐ I sometimes read for pleasure, especially a few favorite authors or magazines.
☐ I look forward to reading and make time for it.
☐ Reading is one of my favorite pastimes. I'm usually partway through at least one book.

How do students view reading? Here are some comments from some struggling sixth-grade readers:

It's kinda boring just sitting there and doing work. Like in a reading class we'll have to read a book and then write a paper on it, read a book, write a paper, like that? If I get into it and it's a good book, I won't stop reading. I'll walk with the book, sittin' there reading it. When it's a book I'm into, but I almost like talk to the person in the book, you know what I'm saying.

It's like at the beginning of the year they place you in a level and then once you're at that level they're not gonna let you go nowhere unless you show them if you're higher. And sometimes even if you ask them and show them sometimes they won't even pay attention.

Right now, both of these students know that reading is occasionally a fun activity, but neither searches for opportunities to read. Too many students view reading as a boring activity. Mueller (2001) quotes a high schooler who had only recently begun to make meaning as he read:

Most of the time reading is a pretty passive thing. Nothing really goes on. Nothing. Well, maybe you're doing something, but it's just not interesting.

93

You are just sitting there and reading words. You are looking at a bunch of letters and paragraphs and sentences. You just read. It is pretty basic. It's boring. It's different for those people that actually like to read. (p. 46)

Somehow, in our struggle to help all children learn to read in time to pass standardized tests, we need to ensure that they *enjoy* reading or we'll fail at the real goal of creating lifelong readers. Hopefully, they'll grasp why reading is better than television:

- There are no commercials.
- You can skip the boring parts.
- Parents don't get as mad when you read for hours.
- You can check out the ending.
- You don't need electricity.
- What else? Get students to brainstorm more ideas.

The lens of Sensing and Intuition—the categorical difference in how people take in information—provides an important framework for reading instruction. In this chapter, we'll look at the following:

- The fundamental differences in how Sensing and Intuitive students learn to read
- Activities that help Sensing students become better readers and are also enjoyable for Intuitive students
- The *content* of what students with different preferences like to read. This provides patterns that teachers can use for creating differentiated choices
- Strategies for differentiation that allow all students to engage in higher level thinking around reading texts.

## HOW SENSING AND INTUITIVE STUDENTS LEARN TO READ

In a study of early reading, Chittenden, Salinger, and Bussis (2001) reported two distinctly different modes of cognition for sounding out words and determining meaning, which they described as Cluster A and Cluster B students.

Cluster A children tended to express their thoughts in imaginative, divergent ways, approach work in a mobile and fluid way, pay attention to several stimuli at once, and engage in parallel sequencing of thought as they juggled diverse ideas and meanings. Note how closely this description matches that of Intuition. Cluster A students emphasized fluidity in reading.

Every child in the group freely offered word substitutions based on memory of the story line, picture clues, partial word analysis, grammatical knowledge, background knowledge, or some combination of these resources. The majority of children gave indication in one form or another that they took in relatively broad spans of print . . . each one of the tactics just described enabled a child to say something when faced with uncertainty and thus to keep the reading performance moving . . . children who exhibited imaginative and divergent preferences appeared to regard text more as guidelines than prescriptions for the construction of meaning. Though necessary in pointing the way, guidelines leave room for deviation. Cluster A children seemed perfectly comfortable in straying from a literal translation of each and every word. (p. 120, 122)

Cluster B children tended to express their thoughts in realistic and convergent ways, approach their work in contained and methodical ways, be more narrow and analytical in directing their attention, and engage in linear thinking processes. Note how closely this description matches that of Sensing. In early experiences, Cluster B students emphasized accuracy in reading.

They usually attended to every word on a page and seemed determined to get each one correct. They rarely showed signs of reading ahead. If they didn't know a word, they tended to wait or ask for help, to remain silent while they tried to figure it out for themselves, or to engage in a head-on struggle of phonic analysis . . . This tendency to balk at adult requests to guess extended to all forms of proffered support, whether the suggested grounds for making a guess were context clues, letter-sound clues, or a supplied rhyming word. The children who paused most often in reading also tended to work in a step-by-step, methodical manner. More importantly, they seemed to organize their thinking in a linear fashion, linking one detail or inference with the next so as to cumulate meaning . . . Had these children skipped steps (words or phrases) in the process, they probably could not have retained meaning so well, nor would skipping have allowed them to build meaning cumulatively in the first place. (p. 121, 123)

These students interrupt themselves for the sake of accuracy and may lose the momentum of the story rather than make mistakes. Imagine the impact on these students if they are asked to read aloud in front of peers before they have confidence in their reading. Myers (1993) described the difficulties of Sensing students when they don't receive the tools to proceed in this step-by-step method.

They are expected to acquire a vocabulary of "sight words" before learning to sound out words. These children clutter their minds with false assumptions: that there is no good explanation of how to read, or surely the teacher would have given it; that a reader must find some way to remember each separate word—a task that gets harder the more one reads; and that there is no way to be sure what a word is until the teacher says it. They learn by the *word-attack method,* that is, they identify a word from its general shape or from its place on a familiar page or by remembering what comes next in the story or by looking at the nearest picture. None of these makeshift techniques is reliable in the actual reading of new material. (p. 141)

A passage from *Dicey's Song* (Voigt, 1982) illustrates the struggles of a Sensing child, Maybeth, who wasn't taught to read in a structured way, as seen through the eyes of her older sister who is tutoring her:

You mean, what Maybeth does is sees—like the beginning of the word and then she guesses. . . . And she's not a guesser by nature. . . . It would make her nervous, and she'd always be waiting to be caught in a mistake, and she wouldn't hear what she was reading, so it would be hard for her to understand what she was reading. Maybeth likes—knowing how to do what she's doing. When she gets nervous, and scared—she can't think about things. (p. 143)

Think about oral reading tests for fluency and specific skills at recognizing phonemes. How might Sensing and Intuitive students perform, given the above information?

In older students who read well, the difference between how Sensing and Intuitive students read can still be pronounced. Sensing students continue to read sequentially, moving through text at a steady pace that remains fairly constant, no matter what they are reading. In contrast, Intuitive students develop two different reading speeds. For factual texts (informational nonfiction or textbooks), especially ones outside of their personal interests, their pace and approach generally matches that of Sensing students. However, they are likely to accelerate pace when engaged in narrative texts, often taking in information in chunks rather than individual words or sentences; they may also unconsciously skip descriptive passages. Because of this, on average Intuitive students are faster readers, although some Sensing people report this same change in style. Sometimes, teachers react by saying, "You can't have read that carefully! Go back and start over." On the other hand, some teachers reward or praise students who read so quickly. Sensing students can grow to feel inadequate if teachers equate speed with competency.

In summary, paying attention to the varying needs of Sensing and Intuitive students is essential if all students are to learn to read *and* find reading enjoyable. Sensing students, without reinforcement of the concept that letters stand for sounds, may struggle to make sense of reading. However, if instruction embeds phonics within reading texts, Sensing students will become proficient readers. A motto for working with Sensing students might be "Help them build the bridge from what they know to what they're learning." This means explicitly teaching strategies through direct instruction.

Clearly, phonics instruction alone is not enough. The National Reading Panel (2004) concluded that "Older children [than first grade] receiving phonics instruction were better able to decode and spell words and to read text orally, but their comprehension of text was not significantly improved" (p. 4). This chapter is filled with strategies for teaching skills *and* helping students create meaning.

## DIFFERENTIATED STRATEGIES FOR SENSING AND INTUITION

### Decoding

In early reading instruction—and in working with older struggling readers—keep in mind the Sensing-Intuitive difference when choosing intervention strategies. Oberkircher (2006) listed successful strategies for each preference.

| *Sensing* | *Intuition* |
| --- | --- |
| Focus on sequences found in words | Focus on word chunks (little words inside big words) |
| Teach word families | Teach context clues |
| Use colors to highlight differences | Use mnemonics |
| Teach phonetic approaches | Teach patterns to manage double consonants or vowels |
| Use manipulatives | Assign lengthy spelling words (Intuitives work harder to master isosceles than ice) |

Note that some of these can be modified to better meet the needs of students with either preference. In brief:

- Sensing students can learn to use Intuitive strategies if they can practice separate from reading for comprehension.
- Intuitive students can concentrate on more repetitive tasks if the teacher adds a kinesthetic component (card sorts, movement, etc.) or friendly competition.

Consider having students work with different genres as they work through these activities, especially in the upper grades, to see which captures their interest. Use sports stories, video game guides, articles on "American Idol" contestants, chapters from the latest "hot" fiction titles for your grade level, how-to selections, nonfiction, and so on.

*Word chunks.* Pull words from a new text. The words should be ones that students understand when spoken but may not recognize when reading them for the first time. Keep these separate from totally new vocabulary. Teach them to find little words within big words, such as *time,* un*time*ly. Can they find syllables they recognize? Note that this allows Sensing students to use a procedure to decode a new word, but then practice fluency in context instead of stopping when they see the word.

A second step would be for them to preread a text, looking only for new words that they would use this strategy with before reading the text as a whole. The goal is to honor the style of Sensing (Cluster B) students while helping them read fluently. Note that most Intuitive students automatically look for word chunks and may grow quickly frustrated with the activity.

*Manipulatives.* Simple manipulatives include alphabet blocks and letters, but these can be used to teach sophisticated skills.

- *Self-stick notes.* Place letters and rimes (a vowel and any consonants that follow it in a syllable) on self-stick notes. Have students combine notes and say the words. For example, you might write "c," "l," "r," "b," "at," "an," and "ug" on the notes. Have students write down the words they find. Then, help them transfer the sound to new words such as "flattery" or "candid."

  Because this activity is hands-on, even middle-school students will engage in it, although they will grow tired of it more quickly than younger students. Intuitive students may engage more readily if the activity is turned into a contest—who can make the most words?
- *Pattern sorts.* Write words on cards and have students sort them into categories by the phonics rule you are teaching. One set might include "cap, cape, fin, fine, rat, rate." Beers (2003)[1] includes several ideas for card sorts.
- *Colors.* Students might highlight words they don't know prior to reading for meaning. Or, they might highlight prefixes in blue and practice reading those words for meaning. Or, they might highlight sight words in a passage to practice reading them quickly.

*Context clues.* Provide opportunities to practice "guessing" meaning by examining context. The goal is to increase the Sensing student's confidence in their guesses.

---

[1]*When Kids Can't Read* by Kylene Beers, although not written with type concepts in mind, contains dozens of strategies that will meet the needs of Extraverted and Sensing readers. Beers developed them through her work with struggling middle-school readers.

Separate this activity from reading text so that students can practice without interrupting flow. This could even be a class warm-up if red card/green card is used so that the students who are adept at guessing don't blurt out the answers. Post sample sentences, underlining one word for which the meaning can be easily ascertained from the sentence. Here are some examples:

- The <u>carillon</u> outside the big church rang out a song at noon each day.
- The movie made me so <u>melancholy</u> that I wanted to cry.
- I stared at the <u>tintype</u>. The eyes of the boy pictured in it seemed to stare right at me.
- The cowboy swung up on the <u>palomino</u>, patted its neck, and cried, "Giddy-up."

*Adjust sight word instruction.* When teaching sight words, include the phonetic instruction, pronunciation rules, and roots and syllables. Tie these drills to making meaning in texts as closely as possible. This is why books such as *Hop on Pop* are so valuable—students are actually reading stories as they learn to decode.

## Active Reading Strategies

Active reading strategies help struggling readers grasp that reading is not a passive activity. Beers (2003) uses "think-alouds" to model how good readers actively engage in text. At first, the teacher reads aloud from a fictional work, inserting comments to demonstrate what goes on in the mind of a reader. For example, a teacher might use the opening paragraph of *Jade Green* (Naylor, 2000) to model, as shown in Figure 7.1.

As one student said, "Well, it's really different, like, you know, like it's like the story has all this stuff in it, that if you really pay attention it's all there or at least there are hints there. But this is really hard work. You do this all the time?" (Beers, 2003, p. 122).

To help students use this technique with classroom or library books as they read silently, consider providing self-stick notes for them to record their questions and statements as they go. Then, these can be transferred to a notebook at the end of class.

**Figure 7.1**   Sample "Think-Aloud"

| Text | Teacher "Think-Aloud" |
|---|---|
| When the carriage turned onto Stone Street, . . . | A carriage? This must take place a long time ago. Stone Street sounds like a cold, lonely place. |
| . . . it was as though the house were watching. There were two gables with a window in each, the curtains slightly parted like cats' eyes, not quite closed, spying. | This sounds spooky. I wonder if this is a mystery or horror story? |
| Earlier that day I had arrived by train in Charleston, and had at once been restless to move about after the tiresome journey from Ohio. Indeed, I felt constrained in my long gray skirt and jacket, a bonnet of gray and blue on my head. I was hungry as well, for in the first few hours I had eaten all the bread and cheese I had packed for the trip (p. 1). | A train. So it's probably after 1850.<br><br>Charleston, that's the south. So an Ohio Yankee down south.<br><br>The narrator is female.<br><br>She had only bread and cheese along? Is she poor? And she packed it herself, so maybe this is an adult. |

---

**TRY THIS!**

Use the red card/green card technique (p. 79) to demonstrate active reading strategies. Prepare a handout with prompts for each strategy for students to use as a reference, such as the following:

- Make a prediction (I wonder if . . . I bet that . . . )
- Ask a question (Why is . . . I don't get . . . Who . . . )
- Clarify something (I think this means . . . Now I get it . . . )
- Make a judgment (I don't like . . . This is confusing because . . . )
- Make a connection (This reminds me of another book where . . . Once I also . . . )

Ask each student to raise a hand and make a comment as you read aloud. Once they've spoken, they turn the red card up until all students have had a turn.

Sometimes a few students don't want to share. Give them the choice of writing down a comment or speaking up; most choose to speak up quickly.

Then, let students continue with the text, working in pairs while using the sample prompts to continue through the text. Note that this also provides a chance for *Extraverted* students to talk about text as they read, honoring the fact that they think as they speak. *Introverted* students might be ready more quickly to continue on their own. However, if the think-aloud has helped them redefine what it means to engage with text, they may wish to practice more with another student.

For primary students, have them practice this technique as you read aloud. Provide red/green cards to five students at a time. The first group of five might all make a prediction and then pass the card to another student. The second group of five might all ask questions. Continue to rotate until all students have used one of the strategies.

---

## Build Interest in Reading a Text

Sensing students (and many Intuitive students) may read more willingly if teachers start with activities that create an interest in the text. Suggested strategies include the following:

*Key word prediction* (National Urban Alliance, 2005). This works well for engaging students in reading nonfiction passages. Choose a word that is central to the theme of a text. Then, choose seven to ten other words found in the text. Ask students to work in small groups (two to four students) to make predictions about how each word might relate to the theme of the article. Have the groups share their ideas for one or two of the words. Then, have students read the text independently. Students pay attention as they check whether their guesses were right. Although teachers sometimes worry that this strategy might result in students remembering their incorrect hunches instead of the text, this doesn't happen. The "aha" moments seem to embed the correct answers in the students' minds. Figure 7.2 was generated for a magazine article on the game Rock, Paper, Scissors.

*Tap a theme.* This strategy uses a circle-frame map (Hyerle, 2004; see further examples at http://www.thinkingmaps.com). On a whiteboard or overhead, write the theme or essential question you want students to grapple with as they read. Draw a circle around the theme and then a larger circle around it (see Figure 7.3). Ask students to make their own map, answering the question "What do you know about ___" in the outer circle. Give them two minutes to do so. Then, have students share a word or phrase from their map; write these on your map.

**Figure 7.2**   Key Word Prediction

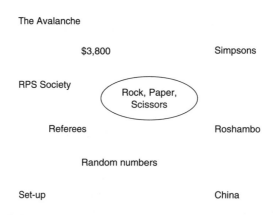

NOTE: "The Avalanche" is a series of "rocks," $3,800 is the prize money in a major RPS contest, Bart Simpson plays RPS, and so on.

**Figure 7.3**   Circle Frame Map

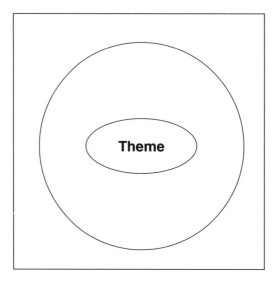

Then, draw a frame around the outer circle and ask students, "How do you know these things?" Students give sources such as school, parents, friends, movies, and other adults.

Before getting into the actual text, you might play part of a song, movie, or news clip that introduces the theme. Have students compare their circle maps to the ideas conveyed in the media clip by adding to their maps in a different color. Let them explain their maps to a partner. Record the different ways students reacted to the clip—what connections they made, their opinions, etc. Encourage discussion that builds interest in the text so they'll eagerly begin reading.

*Prior knowledge stations.* These stations serve a different purpose than learning stations and are fully explained on page 59. Full examples for historical novels are given on pages 60–61. Social studies teachers might use the same kinds of stations to cover the factual part of a new unit: studying maps of a country, exports, famous citizens, foods, etc. Math teachers might have stations for reviewing measurement, basic two-dimensional shapes, tessellations, and other related concepts before moving on to areas of three-dimensional shapes.

*KWL charts* (Ogle, 1986). Although this is a fairly common strategy, think about how it bridges between Sensing and Intuitive styles. Sensing students get to start with "Know," the knowledge they already have about a topic. And, in the "Want to Know" column, Intuitive students get to brainstorm new paths.

Use the chart to give choices. Indicate which "Want to Know" items the whole class will be learning. Then, ask students to choose from remaining items and research them on their own to report to the class.

*Journal entries.* Have students respond to a prompt that introduces a theme or event in a story. Simple ways to differentiate include either giving a choice of two prompts that appeal to different preferences or changing the kinds of prompts over time. Sensing prompts include listing facts, writing about personal experiences, asking what they remember about an event, or describing an object or place. Intuitive prompts include imagining, answering what-ifs, and pretending.

## CONTENT DIFFERENCES IN WHAT STUDENTS LIKE TO READ

Although one positive experience with a book by a specific author or in a specific genre can send a student looking for more regardless of type preferences—and one lousy experience can shut a student down—there are patterns in what people with different type preferences choose to read.

Further, there are striking differences between what teachers and students consider notable books. Although students certainly need encouragement in reading new materials and a core knowledge of some of the classics, go to the Web site for the International Reading Association (http://www.reading.org) and compare the lists of books rated highly by students, "Children's Choices," and by teachers, "Teachers' Choices." In many years, no title appears on both lists!

A few ground rules:

- Grades K–2: Make sure that students have access to fiction, nonfiction, poetry, and magazines. Look for patterns in what struggling readers choose to read. Is a particular genre is more motivating for them? Students might keep log books in which they check off the genre they're reading during choice time. They might also rate their enjoyment of all-class reading selections.
- Grades 3–5: Consider using short stories and articles for all-class readings. If you want to engage the whole class in a novel, choose it as a read-aloud. Provide choices for silent reading. Why? So the non-avid readers aren't stuck with a lengthy story that doesn't appeal to them.
- Grades 6–9: Even with classics, give choices whenever possible. *A Wrinkle in Time* or *Ender's Game, Number the Stars* or *Milkweed, Kaffir Boy* or *Roll of Thunder, Hear My Cry.*
- Grades 10–12: Especially in college-prep classes, reading for enjoyment—humor, science fiction, current fiction—almost disappears. Sherre Sachar, daughter of award-winning children's author Louis Sachar, reported as she finished a high-school career filled with Advanced Placement literature classes, "I haven't

read a book for pleasure in about three years. If I do, it's in the summer, and I might get through only one book because I'm so sick of trying to read. It's not fun anymore" (Strauss, 2005, p. 1). As you read the information below, think of how you might differentiate for the different preferences.

### Sensing Student Preferences in Reading

*Episodic fiction.* Sensing students often enjoy stories they can *finish.* These include short stories and episodic novels (each chapter stands as a story on its own). They feel a sense of completion and accomplishment as they finish reading for the day. Many novels are written this way, from easy readers to adult prize-winning literary fiction. This contrasts with "page-turner" format, with each chapter ending with a character in danger, a mysterious question, or another device that makes the reader want to turn the page. As their reading speed increases, Sensing students may be drawn to realistic page-turners, but episodic fiction can build enjoyment at first and remain a favorite. Many Intuitive students love these books as well.

Besides short stories and collections, examples include the following (in order by reading level):

- Many "I Can Read" books such as *Frog and Toad*
- Beverly Cleary novels (Henry Huggins and Ramona books)
- *Mrs. Piggle-Wiggle* (MacDonald)
- *Pippi Longstocking* (Lindgren)
- *A Long Way from Chicago* (Peck)
- *Who Am I without Him?* (Flake)
- *The House on Mango Street* (Cisneros)
- *The No. 1 Ladies' Detective Agency* (Smith)

*White space novels,* formatted with less text per page, also appeal to Sensing students (and to most struggling readers). These books may have very short chapters, be written in blank verse, use a movie script format, or otherwise break up text in interesting ways. Again, these books can fuel a sense of accomplishment as students add up the number of pages they've read. Examples include the following (in order by reading level):

- *Love that Dog* (Creech)
- *Choose Your Own Adventure* series (various authors, just reissued)
- *Regarding the Fountain* (Klise and Klise)
- *Abarat* (Barker)
- *Bronx Masquerade* (Grimes)
- *Make Lemonade* (Wolff)
- *Keeper of the Night* (Holt)
- *Monster* (Myers)
- *Welcome to the Ark* (Tolan)
- *ttyl* (Myracle)
- *Burned* (Hopkins)

*Nonfiction* is another favorite for Sensing students. They often prefer reading about real life. Sometimes this is satisfied through reading realistic fiction about children just like them, but the preschool tendency of many Sensing children for playing "house," "school," or "firefighter" often transfers over into wanting to read about bugs, firefighters, or helicopters. They enjoy the *details,* not the overviews found in textbooks.

Add nonfiction to "white space" and one might encourage these students to read the following:

- *Ripley's Believe It or Not*
- *Guinness Book of World Records*
- Usborne nonfiction
- Stephen Biesty's *Incredible Cross-Sections* series
- Eyewitness books

*Series books.* Sensing students often like what is familiar and may plow through all of the *Baby-sitters Club* books or other similar series. Although these may never attain literary quality as far as character development or plot, type in a page of a *Hardy Boys* or *Nancy Drew* book and you'll find they're written at about a fifth-grade level. Eventually the student will exhaust a series and turn to something new.

## Intuitive Student Preferences in Reading

*No More Dead Dogs* (Korman, 2002) tells the tale of Wallace Wallace, an eighth grader who didn't like the novel assigned to the whole class. His report followed directions, right down to his opinion that the book couldn't be lousier if it came with a letter bomb. When the teacher insists that the book is a timeless classic, Wallace gives his analysis.

> "What a heartbreaking surprise ending!" [said Mr. Fogelman]
>
> "I wasn't surprised," I said. "I knew Old Shep was going to die before I started page one."
>
> "Don't be ridiculous," the teacher snapped. "How?"
>
> I shrugged. "Because the dog always dies. Go to the library and pick out a book with an award sticker and a dog on the cover. Trust me, that dog is going down."
>
> "Not true!" stormed Mr. Fogelman.
>
> "Well," I challenged, "What happened to Old Yeller?" (p. 4–5)

Soon the whole class joins in. Sounder. Bristle Face. *Where the Red Fern Grows*—two for one.

Here's the problem. Intuitives like Wallace (who also probably has a preference for Thinking) often know exactly what they like to read and why. The more you can channel their energy into reading they enjoy, the better off you'll be as a teacher.

*Science fiction and fantasy.* The majority of science fiction and fantasy fans are Intuitives. Although Harry Potter has vastly increased the popularity of fantasy (partly because Harry, Ron, and Hermione—and their teachers—are just like people students know if one disregards their magical abilities), many Intuitive students continue to read science fiction and fantasy through adulthood, especially Introverted Intuitives and Intuitive Thinkers.

Think about it. Most people will say that they *love* or *hate* science fiction. Few are lukewarm. Despite phenomenal classics such as *War of the Worlds* (Wells), *20,000 Leagues Under the Sea* (Verne), *Ender's Game* (Card), and *A Wrinkle in Time* (L'Engle), adult science fiction books don't win National Book Awards or Pulitzer prizes. This means that science fiction titles disappear in higher level classes, even though the "what-if" philosophical questioning of the great science fiction novels encourages higher level thinking.

*In-depth study.* Intuitive students will also read every book on a subject of interest, perhaps to the exclusion of anything else until they have exhausted a subject. This is especially true of Introverted Intuitives. Often, they'll read more and more difficult materials as they attempt to learn more. Because these students often thrive on independent study—and do far better work when they choose a course of study—teachers will want to give them opportunities to delve into these interests.

*Choice.* Yes, Intuitive students can be required to read certain materials, but they'll engage better with required texts if they also have choices. Further, these students can be quietly stubborn, performing poorly or remaining highly critical of any text that they did not want to read, like Wallace in *No More Dead Dogs*. And, if they've read it before, they're less likely than Sensing students to buy into a teacher's position that they will discover new themes and ideas the second time around. One way to teach an all-class novel, yet honor students who have read it, is to offer choices of two or three longer novels with the same theme. Why longer? Because the students who are only somewhat bothered by rereading will generally choose to stick with the all-class novel rather than do extra work.

## STRATEGIES FOR DIFFERENTIATION

In spite of the differences in instructional needs already noted for Sensing and Intuition, and the differences in preferred reading content, there *are* some strategies that help teachers meet the needs of both Sensing and Intuitive students with varying ability levels.

Silent reading can be tough on students who don't look favorably on reading. Mueller (2001) points out that many struggling readers avoid sustained silent reading periods by acting out, taking too much time to select a text, or staring at a page while daydreaming.

The following strategies are designed to make independent reading more enjoyable and engaging for students with various learning styles. Before dismissing a strategy, consider whether it might appeal to students whose learning style is very different from your own.

> **TRY THIS!**
>
> Go through the lists of reading activities in this section. Count up how many you regularly use for each of the quadrants of the type table.
>
> - IS _____
> - ES _____
> - IN _____
> - EN _____
>
> Do you favor or tend to overlook any of the quadrants in choosing reading activities? Choose a new activity for the quadrant you use the least. Try it at least six times before deciding how well it works. Watch how your reluctant readers react.

### Introversion and Sensing Activities

*Guided reading (silently, looking for answers to specific questions).* These students often appreciate clear assignments. Avoid making all questions fact based. Students might also choose an adjective or quality that best describes a character, make predictions, or chart cause-effect relationships. The following prompts are modeled after the short-answer questions on the Minnesota Comprehensive Assessment.

- Fifth grade
  o Use the information and examples in this poem to compare humans and dogs in at least two ways.
  o Explain why you think this character chose to take a stand. Use three details from the story to support your answer.

- Eighth grade
  o On the basis of the editorial you read, give four pieces of advice that you think the writer might give to a high-school student.
  o The Great Salt Lake is a unique environment. Part A: List three characteristics that make it unusual. Part B: Using facts from the article, explain how each characteristic is unusual.

*Timelines or storyboards.* These students often benefit from identifying the different events in a story. Make this activity more meaningful by having students choose a set number of events from a story or time in history and write a sentence for each to justify why it is one of the most important events.

*Choral reading.* Instead of reading entire texts aloud, have the class choral read some sections. The group process helps Sensing students avoid getting stuck too often on word recognition; they hear other students and continue in the text.

*Journaling.* These students often enjoy journal entries that allow them to connect a story to their own lives. What would they like or dislike about a situation or event? How would they have acted? Which character would they want to have for a friend and why?

## Extraversion and Sensing Activities

*Read with a partner.* In general, students who prefer Extraversion and Sensing struggle the most to sit still and read. *Anything* that involves action or interaction seems more appealing. Allow them to read with other students in any of the following ways:

- Let them sit back-to-back while reading, for companionship.
- Provide alternative spots for reading than sitting at their desks, such as carpet squares or mats.
- Have them read silently with a partner, but allow them to make a comment/prediction/connection about what they are reading every five minutes or so. Help them hold their thoughts by having them write them on self-stick notes.
- Assign parts in chapters heavy on dialogue to read aloud. To avoid the trap of round-robin reading, where children pay attention only to the passage they're going to read, they might read the passage first before knowing which part they will have.

*Picture/caption journals.* Post a question for students to react to. After reading the first chapter of *Breadwinner* (Ellis), the story of a young girl in Afghanistan whose father is arrested by the Taliban, students drew pictures and journaled about three things they would dislike about living as the girl did. Their journal pages looked like this:

To hold student interest, the teacher changed the writing prompts for each chapter, but the format stayed the same.

*Listening to a book on tape.* Because listening while reading engages two senses instead of just one, Extraverted Sensing students often accelerate in reading by listening to passages on tape while following along and then rereading them silently. Note that this may help students with any type preferences, but Extraverted Sensing students may particularly enjoy it as an alternative to silent inactivity.

*Popcorn reading.* This differs from round-robin reading in that students don't know when it will be their turn, so they stay focused on the text. Also, students choose how much or how little they will read. They can stop after one sentence. The teacher designates which student will go first. When that student chooses to stop, he or she calls the name of the next student to read. This keeps all students engaged in the text. The urban students I work with *really* enjoy this practice, although a few (usually but not always Intuitive) students struggle not to read ahead. In some circumstances, the teacher might allow them to do so; they will still be able to participate in class discussions. Teachers might allow popcorn reading in literature circles as well.

*Suspenseful starts.* Read aloud to the class until you reach an exciting part. Then stop and ask the students to continue on their own to find out what happens next.

## Introversion and Intuition

Note that these suggestions assume that the student reads and understands text well. *Usually,* reading comes easily to these students. These techniques help them slow down or review text. When they struggle to read, they still prefer to work at their own pace on activities that will help them improve.

*Imaginative journal entries.* These students often enjoy writing letters to characters (or from characters), imagining themselves in the shoes of a character, retelling the story from the viewpoint of a different narrator, or otherwise going beyond the text.

*Predictions.* These students might enjoy making predictions and justifying them as a way to analyze text.

*Writing new scenes.* Let the students write a new chapter or create an alternative ending, based on reviewing and then changing a choice that a character made.

## Extraversion and Intuition

*Variety of reading approaches.* This group often thrives if a teacher keeps reading interesting by mixing a variety of approaches each week or month.

*Group discussions/debates.* Ask students to form opinions as they read and be ready to discuss them. Here are some sample prompts:

- What should a character do next? Why?
- How would you solve this character's problem? Why?
- Was a character's decision right or wrong? Wise or unwise? Why?

*Role play.* Have students take notes as they read on how to role-play a character in a situation. Will he or she be happy? Defensive? Ready to take action?

*Self instruction, journal choices.* These students thrive on choices, even more so than other types.

## Literature Circles

Many resources exist on effective methods for using literature circles. To ensure that they meet the needs of the various type preferences, include the following practices.

- Designate structured roles for students. If these roles can include activities that meet the needs of different learning styles, students may stay more on task.

Sample roles include the following:

- o Introverted Sensing: Add events to a timeline, identify new vocabulary
- o Extraverted Sensing: Illustrator, drawing key events
- o Introverted Intuition: Connector, recording how the story connects with the real world, other stories, students' lives, etc.
- o Extraverted Intuition: Discussion director, identifying discussion questions

- Choose books at varying ability levels that all share the same theme. This allows for richer analysis within groups as they prepare to share their text, using higher level thinking skills, with classmates. Choices for compassion are listed on pages 85–86. The following chart shows possible texts for four essential questions that can tie the unit together, one set given for each grade level. Note that the lists differentiate for ability and interest:

| Primary grades: What is a hero? (Note: teachers might combine read-alouds and picture books) | Grades 3–5: How can children take a stand? | Grades 6–9: What is an ideal society? Can one be created? | Grades 10–12: Destiny or determination: Which controls our lives? |
|---|---|---|---|
| Stone Fox (Gardiner) | Harry Potter books (Rowling) | The Giver (Lowry) | The Great Gatsby (Fitzgerald) |
| Horton Hears a Who (Seuss) | Behind the Bedroom Wall (Williams) | Ender's Game (Card) | Anna Karenina (Tolstoy) |
| Charlotte's Web (White) | Caddie Woodlawn (Brink) | Fahrenheit 451 (Bradbury) | The Chosen (Chaim Potok) |
| The Story of Ruby Bridges (Coles and Ford) | The Landry News (Clements) | Among the Hidden (Haddix) | Invisible Man (Ellison) |

- Allow for choice. Let students preview four to six books and choose.
- Have the groups set goals. Help both Judging and Perceiving students develop good work habits by cooperatively deciding how they will read the book (independently, popcorn-style, with pauses to share predictions and connections and judgments, or in other ways) and how quickly. Ask them to submit a "contract."
- Have the groups use Thinking Maps or other tools, recording their work on paper large enough for you to see their progress at a glance.
- Suggest the use of conversation sticks (page 82) so that all group members are participating.

## Review Unit Contents Before Immersing Students in Textbook Materials

Both Sensing and Intuitive students benefit from knowing which details they can ignore. Sensing types pick up on thematic material better if the concepts they are to grasp are identified. Intuitive students may not attend to details unless teachers point out which ones are crucial.

Murphy (1992) suggests that teachers walk through textbook materials by looking at pictures and headings and identifying learning expectations. To honor both Sensing and Intuition, identify both themes and details that students will be responsible for. For example, in a unit on the Civil War, details might include the following: Dates for each major battle? Who won? Who commanded the winning army at each battle? Themes they need to grasp might be phrased like this: Picture yourself as a soldier in the war. Why did you decide to fight and what keeps you in the army? Why did the South think slavery was right? Why did the war go on so long? Could the war have been avoided?

### Give Choice

As often as possible, allow students choices in reading materials, in reporting formats, in where they sit to read. On a guided reading worksheet, let them choose nine out of ten questions to answer and cross the other one out. Having choices lets students feel more in control and can be a significant motivator.

Flood your room with desirable reading materials. Some studies suggest that elementary classroom libraries should have about five or six books per student that capture their attention and hold it (Fractor, Woodruff, Martinez, & Teale, 1993). In one such bilingual fifth-grade classroom (Worthy & Roser, 2004), where the teacher also used read-alouds, provided opportunities for students to share what they were reading, and provided instruction in word recognition and comprehension strategies, the researchers reported, "By the end of the year, students' desk stacks held 4 to 12 books—from thin picture books to tomes, some in process, some in planning—much like the bedside table of an avid reader. The students were reading . . . Each of them (save one) passed the end-of-year state examination in reading. That child missed by one question. In a classroom of comparable learners down the hall, the results were much more bleak" (p. 188). A synthesis of "book flood" studies in which teachers were also taught to use the materials showed significant increases in literacy levels (Elley, 2000).

## CONCLUSION

Teachers who employ multiple scaffolding strategies, such as those described in this chapter, *can* help struggling readers actually read advanced texts. Beers (2003) describes how an eighth-grade teacher took her "lowest" reading class through *Huckleberry Finn* when they asked to read what the "advanced" students were reading.

> The teacher did an incredible job of frontloading information students needed to be successful. Students read some sections aloud in paired reading; the teacher read aloud other chapters. Some students with word recognition problems listened to parts of it on tape. Students read independently and stopped often to think aloud their confusions, predictions, or clarifications with peers or the teacher. They kept double-entry journals and used bookmarks and sticky notes to keep up with questions, unusual vocabulary, and comments they wanted to make . . . and they finally finished the book.

At that point, they said they wanted to take the same test that the kids in the advanced class took. They did and all scored between 80 percent and 94 percent on the test. As students looked at their tests with incredible pride, one said, "I guess now we're just as smart as those other kids."

Another said, "Yeah, maybe we're even smarter."

A third remarked, "Being smart is hard work, but it sure feels good once you've done it."

After a moment of silence, another said, "I guess now we've got to keep it up. What's the next book they're going to read?" (p. 262–263)

Those students continued to read the same texts as the advanced class, and the principal changed their report cards to read "Advanced Language Arts." It can be done, but the teacher admitted that she'd never worked so hard.

# 8

# Differentiated Writing Instruction

**Before you read on . . .**

Answer True or False to the following statements:

_____ I consider myself a writer.
_____ Outlining helps students produce better writing.
_____ Students need to process their thoughts individually before writing.
_____ Personal stories/narratives are the easiest form of writing.

**W**hat are you looking for in your students?

One Sensing teacher gave A's on papers that contained detailed sensory descriptions and graded down papers that used exaggeration to make points.

One Intuitive teacher gave assignment after assignment that required students to imagine different endings to famous fairy tales or change the gender of a character or the time period. The same students struggled each time.

One Sensing teacher required students to follow a specific report format. The same students did worse on subsequent assignments that required the same format.

One Intuitive teacher refused to give directions beyond, "Compare and contrast. If I tell you how to do it, all of your papers will look the same."

Our own preferences influence our writing styles and how we evaluate student writing. How did you answer the opening questions for this chapter?

*I consider myself a writer.* People of all personality preferences can become good writers, but they may need different scaffolding. Do you think your needs were met in your early writing experiences?

*Outlining helps students produce better writing.* For fiction, many Judging writers operate this way, but many Perceiving writers find outlining a hindrance.

J. K. Rowling knew what would happen in the final chapter of the seventh Harry Potter book before she finished the first book. Madeleine L'Engle doesn't outline, nor does she begin with the ending in mind; she lets events unfold in her fiction and often completely reworks plot lines more than once. What is required of students in your school? Are there ways to be flexible?

*Students need to process their thoughts individually before writing.* Is there a balance between Extraverted and Introverted activities in your program so that Extraverts can talk through their ideas?

*Personal stories/narratives are the easiest form of writing.* Do you give opportunities for students to write nonfiction, fiction, procedures, and other forms to build confidence in students with different preferences?

Although all types can learn to write, some types naturally excel at some forms of writing over others. Make sure that in spite of state standards or writing tests, you mix the various genres of writing.

- Sensing types often are adept at writing clear facts and procedures, whether detailing steps in a science experiment or explaining what happened in a story or real-life event. They may write with exquisite detail. They often need practice in painting the big picture or drawing conclusions.
- Intuitive types prefer writing forms in which they can express themselves uniquely, unbounded by teacher guidelines. Fiction, poetry, and unstructured journaling are often appealing. They write about great ideas, but may struggle to add sufficient detail or keep things sequential so others can follow their reasoning.
- Thinking types often produce logical arguments, opinion pieces, and persuasive critiques, but struggle to share personal experiences or emotions.
- Feeling types often write personal experience pieces with warmth and sincerity but may lack forceful argument.

If early instruction emphasizes one or two forms of writing, some students will quickly feel inadequate—unless teachers use appropriate scaffolding without overstructuring the task.

Mixing genres gives Sensing students a break from writing short stories or speculating about things outside of their experiences. Stead (2005) found that his second graders grew more excited about writing, and produced more varied texts, when he turned from narrative and fiction to nonfiction. After the class heard a factual read-aloud and a student produced a "fact book" about chickens on her own initiative, he rethought his emphasis.

I realized then that for too long I had kept my students in a world of personal narrative and fantasy by providing demonstrations of these writing forms almost exclusively. When I looked through my classroom library I found that 90 percent of the books were fiction stories . . . No wonder my children wrote the same things every day . . . our own limited knowledge of different writing genres and how they work has made us poor models and guides for our children. (p. 33)

Like reading, writing is usually an Introverted activity. The nature of the writing assignment may call on Sensing, Intuition, Thinking, or Feeling to different degrees. Let's look first at ways to help Extraverts engage in writing and then at ways to help each preference improve writing various forms of text. Probably the most important part of writing instruction is to teach multiple methods for each stage of the writing process and then let students choose which ones work best for them.

*Note: Even at the college level, students struggle to process both content and a new form of writing.*

- If you want students to evaluate literature or present information on a topic with which they are unfamiliar, let them do so in a familiar writing format.
- If your goal is introducing a new writing format—compare/contrast, persuasion, narrative, etc.—let students work with familiar content.

Especially at the high-school level, all too often teachers expect students to be able to do both tasks at the same time. The result? Students fail to develop their writing strategies.

## HELPING EXTRAVERTS GET READY TO WRITE

Key to helping Extraverts write is remembering that they think out loud. Producing text is still a solitary activity, but allowing Extraverts opportunities to discuss ideas and opinions will give them the energy they need to put pen to paper.

### Plot the Thought

For the brainstorming phase of the writing process, allow students to choose whether to work alone or with a partner. Ask each student to write the assignment theme in the middle of a piece of paper. Then, as they generate ideas, through reflection or discussion, they can record them around the central idea, connecting or clustering different thoughts as they occur.

Before beginning to write, students can circle the items they definitely want to include and perhaps number them in the sequence they will write about them.

### Take a Stand

For many Extraverts, writing a persuasive argument seems pointless because a piece of paper is hardly an interactive sparring partner! Begin a unit on persuasive writing by providing students with a text piece or media clip that will spark opinions. You might show pictures of the Alaskan glaciers 30 years ago and their much-diminished size today to get students thinking about environmentalism. The National Public Radio Web site (http://www.npr.org) has recordings of broadcast interviews and speeches from numerous political leaders, artists, and celebrities. Play a clip from *Freedom Song* of the first students of color entering a formerly all-white school to generate discussion on courage. Students might take sides on whether they would or wouldn't want their own child being one of the first in a situation like that.

Allow students on both sides of the issue to articulate the reasons they chose their positions. You can record lists for each group on an overhead or whiteboard, or have students write out their reasons on strips of adding machine paper and then post them. Using strips allows students to reorganize the different ideas.

Then have students write out their own arguments, using a standard five-paragraph format. Emphasize that they need to have topic sentences and evidence that supports their chosen reasons. Obviously, this assignment might be spread out over more than one day.

Afterward, get students to reflect on the process. Have them complete three of the following four journal prompts:

- By listening to students on the other side of the issue, I learned . . .
- To write a good essay, I learned that I need to . . .
- Next time I write a persuasive essay, I will . . .
- I think I could write a persuasive argument about _____ because . . .

## Mobile Outlines

This technique is especially suited to Extraverted and Sensing students because it adds a kinesthetic component to writing. Have you seen children erase holes into their paper as they try to get each word right? Or become frustrated as they outline because they forgot something or decide to change the order? To avoid these dilemmas, have students outline their ideas on self-stick notes, one idea per sheet. Then they can move them around, add, and discard some without feeling that they have to get it right the first time.

Here are sample instructions for writing a narrative story that effectively moved urban students from writing factual, sequential narratives to writing engaging stories. Note that I used the language of Thinking Maps, describing using the note cards as a "flow map" because the students were already familiar with that technique.

For younger students, introduce the steps one at a time, with clear examples. For grades eight and up, the entire assignment might be given at once. Note that these examples provide a step-by-step process to help *Sensing* students form ideas. They also help *Intuitive* students understand where they could fill in more details.

### Your Personal Narrative—From Start to Finish

1. **Flow Map—what happened?** On note cards, record the major events of your story, as shown in the example below. Make at least **FIVE** cards.

*Topic: the first time I went bungee jumping*

| | | | |
|---|---|---|---|
| Grandma took me to the State Fair | We walked by the bungee jump. She said "Bet you'd never do that" | I got in line and paid my money. | An elevator took me to the top of the jump |
| I waited in line as others jumped. | I jumped! | Grandma asked me how it was. | |

2. On each card, use the following cues to write down ideas about how you could expand your description of each event in the story.

   - What did you think or feel? Emotions? Thoughts?

     If I die, I don't want my brother to get my GameCube . . .

   - What did you see? Hear? Taste? Touch? Smell?

     From the top of that platform I could see all kinds of safe, normal things to do at the fair—why hadn't I chosen the Ferris wheel or the whitewater rafts or the camel rides?

   - What did you and others say?

     As the attendant attached the safety harness he quipped, "Don't look so scared. We haven't dropped anyone yet."

   - What were you reminded of?

     Now I knew what a mountain climber felt like when a rope started to fray.

3. Put a **D** in the top right corner of at least two cards—ones that you could write about events in dialogue form.

4. Put an **S** on each card where you could describe the setting.

5. Write an introduction. Choose whether you will start with
   - **Dialogue**. "Bet you'd never do that," Grandma said, pointing at the bungee platform, a hundred feet above us.
   - **Startling statement**. Last summer, only a thin piece of rubber saved me from plunging to my death.
   - **Setting description**. Dust from the shuffling crowd stung my eyes. Ahead, someone screamed. I looked up and saw a body falling, falling, then jerking—it was the State Fair Bungee Jump.
   - **Emotion**. The instant I said, "Sure," my heart started beating so loudly I thought it was going to burst. I watched someone dive off the bungee platform, screaming, and thought, "I'm too young to die!"
   - **Character description**. My grandma is a clown. She never acts her age. Just last summer at the State Fair, she said to me, "Boscobelle, you can't claim to be a man until you've bungee-jumped. Here's $20 if you'll do it." I knew she was joking, but hey, I had to show her I was too old to joke with about something like that.
   - **Other ideas**.

6. Using your cards as an outline, write a draft of your story. Make sure your story includes
   - Dialogue
   - Setting description
   - Your thoughts and feelings
   - Action words

7. Add a conclusion. Make sure it connects with the story. Here are a few ways to start it:
   - After that day, I was different somehow. I . . .
   - Obviously, I'll never forget . . .

- Sometimes I wonder . . .
- Whenever I _____, I remember _____
- Who would have thought . . .
- Perhaps I should have _____ but . . .
- Since then, I _____

8. Check your writing. Where could you add richer words and figurative language? Examples include the following:
   - Instead of "I was really nervous," write "My legs were shaking so hard I thought I'd fall over before my turn came."
   - Instead of "The platform was high," write "The platform was so high in the air that the people in line looked like action figures, not people."
   - Instead of "Grandma hugged me," write "Grandma threw her arms around me and squeezed until I thought she'd break my ribs."

9. Have someone read your rough draft.
   - Are the events in your story clear?
   - Should you add description, dialogue, or information about your characters?
   - Can the reader "see" the experience?
   - Do the characters and dialogue seem realistic?
   - Suggestions for word choice or choice of details?
   - Spelling, grammar, punctuation?

10. Write your final draft. Check it against the assignment requirements.

## Peer Review Sessions

Having chances to talk about writing increases the interest level of many Extraverted students. At the elementary level, these "Author's Circles" might concentrate on the following:

- Helping each other follow a few basic punctuation rules
- Adding adjectives and strong verbs to writing
- Comparing each work to an example provided by the teacher.

In other words, provide explicit guidelines for praise and critique.

In grades four and up, students *can* give effective, timely feedback if peer review sessions are well-structured. For the personal narrative writing assignment described above, the following structure might help students provide helpful suggestions to each other in a supportive way.

- Start with specific, positive statements. Remember, Feeling students need positive feedback, but Thinking students respond best to specific statements that indicate the reader paid close attention to their ideas. "I liked your introduction" isn't as effective as, "The way you described your grandma made me feel like she was standing right in front of me."
- Ask students to provide suggestions on just a few, specific items. In the above assignment, students might help each other with item 8, adding richer words and figurative language. They might also suggest places to add description, dialogue, or more information, one of the items under item 9.

- Once the critiquers have made two or three suggestions, the writer should be able to talk about the ones they like best and why they might not use another one. Build in a pause to allow Introverted students time to process what has been said. You might ask the groups to use red card/green card (page 79) to indicate when they are ready to respond. Again, the writer needs to start with positive comments such as, "Your suggestion about dialogue reminded me that my grandma said . . ."
- Keep students from discussing spelling and grammar errors. Have them either write the correct spelling without comment or underline errors. Otherwise, the entire discussion may revolve around rules rather than ideas.

## Group Writing

The parody station in the poetry lesson described on page 51 is an example of group writing. Various structure elements, such as using conversation sticks (p. 82), can help ensure that all students participate. Teachers might ask groups to complete a process evaluation form, as described on page 82.

Groups often work well in writing texts that will be performed such as skits, dramatic readings, or poems. Perhaps as important as what they write is determining the process they will use to include everyone's ideas. They might record initial ideas on flip chart paper, with each person writing down the ideas they contribute. The group can then consider (or you might point out) who is underrepresented and ask for more ideas from those students.

Build in processing time as well so that the Introverts have a chance to come up with ideas.

## Tag Team Writing

This is an old party game. Form groups of no more than four students. Inform them that they will have a set amount of time, perhaps 20 minutes, to write a story together. Students write the first two sentences in a story and then hand the papers to another student, who writes the next two sentences. Keep passing the papers, watching for attention span evidence. Usually, the students are quite proud of their silly yet lengthy efforts.

To increase class interest in listening to the different stories, consider starting everyone with the same first two sentences. Here are some suggestions:

- I reached for the door handle of our car, still parked in the garage, when I saw something move. A massive shadow shifted along the wall and I took a step back.
- "Class, I have a surprise for you," our teacher said. Groans sounded around the room as students mumbled, "Not another test," but she looked excited, not stern.
- The mist swirled all around me as I stared at the mysterious door. Even though I'd been in this barn a million times, I'd never seen it before.

The goal of each of these activities is to allow students to generate ideas for writing through interaction, helping Extraverts prepare for an Introverted activity. In fact, this pattern puts into practice what brain research shows about retaining what we've learned. Jensen (1998) summarizes how meaning is generated during reflection, writing, or other forms of internal processing time. Conversations, kinesthetic activities, debates, and use of other senses such as sight and sound provide energy to Extraverts that prepares them to go to the less energizing internal world and create meaning for themselves through writing.

# GET STUDENTS STARTED

By definition, writing is like staring at a blank page. "Where do you get your ideas?" is one of the most common questions that people ask authors.

Many of the Extraverted activities just described also provide students with something worthwhile to express. However, Sensing writers may still want more help in getting started. Because over 70 percent of language arts teachers are Intuitive, a general principle that permeates most writing instruction is that being too explicit or structured about what or how students should write will stifle creativity and individual expression. For Sensing students, though, procedures and examples build confidence. They flourish when they know what is expected.

## Explicit Modeling

In teaching college business writing courses, I found that most students needed explicit modeling to write good business letters. Just showing an example and pointing out the elements wasn't enough. Before they attempted to write a letter conveying bad news ("We won't improve your credit rating." "That product is no longer available." "We'll be shipping two weeks later than promised.") I had to take a fresh scenario and walk them through the steps.

- Where did I get the information to form the opening "good news" part of the letter?
- What are possible couching devices, ways to palatably frame bad news? Why did I choose the one I did?
- How did I make sure my answer was firm, with no room for the customer to hope that the outcome might change?

If college juniors and seniors need that kind of instruction, so do elementary and secondary students. There are several ways to do it without stifling creativity.

- Take a look at how you can break the process into steps, as shown in the "Mobile Outlines" example for narrative writing shown above. Note that the goal of the entire assignment was to help students be more creative in narrative writing. Sensing students will use each step as a means to producing a satisfactory product. Intuitive students will skim the steps and use them as a jumping-off place for their creativity.
- Provide graphic organizers or help students construct Thinking Maps, which can be viewed at http://www.thinkingmaps.com. These help students access, in an organized way, the strengths of the preferences they are less confident in using. For example, a Tree Map looks like a standard organization chart: main idea at the top, supporting ideas underneath at one level, with supporting details below each supporting idea. Sensing students benefit by grouping

details to find main ideas. Intuitive students benefit by identifying details that support their main ideas. Feeling and Intuitive students benefit by systematically organizing their data. Thinking students enjoy the logical format.

- Start with "idea menus." To help sixth-grade students focus research for a three-page country report, we asked them to choose three topics from the list shown below. This reassured Sensing students that the topics would be acceptable and sufficient to meet the requirements, yet still allowed choice for Intuitive students.
  - Geography—land features, climate, famous places to visit
  - Family life—roles of males, females, children, how a student might spend a typical day
  - Economics—jobs, trade, money. How does their life compare to life in the United States?
  - Food—everyday and special-occasion foods, and how people cook
  - Clothing—compare how they dress to our culture
  - Shelter—what kinds of homes do most people live in? Who builds them? What materials are used?
  - Transportation—how do people get to work? How do they take long journeys?
  - Government—what kind of government? Democracy, dictatorship, socialist, communist, etc.
  - Arts and recreation—famous authors, sports figures, composers, national sports or games, other pastimes
  - Education—compare to this country's schools.

These menus usually include a place for "other" so that students can suggest unique ideas.

## Examples

As with the bungee cord example above, show students clear examples of how and what they might write. Page 84 shows how one teacher contrasted "right" and "wrong" samples so that students clearly understood her expectations.

The sample introductions shown above are another example. One teacher reported that these immediately moved students away from their too-common start of asking a question ("Did you know that . . ." "What would you do if . . .").

## Progress Checks

"Teacher, is this right?" may be spoken most often by Sensing/Feeling students who want to make sure they're on track. Take advantage of the fact that students write at different rates to offer reassurance and advice—and allow Extraverts a chance to chat with you. You might use red card/green card to do so with a minimum of interruption. Tell students to keep the green side up as long as they are writing well. If they have a question or want feedback, they can turn the red side up.

To make this more effective, provide suggestions for activities while they wait. For example, they might use clustering (page 120) to generate new ideas. They might start another step on a different sheet of paper. For the narrative assignment, a student might begin writing a dialogue for an upcoming scene while waiting for you to check the introduction. They might also check with another student who has "red side up" to see if they can help each other.

### Organized Brainstorming

There is no one right way to brainstorm ideas for writing. Some people love spider maps, whereas others get distracted by the mess. They prefer linear lists. Teach several methods, perhaps one for each writing assignment, and have all students try each one. Then let them choose the one that is most effective for them for future assignments. Note that students might use several of these at different stages of the writing process.

- *Clustering.* Bubble maps, spider maps, and other techniques are variations of this technique. The figure below shows an example for writing on compassion, assigned as an essay theme at a school where compassion was a core value. In some cases, each associated idea might stand on its own. In other cases, students might branch out, adding thoughts to each idea, or connecting them, as shown in the example.

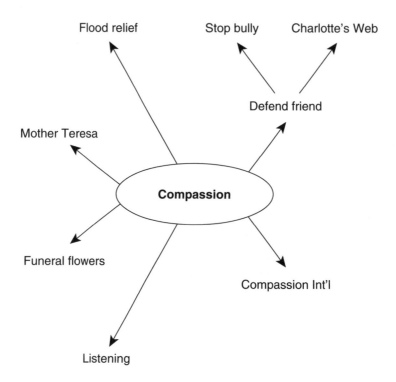

- *Prompts.* Sometimes, students need more help to start the brainstorming process. In the class where we used the personal narrative assignment, past essays had been lists of facts about trips to Disney World, birthday parties, trips to a farm, or other "big" events. The teacher handed out a worksheet with the following prompts in the center to help students think of other kinds of events to write about:
  - The first time I . . .
  - I spent a very special day with . . .

o You may not believe this but . . .

o The best day of my life was . . .

o I used to be afraid of ___ but then . . .

o When I heard that . . .

Consider special occasions, funny events, serious events (an illness or problem), memorable ordinary events such as baking cookies with Grandma, a happy or sad memory . . .

- *Sensing charts.* These charts let students think about possible sensory experiences in a place or situation. Divide paper into five columns, label them "see, hear, taste, touch, smell," and then write ideas under each one.
- *Active imagination* (Loomis, 1999). Have students write out an imaginary conversation with a person or object. In writing workshops, I often use as an example an imaginary conversation with the manikin leg our family passes around as a gag gift:

Me:     Why did we start wrapping you up?

Leg:     Most parties are simply too formal. I help newcomers learn about this family—and get a good laugh.

Me:     Which event was the most fun for you?

Leg:     When your mom got me for retiring. Did you see the look on her face when she found me under that bouquet of roses?

Me:     What's it like waiting for the next event, stashed in someone's closet?

Note that some Sensing/Thinking students may see this exercise as "dumb," so show examples and explain its usefulness in providing you with new ideas. To use this process effectively, the writer needs to (a) relinquish control and (b) LISTEN to the response—what insights do you gain? Often, starting with a question gets the dialogue started.

- *Lists.* Sometimes in the drive for "visual representations," teachers bypass tried-and-true methods. This is one form of a tree map, using it to create a taxonomy. For writing about "The Leg," I might make the following lists:

| Occasions | Disguises | People |
|---|---|---|
| weddings | flowers | mom |
| graduation | fireplace tools | new brother-in-law |
| housewarming | new boxes | grandpa |
| Christmas | multiple boxes | husband |

- *Image searches.* Sometimes an image becomes the best way to express or organize ideas. Poetry is often composed this way, but imagery can also work for personal essays, some persuasive essays, and narratives. In Dickens's *Bleak House*, fog imagery comes in again and again, illustrating the ability of the court system to obscure the truth. Snow imagery helped me tie together a ghostwritten magazine article about a girl in an abusive relationship. Students might compare their lives to waves on the beach, or a basketball game to a roller coaster.

Most students will need concrete examples to get started. Read passages aloud, or examine the poetry of Langston Hughes or Robert Frost or almost any of your favorite poets.

Then, have students cluster or list the attributes of what they are writing about, using adjectives, emotions, and other descriptive words. For a basketball game, they might write:

o Low-key warm-up
o Adrenaline up—other team takes lead
o Anger—ref doesn't see blatant foul
o Hope—Jess drops two 3-pointers
o Helplessness—benched early with 3 fouls
o Hope-fear-hope-fear as lead changes
o Nothing. Buzzer sounds and we're behind

With this list, students can make connections with other events or objects or animals or people with similar experiences. Or, they might focus on one element. Perhaps they take the helplessness of being benched and compare it to watching a floundering boat from shore or letting another teenager drive.

Again, your goal with any of these activities is to provide enough structure to allow students to begin with confidence while still allowing for creativity and individuality. Intuitive students thrive on that freedom and Sensing students often gain comfort in trusting their own ideas by experiencing success with varying processes and techniques.

### Letting Intuitives Loose

In teaching writing, and in designing processes to help all students succeed, the fears of many language arts teachers are important: Overstructuring can stifle individuality. Remember that Intuitive students are *motivated* by words such as speculate, dream, envision, brainstorm, visualize, pretend, and create (see page 48). Further, they are *demotivated* by words such as list, organize, complete, tell, or identify. Intuitive students may struggle just as much as Sensing students as they learn to write, but wise teachers keep in mind the very different ways the two groups are motivated. The reading approaches of Cluster A and Cluster B students (page 94) apply to writing as well. Sensing students want to know they're on track, whereas Intuitive students want to keep going and capture their big ideas.

Use examples from *The Outsiders* for book report ideas. Or, allow for choice within assignments as the "idea menu" allowed for country reports (page 119).

Allow for choice in writing materials. Although you don't have to accept text written in hard-to-read metallic ink, permitting green or purple ink can be a motivator.

Let students design their own writing format. A report on Louisiana in the form of a letter home from the first explorer in that state. A quiz-show-style animal report, with the writing embedded in each right answer. A short fictional story that illustrates political strategies. As one teacher put it, "When Intuitive students come up with their own ideas, at least I know they aren't plagiarizing."

## ACTIVITIES FOR BOTH SENSING AND INTUITION

Because personality preferences do not guarantee skills, students with both preferences usually need to develop several basic skills for writing: grammar, sentence structure, organization, research, and so on. The following techniques help students with all preferences engage in activities that build these skills.

## Cartoon Dialoguing

Practicing punctuation isn't fun, although a few Sensing students might like the certainty that develops with worksheets of punctuation drills. One teacher I worked with developed an idea for using cartoons to teach punctuation.

1. Students find favorite cartoons and then write out the dialogue with proper use of quotation marks, commas, and "Blondie said" or "Dagwood answered."

2. To hold student interest, she then hands them cartoons in which the dialogue has been whited out. Students work in pairs to create new dialogue. They then write it out with correct punctuation.

3. The third step is to have students draw their own cartoons, including proper punctuation for the dialogue.

## Segmented Note Taking

When students begin writing reports, keeping notes organized in a way that facilitates organized writing is a struggle. One helpful strategy is providing a portable filing and organizing system.

Have students label envelopes for each subtopic they will research and one for bibliography information. Then, as they take notes, they record information on sheets of paper that fit within the envelopes and file them in the envelope corresponding with that topic. If they copied a quote, they record the page number on the page.

For each resource they use, students complete a form for recording bibliography information. These go in the designated envelope.

When the student has enough information, he or she can open an envelope, organize the notes into a logical sequence, and begin writing. The envelopes thus serve as a three-dimensional tree map. Dr. Ruby Payne, author of *A Framework for Understanding Poverty* (1996), suggests stapling the envelopes inside a manila folder as a further organizing technique. She also has students make five or so circles on the front of each topic envelope and check a circle each time they add a sheet of notes to that envelope. When all of the circles are checked, the student usually has enough information to write on that topic. I've seen students hold onto those folders as treasures, knowing that they will succeed if they fill those envelopes.

One Intuitive teacher said, "That's too structured. Students will feel like machines." His Sensing team member stood up and gestured, "I'd *want* to make those checks, to see my progress." Indeed, Intuitive students report that the system keeps them from backtracking to find bibliography information and also helps them focus on key topics rather than going off on tangents.

## Sentence Building

Diagramming sentences doesn't help students write better; research shows clearly that those who can already write well master the process quickly, whereas those who struggle to write also struggle to diagram. Instead, Payne (1998) suggests that students use symbols to code their sentences, underlining the subject, using a wiggly line under verbs, placing a triangle around prepositions, and so on, to check whether they've constructed complete sentences and as a guide to creating more complicated sentences. Coded in this way, a sentence would look like this:

I ran quickly along the cement sidewalk after school to catch the city bus.

Another teacher found an engaging way to drill students on sentence elements. She has students write and illustrate a series of steps in expanding sentences. They choose an animal and an action, such as "Bears ate." Then they successively add elements, as follows:

- *Direct object:* Bears ate honey.
- *Rename the subject:* Bears, polar, ate honey.
- *Add adjective and adverb:* Large bears, polar, lazily ate honey.
- *Add a prepositional phrase:* Large bears, polar, lazily ate honey in the forest.

Students form a booklet by illustrating each step in the process. The final picture for the "Bears Ate" is shown below.

## CONCLUSION

Evaluating the writing strategies you provide to students in terms of Extraversion and Introversion, and Sensing and Intuition, can increase student engagement and performance. Even professional writers struggle to generate ideas, organize information, write in a logical flow, and revise their own materials. The more you can meet students' learning styles during the writing process, the more they can grow as writers.

# 9

# Differentiated Math and Science Instruction

---

*Before you read on . . .*

Do you consider yourself a mathematician? A scientist? Check which statements are true for you.

- ☐ I enjoy working with numbers and solving problems.
- ☐ I can master new theoretical concepts easily.
- ☐ I understand algorithms and *why* they work.
- ☐ I often look for the simplest ways to do problems, not the standard way.
- ☐ I work to prove something is true instead of pointing to rules or using examples.
- ☐ I consider not just whether ideas are true or false but under what conditions they prove true or false.

The disciplines of mathematics and science are linked in many ways. Both are open, fluid disciplines that developed through ongoing efforts to explore and understand the world in which we live. One can go only so far in science without good mathematical skills. And both evoke a continuing sense of awe in those who are masters in the field:

> *Mathematics is the only instructional material that can be presented in an entirely undogmatic way.*
>
> —Max Dehn

> *Mathematics is not a careful march down a well-cleared highway, but a journey into a strange wilderness, where the explorers often get lost.*
>
> —W. S. Anglin

*The most beautiful thing we can experience is the mysterious. It is the source of all true art and science.*

—Albert Einstein

But that's not necessarily the way the rest of us view math and science, is it? A math teacher lamented, "Whenever I join friends at a restaurant someone says, 'You're the math teacher. You divvy up the bill.' They'd *never* say, 'You're the reading teacher. Read the menu for all of us.' This whole country is afraid of math!"

In this chapter we'll examine the following:

- Where math anxiety comes from and its implications for elementary mathematics
- Differences in how Sensing and Intuitive students approach math and science
- Patterns in teacher strengths and developmental needs in teaching math and science
- Strategies to help all students think like mathematicians and scientists.

## TYPE AND MATH ANXIETY

"Math anxiety" is an accepted phrase to describe people who are afraid of math—and there are type patterns in who those people are. Huelsman (2002) linked research on brain dominance and personality type and noted the following similarities to type preference descriptions:

Huelsman asked his students to circle the words in Chart 9.1 that best described them. He then compared the word lists of students who did and didn't report math anxiety. He found that *dominant* Feeling students, ones who circled almost no words

**Chart 9.1** Descriptors of the Four Brain Quarters (Herman Brain Dominance System)

| **Left Cerebral** | **Right Cerebral** |
|---|---|
| • Factual | • Holistic |
| • Quantitative | • Innovative |
| • Mathematical | • Conceptual |
| • Analytical | • Imaginative |
| "Thinking" | "Intuition" |
| "Sensing/Judging" | "Feeling" |
| **Left Limbic** | **Right Limbic** |
| • Sequential | • Interpersonal |
| • Structural | • Emotional |
| • Scheduled | • Spiritual |
| • Planned | • Supportive |

from the other quadrants, reported math anxiety in overwhelming numbers. In summarizing interviews with those students, he described their math experiences this way:

> Rote memory and fact regurgitation have become part of a mathematics-course-passing-game that only appears to yield temporary abilities to solve standardized problems. The desire to develop critical thinking skills in a mathematics class appears to have died in these students (p. 31).

In other words, they learned algorithms without understanding why they worked. What is most significant for differentiation is that *the personality preferences of the students identified in Huelsman's study match those of people most likely to become teachers in American elementary schools.*

## MATH ANXIETY AND ELEMENTARY TEACHERS

Step into an elementary classroom. A teacher asks students to solve a simple problem:

$$6/16 \times 8/18 = ?$$

A standard technique is to cross out common factors or reduce the fractions to make the multiplication simpler: $3/8 \times 4/9 = ?$ But one student looks at the equation and writes $1/3 \times 1/2 = 1/6$ and is done in no time. She used the simplest strategy: Switch the 6 and the 8 by using the commutative property of multiplication and then reduce the fractions before multiplying. This is how mathematicians think, yet people with math anxiety, who perhaps are comfortable only with standard techniques for multiplication, may not understand how the student did the problem.

I've shown this problem and solution to elementary teachers and found that a great percentage struggle to find the simpler method. They tend to work from the algorithms they learned. Ma (1999) discovered that only 17 percent of American teachers, compared with 86 percent of Chinese teachers, showed a conceptual understanding of subtraction with regrouping, multidigit multiplication, division of fractions, and approaches to examining a variety of methods to solve problems or test new ideas.

Think about current debates regarding constructivist or algorithmic approaches to mathematics: If a teacher struggles with the abovementioned conceptual understandings, how can he or she guide student thinking during constructivist investigations that are designed to help students unearth those very concepts?

Instructional approaches to both math and science make a difference in long-term student achievement. Kamii and Dominick (1998) found that teaching algorithms harms mathematical development in children. The algorithms prevent them from constructing an understanding of the distributive, commutative, and associative properties of multiplication that are foundational to algebra. The students turn into technicians, not noticing whether their answers make sense or if their procedures could be simplified; note how this description matches Huelsman's (2002) description of people with math anxiety!

Yet around the country, parent groups and many educators are insisting that our children be taught algorithms through "traditional" math curricula. Why? Because they see a lack of computation skills in children. If constructivist math is best, and produces number sense in children, why isn't it working?

Because many elementary teachers, as shown in Ma's research, don't have the number sense themselves to teach in that way. Fosnot and Dolk (2002), who have been training teachers in New York City to teach in a way that supports mathematizing—calculating with number sense—say that for teachers to develop that understanding takes time.

> Sometimes, parents have responded by hiring tutors to teach their children the algorithms—a solution that has often been detrimental to children as they grapple to understand number and operation. Sometimes, as teachers have attempted to reform their practice, children have been left with no algorithms and no repertoire of strategies, only their own informal, inefficient inventions. The reform will fail if we do not approach calculation seriously, if we do not produce children who can calculate efficiently. (p. 107)

If we think in terms of type, we can surmise that what we have is a preponderance of Sensing and/or Feeling elementary teachers (see Table 2.1, page 22) who either approach math procedurally, or experience math anxiety, or both. When we ask them to teach for number sense, can they really evaluate what students are doing if they weren't taught the concepts themselves?

The algorithm-versus-constructivism battle in mathematics instruction is identical to the battle that raged for years over phonics versus whole language instruction in reading. Sensing teachers *tend* to take a step-by-step, parts-to-whole approach to math and science instruction, similar to phonics instruction. Intuitive teachers *tend* to take a more open-ended, constructivist approach to math and science instruction, similar to the whole language method.

Do all Sensing teachers prefer algorithm instruction? No. One Sensing/Thinking middle-school teacher told me, "When I started working with the constructivist curriculum, I realized that I hadn't understood math in high school. I needed this kind of exploration to connect those procedures with concepts." Do all Intuitive teachers prefer constructivist instruction? No. Some grasped the concepts through algorithmic instruction and assume their students will do the same.

What we want to do is break the cycle—stop producing teachers with math anxiety who can therefore help students develop number sense. New York's Mathematics in the Cities program (Fosnot & Dolk, 2002) works with teachers in this manner. On the New York State standardized mathematics test, the mean score of students taught by teachers in their program fell within level three, the level considered proficient by the state. The mean of traditionally taught students fell within level two. An item analysis of fifth-grade students showed that the program's students rated significantly higher on number understanding, geometry, measurement, data, and problem solving. One teacher journaled after a training session,

> Math was never like this for me. I remember hating it. There was only one way to get an answer and it was the teacher's way. That's why I majored in English literature . . . math now seems creative. Today we imagined in math; we explored relationships; we tried to understand and prove our ideas to each other. I don't want my kids to see math as I did, to hate it and think only the answer matters. Today I feel like a mathematician and I want my kids to have that same feeling. I want them to debate, think, inquire, and prove. I want them to see math as creative, as philosophy, as art! (p. 157–158)

Look back to the reflection question at the beginning of the chapter. These are a list of how mathematicians and scientists approach their disciplines. To reach this level, though, students (and teachers) need a solid foundation.

# SENSING, INTUITION, AND PROBLEM SOLVING

Remember that Sensing students learn in a step-by-step fashion. If a step is missed or the process breaks off before they reach a clear conceptual understanding, they struggle to put the pieces together. If they don't understand that the size of 1/4 depends on the size of the whole, or that 1/4 is bigger than 1/8, even though 8 is bigger than 4, they may need to start from scratch when the topic of fractions rolls around again the next year. They may understand a procedure and memorize it for the test, but they can't file the procedure away because they haven't connected it to the big picture. *Many* Sensing students master math by becoming outstanding technicians with algorithms. This is different, though, from conceptual understanding.

- Sensing types who also prefer Thinking may master the algorithms more quickly because they are usually quite logical or orderly. Sensing types who prefer Feeling struggle the most. After all, math is seldom presented as a means to helping people, a key motivation for Sensing/Feeling types. They don't grasp the big picture, they struggle with procedures, and end up with math anxiety in disproportionate numbers.

  Most math teachers prefer Thinking, decreasing the likelihood that Feeling students will experience a math classroom that closely meets their needs.

- In general, Intuitive students grasp the big picture more easily than the procedures. If they forget an algorithm, they can usually look at an example or two and remember how to solve a problem because they still remember the general idea of how it works. They also can easily make connections between different problems, for example applying the commutative property of multiplication to whole numbers and fractions. Add Thinking to Intuition and students often enjoy playing with numbers and mathematical models.

## Providing a Solid Foundation

More than any other subject, math topics build on each other. Although one can think at higher levels without mastering times tables and regrouping, calculations become arduous, making mathematics less and less fun. As with reading skills, certain techniques work better for students with different learning styles as they master math facts.

Whether you are working with young students or secondary students who are missing significant foundational pieces of math knowledge, make learning the facts useful and fun by considering the needs of different learning styles. Chart 9.2 can be used to add variety to whole-class instruction or to provide students with choices as to how they might learn.

In science, students have natural strengths—activities that help them grasp scientific concepts Chart 9.3 shows how different science activities fit into the four learning style quadrants. Consider where the majority of science activities fall in your classroom.

In many ways, the higher the level, the more math and science favor Intuitive and Thinking students. As we look at what Sensing and Feeling students need in math and science, our overarching goal will be to help them view themselves as mathematicians and scientists. Fortunately, research exists that can help teachers ascertain whether they are moving their students in this direction.

**Chart 9.2**     Learning Styles Strategies for Mastering Basic Math Skills

| Introversion and Sensing | Introversion and Intuition |
|---|---|
| • Have each student make a progress chart so they can color in the math facts they've memorized. | • Let them set their own goals and challenges for learning. |
| • Provide manipulatives until they master a concept, such as making an array of three fives to understand that $3 \times 5 = 15$ | • Have them design a game to help themselves and others learn facts. |
| • Have them fill in blank multiplication tables, starting with the facts they're sure of. They might make flash cards to practice the remaining ones. | • Prepare independent drills for them to use. |
| • Provide worksheets or handheld devices that let them drill their facts. | • Let them write multiplication stories. |
| **Extraversion and Sensing** | **Extraversion and Intuition** |
| • Teach or let students come up with rhythms/raps to learn their multiplication tables. | • Let them work as a group to design a math game. |
| • Incorporate physical movement into math drills. | • Let them tutor or help others learn their facts. |
| • Have each student make a progress chart so they can color in the math facts they've memorized. | • Use group games to teach the facts. One teacher uses "math volleyball." She writes a number on each stripe and students have to compute the fact for the stripes their hands touch as they catch the ball. |
| • Hold a contest. Perhaps study groups might compete to see which group can master the highest percentage of facts. | • Set up a competition, perhaps seeing which students improve the most. Or, have them chart their own best scores on a computer math game. |

**Chart 9.3**    Learning Styles Strategies for Mastering Basic Science Skills

| Introversion and Sensing | Introversion and Intuition |
|---|---|
| • Experiments with accurate, step-by-step procedures | • Open-ended exploration |
| • Guided reading | • Independent study |
| • Observation | • Forming and testing hypotheses |
| • Recording data | • Brainstorming |
| • Memorizing facts | • Background research |
| **Extraversion and Sensing** | **Extraversion and Intuition** |
| • Experimenting before learning the theory | • "Open" labs to explore a concept |
| • Hands-on demonstrations and labwork | • Group contests |
| • Connecting knowledge with real-life applications | • Analysis that requires compare/contrast |
| • Game-oriented experiments | • Nonrepetitive labwork |

# MAINTAINING THE COGNITIVE DEMANDS OF THE TASK

The National Council of Teachers of Mathematics (NCTM) identified several essential conditions for cognitively complex tasks that correlate with effective math instruction. Because the study emphasized constructivist mathematical tasks, the results also apply to inquiry-based science instruction.

Chart 9.4 synthesizes the information from the NCTM (Stein & Smith, 1998), how teachers with different preferences struggle with these factors, and how the techniques provided in this chapter to address this area of instruction. The teacher comments came from a group of 25 math teachers who knew their type preferences.

Although teachers struggle with different aspects of constructing solid math and science instruction, several key elements are in the best interests of all students. These include the following:

- Teaching students to think like mathematicians and scientists
- Emphasizing universal thinking tools rather than specific procedures
- Planning appropriate warm-up activities
- Anticipating scaffolding needs
- Planning roaming strategies
- Avoiding busywork
- Selecting problems that are relevant to students' lives

We will look at each of these strategies in turn.

## Teaching Students to Think Like Mathematicians and Scientists

As discussed above, most people think of math as a series of facts or procedures to master. In a review of several books on teaching mathematics, I compiled the following list of how mathematicians operate. Scientists are similar. They

- Describe the world with numbers. Every teacher in a school can reinforce this perspective on mathematics. If a student is late to class, ask, "You're 10 minutes late. What percentage of class have you missed?" When a student brings treats, ask, "Four boxes with six items in each box. How can we figure out the total number?"
- Look for patterns. Games, artwork, poetry, weather information, sports statistics, fabric, architecture, and countless other activities and objects display patterns. Learning to recognize patterns is essential for factoring, for remembering math facts, for relating new problems to old problems, and for countless other mathematical tasks.
  - *Set*, a card game from SET Enterprises, Inc., uses cards that show different combinations of three shapes, colors, and fill patterns to promote pattern recognition. Play a sample game at http://www.setgame.com.
  - Students might color geometric designs using patterns, especially as they learn to calculate surface area or volume.
  - Have students analyze games for patterns. Which opening move wins most often in tic-tac-toe?

**Chart 9.4**  Maintaining the Cognitive Demands of a Task

| Factors present in high-level cognitive tasks | Teacher comments about their skills | Strategies |
|---|---|---|
| 1. Students have sufficient information to engage in thinking and reasoning; teachers scaffold but avoid overstructuring. | *Sensing teacher responses* <br><br>• I jump in too soon with alternate processes, details. <br><br>• I struggle with "overprocedurizing." Many students don't grasp a concept even after following the six step process that I had them do. Others . . . can go straight to the big idea. <br><br>• I am likely to specify procedures in an effort to help students succeed—I often think I've discovered the "best" method for tackling a problem. | • Thinking tools <br><br>• Roaming strategies (methods for prompting student thinking without decreasing the cognitive demands of the task). |
| 2. Teachers go beyond accuracy to concepts and meaning, pressing students to justify, explain, and reason by questioning them and providing feedback. | *Sensing teacher responses* <br><br>• I have problems pushing past correct answers to meaning. <br><br>• I look for all problems completed, thinking after students have tried problems questions will come. <br><br>• I do tend to look for accuracy first. <br><br>*Intuitive teacher responses* <br><br>• Sometimes it is hard to explain/justify an answer because it just is and I don't always know how to break it down. I move very quickly through solutions, especially on concepts I think are easy. If a student does not understand something I'll present them with an idea on how to work it. <br><br>• I don't let incorrect thinking go unrecognized but I sometimes allow students to get away with not applying high-level thinking. | • Clear goals for each lesson, including concepts to be drawn out and emphasized. <br><br>• Have students write out their justification to improve clarity and meaning. |
| 3. Teachers provide sufficient time for exploration (not too much or too little). | *Judging teacher responses* <br><br>• The stressed need to "Summarize" lessons keeps me "on clock." <br><br>• I don't want to be the teacher who gets through only 4 instead of 6 topics because I was so caught up in mastery for each investigation. | • Preplan both scaffolding techniques and extensions to keep all students engaged. |

*(Continued)*

**133**

**Chart 9.4** (Continued)

| Factors present in high-level cognitive tasks | Teacher comments about their skills | Strategies |
|---|---|---|
| | *Perceiving teacher responses* | |
| | • I want students to experience the math and in turn cut the summary short because students are engaged. | |
| | • Class time is overfilled for the students. Often we do not get to review, recap, or ponder and they leave class late. I sometimes misjudge a problem's complexity or assign homework that takes more time than I intended. | |
| 4. Teachers structure tasks to build on student prior knowledge and interests to create motivation. | *Intuitive teacher responses* | • Plan appropriate warm-up activities. |
| | • I don't always preevaluate prior knowledge enough (I think I have!). | • Focus on clarifying or restating problems or question being asked. |
| | • I'm usually giving instructions as the class period moves forward. | |
| | *Sensing teacher responses* | |
| | • I struggle to stray from curriculum. | |
| | • It's hard to keep separate whether students don't like me or whether they don't understand a task! | |
| 5. Teachers or capable students model higher-level performance. | • No significant differences among teachers with different personality preferences. | • Model good reasoning, |
| | | • Ask students to explain reasoning to you before they explain to the class. |
| 6. Students are provided with means to monitor their own progress. | • No significant differences among teachers with different personality preferences. | • Students identify areas for improvement and set goals. |
| | | • Answer keys or problem-solving strategies. |
| | | • Helping students monitor progress on |

o Provide frequent practice in discovering number patterns. Point them out on clocks, calendars, school supply lists, and anywhere else that students can begin linking patterns with number sense.

Practicing looking for patterns is especially helpful for Sensing students. Intuitive students do it more naturally, but find it an enjoyable activity.

- Look for efficient strategies. Fosnot and Dolk (2001) use "mental math strings" almost daily to help students work with numbers more efficiently. The following are sample strings, introduced to a class one problem at a time for group discussion (p. 128). Think about how the first problems in the string can be used to introduce strategies for solving the other problems:

| | | |
|---|---|---|
| $5 \times 6$ | $1/5 \times 1/7$ | $3/8 \times 4/9$ |
| $30 \times 6$ | $3/5 \times 4/7$ | $5/6 \times 3/5$ |
| $35 \times 6$ | $4/6 \times 3/7$ | $4/5 \times 5/8$ |

These students are in fourth grade. Eventually, students understand that mastering some of these ideas leads to efficiencies, and they engage even more.

- Work to prove something is true instead of pointing to rules or using examples. Ma (1999) reports that Chinese teachers expand a common proverb, "Know how and also know why," to apply to their own practice: Know how to carry out an algorithm and know why it makes sense mathematically. In the United States, most of us commiserate with Billy in a *Family Circus* cartoon. When the teacher asks him if he can justify an answer, he says, "No, I think it was Divine Intervention."

To build greater understanding, and to apply the knowledge more readily in new situations, Intuitive students need to be able to justify their answers. They are often adept at guessing, working backward, or otherwise getting right answers without knowing how they did it. Sensing students may memorize procedures without understanding why they work.

Don't let students fall back on answers like, "The textbook says so." "We learned it last year." "I tried some examples and they worked." Instead, have them explain logically, using correct terms and argument. Here are some ways to engage students in reasoning:

o Journals. Have them practice reasoning by writing out their understanding of terms, operations, and techniques.
o "Safe" justification. Have a student explain their reasoning to you before informing the entire class. This prevents having to undo incorrect explanations and also allows you to correct or prompt privately, or to press a small group to explain their work while they can easily turn to each other for deeper understanding.
o Model good reasoning. At every opportunity, point to prior learning, concepts, or theorems the children understand conceptually to justify how you solve a problem.
o Prove how new understandings follow from old concepts. For example, one might prove mathematically how $6/16 \times 8/18 = 1/3 \times 1/2$ as well as citing the commutative property of multiplication. Create science labs that introduce new concepts by building on what students know.

o Have students show work in ink rather than using pencils. In this way, you can see their thinking process.

o Writing new problems. Ask students to write their own word problems that use the concepts they've learned. Insist that they check for reasonableness. For example, answers can't produce half a person.

- Solve problems in multiple ways, and work to solve complex problems in simpler ways. When students work problems in different ways, point out these differences to the class. Emphasize that different paths involve different reasoning. Let the students ponder whether some methods are easier or more efficient.

## DIFFERENTIATION STRATEGIES

### Emphasize Universal Thinking Tools Rather Than Specific Procedures

Universal thinking tools are strategies, problem-solving techniques, or tools that can be used in solving multiple problems, whether students are working on arithmetic, algebra, calculus, geometry, scientific investigations, or real-life problems. They help Sensing students connect prior knowledge with new situations. They help Intuitive students provide better justifications of their answers because they will create visual aids to make their reasoning more concrete.

Introduce the strategies one at a time, in the context of a problem for which the tool is an optimal strategy. Then, post the thinking tools on signs around the room. When students aren't sure how to approach a problem, remind them to consider which thinking tools might help. Many writers include similar lists of strategies. Referring to thinking tools then becomes an essential **roaming strategy,** a way to provide students with help without decreasing the cognitive demands of the task. Other roaming strategies are described on page 139. Thinking tools include the following:

- *Looking for patterns.* Sensing students often need more practice in finding patterns. In some cases, you may need to assist students in making a chart so that they spot the patterns. This tool plays an essential role in helping students construct an understanding of algebraic equations.
- *Restating the problem or question to be answered.* When faced with a rather lengthy word problem, restating the question in simple terms may help students focus on the essential information.
- *Looking for connections to past problems.* Sometimes it seems as if students who lack confidence in their ability to solve problems don't transfer knowledge from one problem to another even if the only element that changes is that the problem deals with milk rather than orange juice. Using key activities to introduce concepts (such as the "bouncing ball" problem described on page 49) allows for better recall by students. They worked with the problem long enough to make meaning with it.
- *Organizing data into tables.* These help Sensing students look for patterns and help Intuitive students be more systematic.
- *Using graph paper for graphs or arrays.* Modeling on paper helps students bridge from concrete manipulatives to abstract concepts.

- *Drawing a picture, making a model, or using manipulatives.* All of these techniques help Sensing students visualize abstract concepts and Intuitive students concretize their reasoning. Sometimes, teachers see using manipulatives as evidence of lower levels of thinking when in fact they can scaffold a student's ability to stretch themselves or to think independently. For example, math students who struggle with calculating surface area using diagrams of three-dimensional geometric figures may grasp the concept of the "hidden" sides of the figures by holding a cube while doing the calculations.

  Make sure that students' use of manipulatives reinforces the concept you are trying to teach. For example, if students count out 20 blocks, take 7 away, and recount the remaining blocks, they aren't learning to regroup. And, watch that students don't get lost in drawing the perfect slice of pizza, missing the mathematics involved.

- *Substituting friendlier numbers.* Often, students can develop a conceptual understanding of a problem by thinking of it in terms of money or time (pennies, quarters, and dimes lend understanding to fractions, decimals, and percentages, as do minutes and hours). Or, one might work through a fractions problem by using a friendly "whole"—calculate the fractions as part of 100 or 10 or 20 or whatever number results in simple calculations.

- *Estimating or checking answer for reasonableness.* Horror stories abound of students using calculators, coming up with totally unreasonable answers, and writing them down without thinking. Teach students to check work, estimating $4 \times 37$ by saying, "Well, I know that $4 \times 40$ would be 160." Such problems could be used as problem strings. Or, they might use friendlier numbers to see if an answer is reasonable.

- *Working backward.* Some problems are best solved this way. An example might be, "Lyssa came to class with several candy bars. She gave two to Ben, five to Sara, and one each to Jamal, Eric, and Jasmine. Now she has four left. How many did she start with?"

- *Double number lines.* This thinking tool works for problems such as, "How many miles of a 30-mile bike race has Jon completed when he finishes 1/3 of the race? 5/6 of the race?" Students mark the fractions on the top side of the number line and the miles elapsed on the bottom side.

## The Scientific Method as a Universal Tool

Science teachers can increase student expertise with the scientific method by helping them understand how to use the skills of the various personality preferences at different steps in the process.

- *Forming a question.* Sensing, Intuitive, Thinking, and Feeling students *all* wonder about the world around them. Often, Sensing students form better questions through observation. If you want them to come up with their own research question for a science fair project, direct them to observe the real world—their backyards, their favorite activities, etc. Intuitive students might also benefit from this approach as they search for a topic of interest.

- *Stating a hypothesis.* Predicting is a natural activity for Intuitives. Sensing students will benefit from relating the question they are investigating to things they already know about, through analogies or comparisons. For example, to investigate reflex responses in students, students examined what they knew about friends who played video games a lot. What would their reaction times be like?

- *Methodology.* Most Extraverts like to jump into experiments without thinking through needed procedures. A demonstration of one thing that could go wrong often helps them begin brainstorming about how to set up an experiment. Intuitive students may gloss over considerations for keeping experiments consistent; a few key questions from the teacher can guide their thinking.

- *Data gathering.* Sensing students often excel at gathering accurate data, with Thinking students close behind. Intuitive students might benefit from comparing partial data sets with other students to check on their accuracy, before continuing with more observations.

- *Analysis.* Intuitive and Thinking students often find this part of the process most enjoyable. Clarify the process for Sensing students:
  - o Did you answer your question?
  - o Was your hypothesis right? Why or why not? What data supports your conclusion?
  - o How might you revise your experiment for better results? To test a different hypothesis?

## Planning Appropriate Warm-Up Activities

Many mathematics and science programs emphasize using appropriate "launch" or introductory activities before introducing concepts. Well-designed introductory activities help Sensing students connect more easily with prior knowledge and help all students begin to think mathematically or scientifically about a situation. Here are some examples:

*Demonstrate.* To remind students of fraction concepts, a teacher once offered half of a king-size candy bar to me and half of a regular candy bar to another math coach. The students immediately pointed out that that wasn't fair, allowing the teacher to emphasize that fractions are parts of wholes, not absolute values.

*Tell a related story or, if possible, use a real situation.* "We have an opportunity to make bead bracelets and sell them at the school fair to raise money for a field trip. We have to decide what kinds of beads to use. Now, these seem prettier to me but they cost more, so we'd have to charge more for the bracelets. These cost less, but I'm not sure we'd sell as many. How can we figure out what to do?" Make sure the story isn't too long or the students may miss the problem being stated.

*Create a mystery.* Place simple problems that review concepts needed for a lesson in a bucket covered in interesting paper. Have students work in pairs to draw problems, read them to the class, and provide the answer.

*Review vocabulary.* Use a bingo or Jeopardy-style game to review basic vocabulary that students should remember from past units.

*Choose a problem from the prior year's curriculum.* If you're teaching fifth grade, take a problem on the topic of the day from the fourth-grade curriculum.

The key to introductions is making them relevant to the day's work and making them interesting.

## Anticipating Scaffolding Needs

Actually, many of the above techniques *are* scaffolding techniques. Accessing prior knowledge, providing universal tools, and preparing prompts and hints to nudge along a student's thinking are all ways to differentiate for ability.

Look back to Chapter 5, "Key Differentiation Strategies," for examples of ways to meet the needs of the various quadrants.

Perhaps even more important for mathematics instruction, though, is meeting the needs of Feeling students, those most likely to develop math anxiety. If your preference is for Thinking, make sure to include the following strategies.

- Establish a relationship. Remember that Feeling students need to know that a teacher likes them.
- Provide positive, immediate feedback. It may seem as if these students are asking, "Is this right?" after they complete each problem. Receiving this reassurance may build their confidence. If they did work a problem wrong, they, more than other students, might need assistance so that they don't start to believe they can't grasp the concept. You can "wean" them from asking you to check every problem by asking them to compare work with a friend or to work three problems before showing their work to you.
- Connect math to helping people. Recipes for class gatherings, fundraising calculations, and problems that involve sharing are sample ways to connect math with people.

## Planning Roaming Strategies

Planning ahead for how you will help students solve problems is crucial for maintaining the cognitive demands of the task. Otherwise, it's too easy to give a hint that tells them exactly what to do, rather than encouraging them to think and draw connections. Planning ahead also allows you to think through the strategies students might use and the common mistakes you might need to steer students away from. When students will be involved in a lengthy investigation, think through what you might see, hear, say, and do as you roam the classroom to answer questions, observe student work, and press for justification and reasoning.

- Prepare hints that maintain the cognitive level of the task. For example, the following questions prompt student thinking by reminding students of strategies they've used before rather than telling them how to proceed. These prompts might also focus them in a new direction.
  o Is there a thinking tool you can use?
  o Is there another way to diagram it?
  o Is there another way to organize your data?
  o Tell me again what you're looking for. What is the question you're trying to answer?
  o What facts do you know in this problem?

- Think ahead to prepare questions to help students revisit false reasoning, such as these:
  - o What if the numbers were . . .
  - o Explain your reasoning.
  - o Did you check it? Does it work?
  - o Explain it to me as if I were your little sister (or brother).
  - o Does your answer make sense? Is it reasonable?

    If two groups are close to being on track, but their reasoning is off, pair them up and have them justify it to each other. See if they can correct their own thinking.
- Look for models of high-level reasoning. Ask those students to prepare to present their solutions to the class.
- To encourage justification, consider what prompts might be effective for a given problem:
  - o How do you know . . .
  - o Where does that concept come from?
  - o Where did you get that number?

The more you work with these strategies, the more automatic they become. However, the big benefit to planning roaming strategies is that they help *teachers* avoid their natural pitfalls in maintaining high-level thinking in their classrooms. Sensing teachers are ready to look beyond right answers and avoid overscaffolding. Intuitive teachers are prepared to require students to justify their conclusions and are clear on lesson goals and directions.

## Avoiding Busywork

*Practice problems.* Let's look at how students with different learning styles might approach a worksheet filled with practice problems, perhaps three-digit multiplication or practicing scientific classifications.

**Chart 9.5**   How Different Learning Styles Approach Practice Problems

| **Introversion and Sensing:** | **Introversion and Intuition:** |
|---|---|
| • These students often enjoy practicing their skills, knowing careful work brings a good score (some adults have told me that they hated it when teachers would assign only the even problems because they knew they could get them all right). | • These students might do several problems correctly. Then, they may stare off into space, losing interest, or rush to complete the worksheet and make several errors. |
| **Extraversion and Sensing:** | **Extraversion and Intuition:** |
| • These students usually get to work, finishing five problems, then getting up to sharpen a pencil, working two more, then stopping to see what's making noise out side, finish another and . . . | • These students may work in spurts on the problems. Or, they may finish 10 and hand the paper in, saying, "These are all correct and I'm not doing any more." |

Thus, what helps one student hinders another.

Although "traditional" math curricula are generally viewed as more repetitive and therefore filled with busywork, exploration-based problems can fall into the same trap by, for example, requiring students to perform dozens of calculations to come to the understanding that the accuracy of a sample's predictive power increases through multiple trials. No one, not Sensing, Intuitive, Thinking, or Feeling students or adults, really wants to recalculate the cumulative number of matches on the shake of a die over the number of shakes for 25 shakes! Instead, turn it into a group assignment, giving each group member specific roles to move the task along while still letting students experience the concept.

*Note taking.* Another danger occurs when teachers require students to take notes. Note taking is essential, providing Sensing students with a "map" for how to proceed and "guidelines" for Intuitive students to refer back to as needed. However, the same students who struggle with math may also struggle with reading and writing. As they take notes, their attention may go toward spelling words correctly, keeping items in straight lines, or drawing accurate geometric figures or other diagrams. They may fail to grasp the concepts being taught.

Here are some strategies for avoiding this danger:

- Separate vocabulary and concepts during lectures. If students are to copy vocabulary words, front-load this at the start of the lesson or unit. Then concentrate on demonstrating a problem.
- Use visual aids as well as two-dimensional representations. Students will watch you manipulate a sphere instead of getting lost in detailed notes. Get 12 students on their feet to demonstrate fractions. Stack pop cans into arrays. Better yet, have the students who struggle to sit still stack those cans for you.
- Provide fact sheets with some of the notes already intact. This will help English language learners concentrate on the concepts.
- Pause for students to come up with the next step. When working sample problems, ask students to complete a step. Walk around to make sure everyone is following along.

## Selecting Problems That Are Relevant to Students' Lives

No curriculum is perfect, but teachers need not start from scratch, either. Simple adjustments often make problems more interesting. For example,

- Instead of solving a problem about hair ribbons, ask students to calculate how many pants cinches (to hitch up low-riding jeans that fail to meet dress code) a teacher could cut from several yards of duct tape.
- Calculate profits on the sale of trading cards, and what to do with the profits.
- Have students calculate the amount of material needed for a project that will actually happen at school, be it display boards for the science fair, new library books to buy, construction of a prairie habitat, pizzas for the school party, or other problems that demonstrate that math and science are useful and that generate interest.

## CONCLUSION

Probably most important, make sure that students begin to view themselves as mathematicians and scientists. Like the teacher quoted on page 128, we want students to view math and science as creative endeavors, and learning basic skills as a pathway to adventure.

# 10

# Differentiating for Students From Other Cultures

*Before you read on . . .*

- How diverse is the population of your school?
- How easy is it for teachers and students to talk about differences in race and culture?
- What gets in the way?
- Which students struggle to succeed academically?

**W**hich type preferences are honored in the United States?

We worry about shy children, we grade on class participation, and in a preponderance of business situations, people are rewarded for brainstorming during meetings, being able to quickly articulate new ideas, and networking broadly. Decades of type research confirms that our cultural *archetype* is for Extraversion.

- *Archetypes* are ways of being or expected behavior that people within a culture tend to view as desirable.
- *Stereotypes,* in contrast, are sweeping generalizations about all people within a culture.
- *Modal types,* the most frequent type in a population, may or may not match the archetype or stereotype.

To illustrate the difference, the percentage of Extraverts and Introverts in the United States is approximately equal—the modal type is unclear. However, our *archetype* for Extraversion does match the *stereotype* other cultures hold of the United States—the loud, pushy American.

Are all cultures Extraverted? If I as an American try to determine the archetype of another culture, I run the risk of stereotyping. Fortunately, the Association for

**143**

Psychological Type International has chapters or affiliated associations in Britain, Europe, South Africa, Japan, Korea, Australia, New Zealand, Brazil, Chile, Indonesia . . . type goes around the world. Their Web site, http://www.aptinternational.org, has links to the other type associations.

Type experts within various cultures have analyzed their own cultures and determined the archetype, stereotype, and modal type in their countries. They've also developed their own official versions of the MBTI, to help people sort their preferences. The United States version of the MBTI can't even be used in Britain because of cultural differences and archetypal notions of the preferences.

It's easy to think of the stereotypes we have for different cultures around Extraversion and Introversion (England, Italy, Ireland, Finland . . . ), but stereotyping does little to promote understanding. At recent international type conferences, various experts from around the world have shared their understanding of their own cultures.

Why does this matter? Because *all* preferences are equally valuable ways of being. Understanding the archetypes within a culture provides a bridge to comprehending what is valued and how their way of life is effective and valuable. Consider Judging and Perceiving for example, our approach to life. The American culture honors Judging. We expect people to be on time, orders to ship as scheduled, train timetables to be accurate, meetings to end when posted. What happens when Americans travel to Perceiving cultures? Many African and Latin American cultures have an archetype of Perceiving. The needs of the moment are more important than schedules. When an American had waited over an hour at an airport in a Perceiving country and still saw no indication that his plane would be taking off soon, he approached the ticket counter. The attendant said, "The schedule is mostly for Westerners. Here, the plane takes off when it is ready." That's a Perceiving way of looking at life. It's also a really good idea to wait until a plane is ready before it takes off.

The American culture also values Sensing. We take a realistic, matter-of-fact, practical approach to most situations. It's also our modal type; 65–70 percent of Americans prefer Sensing. We also prefer Thinking. The scientific method of investigating hypotheses, logical argument, and objective decision-making are valued in schools, businesses, and politics. Thinking is the modal type for males in this country; 60–65 percent of males prefer Thinking, but 60–65 percent of females prefer Feeling. In general, the culture isn't particularly kind to Feeling males or Thinking females; derogatory labels abound.

Extraversion, Sensing, Thinking, Judging. ESTJ is the American archetype.

## TYPE, MULTICULTURALISM, AND SCHOOLS

What does this mean for educators?

First, schools also have an archetype surrounding type preferences. This influences our expectations of student behavior and learning styles as well as our definition of intelligence. The school archetype is discussed on page 146.

Second, our classrooms are filled with students from cultures with archetypes that differ from the U.S. norm of ESTJ. Because of type's universality, it can become a tool for bridging among cultures within a school, distinguishing between the stereotypes we have and real differences in what is valued within a culture. Although teachers still need to be aware of very real differences in other aspects of a student's culture, type is a starting place for viewing each culture positively, a crucial first step in culturally responsive teaching. Nieto (1999) points out

> There is ample evidence that some educators believe that bicultural students have few experiential or cultural strengths that can benefit their education. Teachers consider them to be . . ."culturally deprived" just because they speak a language other than English as their native language, or because they have just one parent, or because of their social class, race, gender, or ethnicity. Rather than begin with this deficit view of students, it makes sense to begin with a more positive, and, in the end, more complete view of students and their families, and to accommodate school policies and practices to reflect those positive beliefs (p. 85).

There is a profound difference between saying, "That student constantly blurts out in class" and "That student comes from a culture that values Extraversion and therefore thinks out loud. She may need strategies for holding thoughts." Or, "That child is needy, always looking for praise" versus "Positive affirmation is key in that child's Feeling culture."

Further, using type as a bridge for understanding culture can move educators away from the dangers of checklists that describe how students from various cultures learn. Nieto (1999) found that such lists are often used for determining the learning capabilities of students and argued that "such lists can perpetuate the notion that culture is passive, fixed, and equally distributed among all members of a group" (p. 9).

In contrast, experience with type and culture points to the innate yet malleable nature of the preferences.

- Individuals are born with certain preferences.
- How we manifest those preferences is influenced by the archetypes in our cultures and families of origin. Extraverted children in Introverted households are generally quieter than Extraverted children who are raised in Extraverted households. My Extraverted friends from England, where the cultural archetype is for Introversion, point out that they are more reserved than their Extraverted American friends and business associates.
- Only a small percentage of the population actually shares the preferences of the modal type. For example, although the American modal type is ESTJ, meaning that there are more ESTJs than any other type, they still represent only 12–16 percent of the population.
- Therefore, teachers who understand these factors expect that students will be influenced by their cultures but will still be individuals.

Gay (2000) describes the differences in how students express their cultural heritage as a continuum that is influenced by gender, age, social class, individuality, and other factors. Her discussion of cultural influences on teaching and learning

> . . . focus[es] on core characteristics, as manifested on a range of clarity, specificity, purity, and authenticity that is closer to the "high" end of the continuum. The imagined individuals exhibiting these cultural characteristics are *highly ethnically affiliated with a strong cultural identity* . . . furthermore, cultural features are *composite constructions* of group behaviors that occur over time and in

many different situations. They are not pure descriptors of specific individuals within groups or behaviors at a particular point in time. Instead, *descriptions of culture are approximations of reality—templates, if you will—through which actual behaviors of individuals can be filtered in search of alternative explanations and deeper meanings.* (p. 11–12)

That is the goal of using type as a framework for understanding cultures. Instead of using a deficit model, either consciously or unconsciously, differences in archetypal preferences can be used to explore behaviors and academic needs from a positive standpoint. Further, most teachers will share at least one of the preferences honored in different cultures. This provides a starting place, although by no means a complete basis, for understanding.

# TYPE AND CULTURALLY RESPONSIVE TEACHING

One area of agreement about culturally responsive classrooms is that teachers who create these environments use strategies that meet the needs of a variety of learning styles (Shade, Kelly, and Oberg, 1997; Gay, 2000; Nieto, 1999).

Paying attention to the needs of Sensing and Intuitive students honors the profound difference in how students access the information they are supposed to be learning, a profound difference recognized in cultures throughout the world.

Paying attention to the needs of Extraverted and Introverted students ensures that all students find the classroom an energizing, appealing place that honors the style of their home culture.

Paying attention to the needs of Thinking and Feeling students helps teachers bridge between cultures that value competition and achievement and those that value group affiliation and cooperation.

Paying attention to the needs of Judging and Perceiving students helps teachers devise strategies to aid students from Perceiving cultures navigate the very Judging worlds of American schools and workplaces.

Before turning to individual cultures, let's look at the archetypes of two very different cultures that are often strikingly in conflict: the culture of school and students living in poverty.

## The Culture of School

Although the American archetype is Extraversion, Sensing, Thinking, and Judging, and people with ESTJ preferences are overrepresented in successful business positions, this is *not* the archetype of our schools. In fact in many studies, ESTJ students are at the bottom of measures of academic performance, racking up low GPAs and standardized test scores (Myers, McCaulley, Quenk, & Hammer, 1998). What *is* honored?

*Introversion.* Even though we grade on class participation, most classrooms still emphasize limited movement and long periods of listening or working silently. Teachers do use group work, cooperative learning, discussions, and debates, but complaints usually arise over noise, not silence. Teachers complain when students come back from physical education class or recess "wound up" instead of recognizing that the Extraverts are reenergized! Quiet *is* a good thing—after all, studies show that almost half of the students in any school are Introverts, but teachers tend to see noise as misbehavior and use discipline to curtail it rather than seeking to teach to the Extraverted style of learning.

*Intuition.* Yes, our society values Sensing, but in school, the Intuitive style of making connections, displaying creativity, taking unique approaches to problem-solving, and synthesizing is defined as "higher level thinking." Our standardized tests are biased toward Intuitives, who outperform Sensing types by 150 points on average on the PSAT (Wilkes, 2004). They also consistently achieve higher GPAs on average than Sensing students.

*Thinking.* Even humanities classes are taught in a Thinking style, with an emphasis on critical analysis, logical reasoning, and objectivity. Because of the necessity of consistency, school rules and discipline policies can seldom take individual differences into account to a great degree. There is a tendency to consider math and science classes as the height of intellectual endeavor.

*Judging.* Bells, not process, tell us when learning is done. The calendar year marks benchmarks in student growth. Pacing schedules often loom large in teacher consciousness and decision-making. Teachers can seldom accommodate varying needs of students in setting due dates; promptness, attendance, and completeness count.

Is it any wonder that people who prefer Introversion, Intuition, Thinking, and Judging (INTJ) have the highest GPAs and the highest standardized test scores? (Myers et al., 1998) Or that Introverted Intuitives account for 32 percent of our college professors even though only 12 percent of the population prefers Introversion and Intuition? School is designed for these people—and to a large extent, *by* these people as the colleges of education determine our models for pedagogy and curriculum.

Let's look first at one culture that tends to do poorly in American schools, the culture of poverty.

## The Realities of Poverty

Payne (1996) developed her understanding of poverty from her experiences with her husband's family and the neighborhood where he grew up. His own father died when he was six, so he grew up in an area where culture was defined by generational poverty. Payne found that these experiences helped her "translate" for middle-class educators like herself why student behaviors happened. Note that Payne has been criticized for stereotyping and thus continuing the deficit view of these students. Consider how using the language of type can move past the stereotypes. Her descriptions of poverty indicate the following patterns in preference archetypes.

*Extraversion.* "Almost always the TV is on, no matter what the circumstance. Conversation is participatory, often with more than one person talking at a time" (p. 68). She also cites an oral rather than written language tradition and kinesthetic communication, another Extraverted tendency. Further, they value a person's ability to entertain others through storytelling or humor.

*Sensing.* The emphasis on day-to-day survival leaves little room for abstract thinking. Further, people in poverty tend to hold clear opinions without examining them; polarization of positions is the norm, an exaggerated form of the Sensing preference for clarity.

*Feeling.* Relationships are of utmost importance because other people, not money or things, are their primary resources. Further, a high percentage of people in generational poverty in this country are members of ethnic cultures that value the Feeling tendencies of cooperation, collaboration, and community (Gay, 2000). They also often consider personal opinion of as much value as facts or logical reasoning.

*Perceiving.* Payne describes "Time occurs only in the present. The future does not exist except as a word. Time is flexible and not measured. Time is often assigned on the basis of the emotional significance and not the actual measured time" (p. 69). They tend to live for the moment, not setting goals or being proactive. They seldom have systems for organizing papers or other household items.

Extraversion, Sensing, Feeling, Perceiving, ESFP. The exact opposite of the INTJ world of schools. School for many students living in poverty thus seems like a foreign culture. How do they frustrate teachers? By being disorganized, by not being self-starters, by attempting to entertain their classmates, by talking back or participating too much, by refusing to work if they don't like a teacher. Traditionally, teachers have seen the deficits and not the assets of these students.

In my experience, when teachers begin viewing students through the lens of type rather than exclusively through the lens of poverty, they start to see more ways to help these students navigate the school system.

Teachers often ask, "Don't these students need to learn the rules of school? That's the real world so why should I change my style?" This tendency grows stronger in middle school and high school. Nieto (1999) points out the fallacy in this reasoning: It excuses teachers and schools from examining their own practices and how those might contribute to failure in those students. Demanding that these students adapt has resulted in behavior problems and academic underachievement.

Further, one isn't simply asking them to change a "style" or flex on a cultural value. Instead, when one expects these students to assimilate, the very real differences in the needs of Sensing and Intuitive students are ignored. They are at a perpetual disadvantage, "writing with their nonpreferred hand" day in and day out at school.

## TYPE AND OTHER CULTURES

By now, you are probably thinking about other information you've read or common behaviors you see in students from different ethnic groups. Specific information on each culture remains crucial; type gets only at part of cultural differences. However, in several of the schools I work with, teachers have students from several cultures. The job of creating culturally responsive classrooms seems overwhelming, especially when some of the cultures have seemingly opposite values. That's where type provides a starting place, a way to pinpoint bridges among cultures instead of gulfs. Students from Extraverted cultures realize that individuals in other cultures may be

Extraverted too—or that they themselves may be Introverted. Teachers know that if they are meeting the needs of the various type preferences, they have taken a giant step forward in meeting the needs of learners from different cultures, even as they continue to learn more about different cultures and individual students.

In the following descriptions of the archetypes for each culture, I will point to existing research and compare internal descriptions of those cultures with type preference descriptions. Again, a cultural archetype is just one influence on the personality, learning style, and behavior of any student, but it is central to understanding that student's relational, motivational, and informational needs.

## The African American Culture

There isn't just one African American culture, just as the United States culture varies from region to region. However, several studies on African American learning styles (Delpit, 1995; Fiske, 1991; Hale-Benson, 1982; Ladson-Billings, 1994) point to successful techniques in working with these students that parallel suggestions given by type experts for working with Extraverted and Sensing students. The following list of descriptors of African American learning styles comes from Shade et al. (1997). Test your understanding of type preferences by covering the right-hand column and thinking about which of the preferences each descriptor might correspond with:

| *African American students learn best from:* | *This corresponds with a preference for:* |
|---|---|
| Bodily movement | Extraversion (correlates with kinesthetic learning) |
| Equal talk time for teachers and students | Extraversion |
| Material presented with social/emotional context rather than impersonal | Feeling |
| Social rather than object cues | Feeling |
| Use of multiple senses—touch, sight, hearing | Sensing |
| A variety of information presented at a constantly changing pace | Perceiving |
| Environments where they don't feel criticized personally | Feeling |

Studies show mixed results on the modal type of African Americans. Nuby and Oxford (1998) presented detailed information on the psychological types of African American high-school students. They most often preferred Extraversion, Sensing, and Thinking, but were evenly split on Judging and Perceiving. Robinson (2001) points out that African Americans tend to report their "doing" selves rather than their "being" selves when taking the MBTI tool. Robinson asserts that the needs of African Americans and their view of type must evolve from within a setting that optimizes their innate abilities. He postulated that within his culture, Perceiving is the archetype, but many "mask" Judging to navigate the majority culture.

Melear and Alcock (1998) found that high-school African American students in upper-level science classes showed preferences for ST and SP, whereas sixth-grade students showed a higher preference for Feeling. However, more study is needed to determine whether students with Feeling preferences are less likely to pursue science or if younger children are more likely to report a Feeling preferences, as Murphy and Meisgeier's (1987) data suggest. The higher numbers of African American male students reporting a preference for Perceiving supports Hale's (1994) findings that these students tend to prefer more flexible environments.

In summary, most studies, both of learning styles and personality type, seem to indicate that the archetype in African American culture is Extraversion, Sensing, and Perceiving. Recall (p. 22) that few people with these preferences go into teaching, nor are there high percentages of African American educators, meaning that these students may seldom be in classrooms where teachers share their natural style.

## The Latino Culture

Although analyses exist on the type preferences of countries such as Brazil and Chile, little has been gathered about the Latino culture in the United States. Shade et al. (1997) make the following statements about the learning styles of these students, which can be matched with type preferences. However, more research is needed.

| *Latino students learn best from:* | *This corresponds with a preference for:* |
|---|---|
| Clear hierarchies and roles, orderliness | Sensing |
| Atmospheres where sensitivity toward others' feelings is shown | Feeling |
| Success measured by cooperation rather than competitive individualism | Feeling |
| Chances to interact with others | Extraversion, Feeling |
| Avoidance of arguments which are considered rude and disrespectful | Feeling |
| Activities that incorporate the arts, of high value in their culture | Art is of value to both Sensing and Intuitive cultures |

## The Hmong Culture

Trueba, Jacobs, and Kirton (1990) highlighted some of the cultural differences in the Hmong community. Of particular importance were the traditional high regard for educators, resulting in a reluctance to any questioning by parents of teachers; parents' lack of schooling in Laos, where usually only one child per family attended schools with rigid discipline; and a cultural tendency to never brag, resulting in comments such as, "My child is slow," which educators took literally. Trueba gave the following descriptors of the Hmong learning style:

| Hmong students learn best from: | This corresponds with a preference for: |
|---|---|
| Demonstration-based, related to real life | Sensing |
| Oral communication of ideas | Sensing (ideas not bound in symbolic world of writing) |
| Emphasis on correctness, not speed | Sensing, Perceiving |
| Material presented with social/emotional context rather than impersonal | Feeling |
| Collective action activities (group process) where process is important | Introversion (preferring to blend in to group) and Feeling |
| Environments where they don't feel criticized personally | Feeling |

Other sources emphasize the Sensing preference in learning. Bliatout, Downing, Lewis, and Yang (1988) suggested

> There is a great deal of pattern to the speaking done within the society; a person learns the appropriate structure, vocabulary, and "flower words," then varies the text to give it a personal signature. Student will fare better in preparing speeches, reports, letters, or essays if they are given a sample, which can be memorized and then varied to suit the specific circumstances and personal style. This technique runs counter to American teachers' desire not to stifle creativity, but provides a structure . . . (p. 19)

Another important cultural factor is the hierarchical nature of Hmong society, in which elders and experts are not to be questioned. This is more common in cultures with Introversion and Sensing archetypes. Lee (2002) found that adolescent Hmong students are consciously choosing, more so than many other students, whether to do as their parents ask or rebel. Teachers might use type to help students understand the values of tradition and the importance of the collective good in their own culture, as well as how it differs from the American culture, shedding a positive light on the dilemmas these students face.

## Native American Students

Jung himself looked at how type appeared in other cultures, partly through anthropological expeditions to the Pueblo Indians of New Mexico and the Elgoni of Kenya. In his *Memories, Dreams and Reflections* he recounted a conversation with a Pueblo chief, who was disturbed by white Americans.

> "The whites always want something; they are always uneasy and restless. We do not know what they want. We do not understand them. We think they are mad." Jung asked him why he thought the whites were mad. "They say that they think with their heads," the chief replied. "Why, of course. What do you think with?" Jung asked him in surprise. "We think here," the chief said, indicating his heart. (Stevens, 1991, p. 272)

This description seems to indicate a Pueblo cultural value around using the Feeling function, rather than the Thinking function. Some common descriptors regarding the learning style of Native Americans include the following (Shade et al., 1997):

| Native American students learn best from: | This corresponds with a preference for: |
| --- | --- |
| Cooperative learning groups | Feeling |
| Getting the big picture before isolated skills | Intuition |
| Settings full of encouragement | Feeling |
| Artwork, metaphors, images, analogies, and symbols rather than dictionary-type definitions | Intuition |
| Visual/special orientation rather than verbal | Introversion |
| Brainstorming, open-ended activities | Intuition |
| Student-designed games | Intuition |
| Lessons and exercises that include discussion of values | Feeling |

Kaulback (1984) found that Native American children, regardless of nation, learned best through visual techniques rather than oral techniques. Children are encouraged to watch and then do. Shade et al. summarize,

> The ethnographic studies of the communities tend to suggest that Native American children are taught to focus their attention on everything in their environment at the appropriate time. This includes both the people and the physical objects who are in their environment. Researchers report that Native Americans can perceive the slightest movement in gestures and eye expressions and can identify relatives or others from great distances. However, their general personality orientation would probably be toward introversion because they are autonomous, analyze what they perceive, and concentrate their attention on understanding how they fit into the scheme of things. (p. 74–75)

Nuby and Oxford (1998) found that Native American students were over three-fourths Perceiving and had a larger percentage of Intuitives than the general population. In a workshop I conducted with a group of Native American educators, we talked about the similarities and differences in the United States and Native American archetypes throughout the day. They concluded that their own culture's archetype was Introversion, Intuition, Feeling, and Perceiving (INFP)—the total opposite of the larger U.S. culture. One of the leaders quipped, "Right, all these centuries we kept thinking you'd listen. . . ."

The point was not to stereotype all Native American students as INFP (any more than all white American children match the cultural stereotype/archetype of ESTJ; only about 12–16 percent do). Instead, we were working on using type as a vehicle for helping the students navigate between the two cultures. The educators pointed out that although the descriptors above rang true for Native American traditions, many of their students had lived in the inner city so long that they didn't know much about their own culture. The group hoped that type could help the students "translate" among their cultural values and traditions, their daily life, and the school culture they'd need to negotiate to finish high school.

A study of the personality types of Native American students in Alberta, Canada (Rosin & Boersma, 1993) indicated that Native American students are more likely to have preferences for Introversion and Feeling. Cree males were 65 percent Introverted, compared with 47 percent for the non-Native comparison group. The Cree males were also 4.5 times as likely to have a preference for Feeling as the non-Natives. For Cree males and females, the modal type was ISFP, almost six times as frequent as in samples of general populations. The Native sample also showed higher numbers of Perceiving students. IFP students do best in smaller environments where they can have a few close relationships, where teachers know them as individuals and encourage their uniqueness, and provide ways to meet the Perceiving needs for flexibility, openness, and exploration.

Many studies indicate that perhaps Native Americans struggle more in high school than any other ethnic group. Look back at the description for Introverted Feeling students on page 37. Why might high school be such a struggle?

# WORK COMPLETION STRATEGIES FOR STUDENTS OF POVERTY AND OTHER PERCEIVING CULTURES

One success story is our use of type to help students from Perceiving cultures complete major projects in the very Judging world of school deadlines. Several urban middle-school teachers and I joined forces to reduce the number of failing grades their middle schoolers were receiving. By implementing the following "No More F's" strategies, we succeeded in getting 95–100 percent of our students to receive a C or better on major projects, compared with failure rates as high as 30 percent without the strategies.

The scaffolding techniques are designed to meet the needs of Perceiving students. Review the "Behavior Clues" for Perceiving students on pages 25–26; often these "symptoms" surface in greater strength as students enter adolescence and have (a) more teachers and (b) projects to complete with a greater scope, such as science fairs, long reports, or other major assignments.

## Strategy 1: The Expectation of Achievement

Expecting students to achieve is different than having high standards. On a daily assignment, teachers with high standards might give F's to all students who don't engage and therefore fail to complete the work. The problem with this approach is that adolescents are immature and think they're getting away with not doing work.

Teachers with high expectations walk around and nag until every student has pencil and paper and is writing. Usually within a few class periods, students understand that they are expected to do the work. This practice is consistent with what Wilson and Corbett (2001) found:

Students . . . wanted to be in classrooms where:

- The teacher "stayed on students" to complete assignments.
- The teacher was able to control student behavior without ignoring the lesson.
- The teacher went out of his or her way to provide help.

- The teacher explained things until the "light bulb went on" for the whole class.
- The teacher provided students with a variety of activities through which to learn.
- The teacher understood students' situations and factored that into their lessons.

> When we say "students wanted" these qualities present in their classrooms, we mean that the overwhelming majority of students reiterated these characteristics at every opportunity in the interviews over the three-year period. These are not "the survey says" kinds of answers. Offering the percentage of students who responded with these "wants" is not very meaningful because the number of dissenters would be in the single digits—in absolute numbers, not percentages. Essentially we interpreted students to be saying that the effective teachers adhered to a "no excuses" policy. (p. 63–64)

## Strategy 2: Planning for Completion

Completing a project requires the strengths of the Judging preference: understanding the steps involved, the amount of time each will take, the time available, and the requirements of the task.

*Identifying project steps.* Teaching students to complete "step sheets" is time-consuming and frustrating, yet it illustrates why so many students fail to finish what they start—they don't know how to get from start to finish! Even with clear examples of the steps involved in a project, students often list two steps: (1) Start project, (2) Finish project.

Kneel beside them and say, for example, "You've chosen to create a board game to show what you know about the story. What's the goal of your game?" "To win." "Well, think about board games and *how* you win them. Reach the last square first? Collect the right game pieces?" Then help them identify the *many* steps: choosing a format, writing out the rules, checking them for errors, drawing out what the game will look like, using the story to generate moves or questions, etc.

To develop planning skills, students need to write out the steps themselves. If everyone will be doing the same project, generate the steps as a class. Because the steps will later be used to mark their progress on the assignment, a detailed list provides more opportunities for students to feel successful.

Two things happen during the step sheet process. First, on assignments with choices, students evaluate whether they can complete the task they chose by the deadline. Is it too complicated? Can they get the materials? Can they find enough information? Sometimes they change to a more realistic task for them after grasping what is involved.

Second, the step sheet helps them plan out their real deadlines. For example, knowing that the papier mâché features on your game will need to dry for a day before you can paint them changes the start date for constructing the game board.

*The calendar.* The second part of planning is having students fill in a calendar that shows when they will complete each step. Have the students work *backward* from the deadline. It helps them see why the mini-deadlines are important, for example providing time for that papier maché mountain to dry. The calendar also includes teacher deadlines. One deadline is turning in the step sheet, which counts toward their total points on a project. Another might be a draft plan for the project or a rough draft of a paper.

Again, to develop the skills, have students make their own month-at-a-glance calendars for the days they have until the project is due, including weekends. Together as a class, record the final deadline for the project and any other mini-deadlines.

Next, students fill in other events in their lives: Wednesday night religious commitments, babysitting, soccer games, family events, etc. Finally, they fit their own project steps into their calendars, starting with the last step.

Ask students to take their calendars home and have a parent or guardian sign them. Parents tell us, "Even if my child fell behind, I knew where they were supposed to be on the project. That helped me know whether to insist that they set aside time to work on it." Again, handing in the calendar is part of the project and part of their grade.

*Clear deadlines.* Many teachers think they have clear deadlines, but students are fully capable of not listening. One teacher told her class that notes for their speeches were due a week before the presentations would start. She also wrote that fact in bold letters on their instruction sheets. However, when she asked them to complete the calendar, not one student in three sections of her class remembered to write the due date in the notes until she pointed it out yet a third time!

Whenever possible, put "teeth" into mini-deadlines. For example, students might need to turn in the rough draft of their speeches before starting the art project their speeches will explain.

*Goal setting.* Students can use their step sheets to set their own goals for class time. What are they going to accomplish today? Have them leave their goal sheets on their desks during class so that you can see easily whether they are on task. Further, this gives them a concrete reminder of what using their class time wisely will look like.

*Reflection.* Periodically, ask students to reflect on their progress by rating themselves, on a scale of 1–5 stars, how confident they are that they will make the deadline. Then have them journal on how well they're using their time, how they will adjust their work habits, and in some cases, whether they need to switch projects if they chose something too complicated.

Work behavior definitely improves after these reflection exercises. The students who choose to change projects are frequently the ones who struggled to complete projects in the past. The goal is to help them feel the success of completion as well as to help them manage their time well. These student reflections were submitted with the final project.

> I used the first half of my time wisely and I wasn't going to start over after that. But then it was like, "Oh I'm almost done and I still have a long time" and I started watching TV. If I had used the time I spent watching TV to write the directions, I would have finished on time.

> I did get to do the project I wanted but it took a little more effort than I thought it would. I think I managed my time okay but I could have done it better. We got it in at the last second, but we had to come in for lunch and type two pages the day it was due.

### Strategy 3: Choices—or the Alternative Assignment

Providing an alternative assignment to any student who does not complete the original project requires them to do something rather than allowing them to do nothing. If they stay on schedule, they can stick to their original choice of assignment. The further behind they fall, the fewer choices remain. Often, to avoid doing the teacher-chosen alternate assignment, students ask for lunchtime passes, leave messages on their home phones as reminders of what they need to do, work feverishly during class—anything to avoid the fallback assignment, the design of which is a strategy in itself. There are two keys to making this strategy work:

1. The alternative assignment needs to simulate the initial assignment if possible. For example, if students failed to write a report, then the alternative assignment might require note taking from text excerpts, writing an opening paragraph based on those notes, completing bibliography entries for given resources, answering questions about where certain kinds of information might be found, and so on.

   Other alternative assignments include using commercially available worksheets or tests. Or, students who fail to complete their science fair project might complete a standardized experiment chosen by the teacher.

2. The students need to feel the pain. Because administering the alternative assignment often requires class time, teachers might assign the rest of the class a curriculum-based enrichment activity such as an art project. One science teacher set up an experiment that tested the properties of different kinds of chocolate, including a taste test. Students working on the alternative assignment missed the fun.

Again, the goal is to help students experience academic success. Simply giving F's leaves some children behind. Teaching them to plan *how* to complete a project and meet their goals helps them develop the skills they need to be responsible students in the future. Requiring them to do something rather than allowing them to do nothing helps them increase their expectations of themselves.

A few students will still slip through the cracks because of major suspensions or transportation problems for make-up opportunities or other uncontrollable factors. However, many more will experience the satisfaction of being successful students.

## CONCLUSION

The goal of using type to differentiate for culture is *not* to stereotype, nor to ignore other critical values, differences, or norms within other cultures. Instead, type can provide the following:

- An entry point for teachers to gain insights into other cultures through a positive framework rather than through deficit models
- A bridge among the multiple cultures present in many schools today
- A framework for meeting the needs of various learning styles honored in those cultures.

More research is needed, and is occurring, but type can serve as a tool for meeting the goal of culturally responsive teaching: helping all students learn. Nieto (1999) describes the light in children's eyes when they become excited about learning.

> There is nothing quite as dazzling as this sight. Once we have seen the look of discovery and learning in students' eyes, we can no longer maintain that some young people—because of their social class, race, ethnicity, gender, native language, or other difference—are simply unmotivated, ignorant, or undeserving. The light in their eyes is eloquent testimony to their capacity and hence their right to learn. (p. xix)

# 11

# Differentiating by Grade Level

**Before you read on . . .**

Think back to your experiences as a student at the grade level you teach.

- What do you wish you had known about your personality and learning style?
- What do you wish your teacher had known?
- Why might you introduce type to your students?
  o To learn more about your students as individuals?
  o To help them be more accepting of each other and different classroom activities?
  o To help them learn to advocate for their own learning needs?
  o To develop a common language in your classroom around teaching and learning?

**Y**ou can use just about all of the differentiated instruction and classroom management techniques described in this book without teaching your students about type. However, giving students a language for thinking about how they learn adds power to the strategies.

Goals for teaching type may vary by classroom, grade level, and student needs. In this chapter, we'll look at type development, classroom objectives for type instruction, and exercises for introducing students to type.

*Learning about type was affirming for students—they weren't defects. So many kids wonder what's wrong with them that they don't care about deadlines or that rewriting makes a difference. They learned, "It's not that I'm a bad student. I just need to work on these skills!"*

—Middle-school teacher

## KINDERGARTEN TO SECOND GRADE

Perhaps you've heard of the little girl who announced after her first day of kindergarten, "School's a waste of time. I can't read and they won't let me talk." Picture a

Pippi Longstocking or an Eloise, with big ideas and a penchant for freedom, in the average primary classroom. Type concepts can help both teachers and students better negotiate the line between exuberance and misbehavior. Teachers can use them to do the following:

- Help students meet classroom expectations. The literature-based activities for introducing the learning styles, described in this chapter, help them understand that different students have different needs, and that "doing school" requires that they have some skill with every style.
- Ensure that their classroom environments and overall program meet the needs of diverse learners. The students themselves often lack the self-awareness necessary to identify their own preferences. However, they *are* aware of the kinds of activities they do and don't enjoy.

Spotting type preferences in five- to seven-year-olds, especially Extraverted children, can be easier than in older children because the school socialization process tends to cause children to mask their natural personalities. A kindergarten teacher might become aware of students with preferences for the following:

- Sensing as they struggle with "Don't touch" or hesitate at unclear directions
- Intuition as they make up their own rules for games or imaginative play
- Thinking as they voice opinions or pursue one or two deep interests
- Feeling as they look out for the underdog and yearn for positive feedback.

Primary-grade teachers might also keep in mind three important factors concerning Sensing and Intuition. First, written words and numbers are *symbols*—the natural realm of Intuitive, not Sensing students. Planks are easily knocked out of the Sensing bridge to literacy by seemingly innocuous activities. Take learning the Alphabet Song. If students have learned the song, the letters C-A-T spell "sate," not "cat."

Second, Sensing students prefer step-by-step instructions and clear examples. For arithmetic, you might see them spend more time counting blocks before agreeing that 2 + 2 + 2 = 4 + 2. Numbers are symbolic; they're testing the reality of what they're being taught.

Third, Intuitive students may struggle with or rush through structured tasks or repetitive assignments with little room for the imagination. Teachers may quickly label them as sloppy or poor listeners. Intuitive students also naturally focus on tangents that may not fit a teacher's plans! To grow in academic confidence, Intuitive students need affirmation of their leaps of faith, ability to make connections, and original thoughts.

## THIRD TO FIFTH GRADES

Our educational system expects that by grade three, all students will have mastered basic reading, addition, subtraction, and writing skills. Deep inside, though, we know that this won't quite be the case. Those students who move at a slower pace feel themselves slipping behind. Fears mount—inside teachers, administrators, parents, and students—as high-stakes tests loom. In my experience, the more intense the school, the earlier this happens. I've heard seven-year-olds declare, "I can't do math."

Innocence begins to evaporate on another front as well. MacKenzie (1996), who speaks on creativity, reports that when he asks first graders whether they are artists, every hand shoots into the air. By third grade, perhaps a third of the hands go up.

The higher the grade, the fewer children raised their hands. By time I reached sixth grade, no more than one or two did so and then only ever-so-slightly—*guardedly*—their eyes glancing from side to side uneasily, betraying a fear of being identified by the group as a "closet artist." [He tells students] "I think what's happening is that you are being tricked out of one of the greatest gifts every one of us receives at birth. That is the gift of being an artist, a creative genius." (p. 19–20)

Teaching type has essential pay-offs for students in these grades as we structure classrooms and lessons to help every student value his or her unique academic and creative abilities. Focusing on three goals can bring this about.

## Goal 1: Building Academic Confidence in *Every* Child

Resnick (1995) points out that "What we learn is a function of both our talents—our aptitude for particular kinds of learning—and how hard we try—our effort" (p. 55). Effort creates ability, and the framework of type helps teachers and students realize that factors other than intelligence affect how quickly we finish many academic tasks. For example, page 96 described the two speeds Intuitive students use for reading. If teachers measure free reading by pages read rather than time spent reading, they are favoring Intuitive students. Teachers can help all students feel successful by honoring accuracy, thoroughness, and reflection, as well as speed.

Further, Sensing and Intuitive students need different information to proceed confidently on tasks. With young students, we want to be careful about labeling certain practices as "crutches" or examples of lower level thinking. For example, using manipulatives and drawing diagrams helps both Sensing students and visual learners process new ideas. In affirming classrooms, students know,

- I can think like a mathematician if I draw pictures (and this holds true right through calculus).
- I can be creative if I see examples of what other students have done.
- I can succeed if I work at my own pace instead of judging myself by how fast or slow others go.

## Goal 2: Building Bridges to Higher Level Thinking

Remember that students who are good technicians in the early grades, often Sensing students, frequently struggle to move from concrete tasks to evaluation and synthesis. Establish classroom norms:

- It is okay to start with either the details and examine them to find the big ideas *or* start with your hunch and look for details to back it up or contradict it.
- Your opinions and ideas are as important as the facts and viewpoints in textbooks. Some assignments have no right answers or procedures.

## Goal 3: Identifying True Academic Difficulties

As differences in student progress become evident, educators want to ensure that each child receives the help he or she needs to succeed. Making the right diagnoses—dyslexia, ADHD, or clinical depression—and providing the right services are essential.

Yet children are overdiagnosed with these difficulties. Looking first for *normal* differences can decrease this tendency. Is the student really withdrawn or an Introverted student with one or two special interests? Is the child truly oppositionally defiant or an Extraverted Thinking child who is far too often being told to "Sit! Stay! Heel!"?

In short, in grades three through five, teachers need to make every effort to ensure that students discover the strengths of their learning styles, yet get extra help if needed.

# THE MIDDLE-SCHOOL YEARS: HELPING ADOLESCENTS SEE THEMSELVES AS STUDENTS

Many middle-school teachers view their role as readying students for later learning and life. This translates to tough homework policies and, sometimes, less readily available help. Student questions may be interpreted as signs of laziness ("Go back and reread the directions") or inattention ("If you'd been listening you'd know.")

However, the truth about adolescents is that *by definition they are immature!!!* The most current research shows that the very last part of the brain to develop fully is the prefrontal cortex, which controls planning, setting priorities, and pondering what different courses of action might bring. During adolescence, as the amygdala swells and students are more emotions-driven than reason-driven, they all lean toward Perceiving. Adolescent Perceiving students need scaffolding, not penalties, to grow in organizational skills. In many studies of at-risk students, a high percentage have a preference for Perceiving—82 percent at one school I worked with.

Further, a preponderance of middle schoolers, even those who will later easily graduate with honors, slip up for a while somewhere in seventh or eighth grade. Although for many this period is just a "blip" on their school record, for others, the penalties and repeated failures change their outlook on school for good. Our overall objective needs to be helping middle-school students view themselves as successful learners.

## Preference Clarity—Do Middle Schoolers Know Who They Are?

Students from third grade on will understand type concepts, but middle schoolers are at the beginning of the struggle for adult freedom . . . and usually use that freedom to try to be like every other middle schooler. The archetype of middle school—the personality most admired—seems to be Extraversion, Sensing, and Perceiving.

- *Extraversion.* It may take several weeks of repeating, "This preference pair is about energy, not about how many friends you have" before 12- and 13-year-olds grasp the definition. Although a solid group of Introverts are relieved that there is a name for their disposition, students may need several quiet, reflective experiences before understanding the value of Introversion.
- *Sensing.* The media has a heyday with Intuitives. In the movie *Galaxy Quest,* the geeky boys who have computer-modeled the starship NSEA Protector are Intuitives. Hermione Granger is an Intuitive. Most science fiction readers are Intuitives. It is not cool to be an Intuitive, although the increased popularity of fantasy and science fiction resulting from *Harry Potter* has helped these students blend in a bit.

- *Thinking* and *Feeling*. Adolescents are often very good at stepping into the shoes of their friends and understanding their needs, the realm of Feeling. However, the overall culture of adolescence has a Thinking side, based on rules more than values. There are right and wrong ways to walk, talk, dress, smile, and so on. Further, they're likely to argue back with adults.
- *Perceiving*. In a nutshell, it is countercultural for middle schoolers to tackle homework quickly, finish reports on schedule, or keep track of assignments in planners. However, multiple experiences with the concepts help Judging students realize their discomfort with last-minute efforts.

In summary, middle-school students feel pressured to be like everyone else, but as they learn about type, they grow to recognize and embrace their own preferences. Teachers can help students think about learning styles so they can process, "If I have to work out of my style, I can compensate or even flourish by taking these actions . . ."

# THE HIGH-SCHOOL YEARS: HELPING TEENS MAKE THEIR FIRST LIFE DECISIONS

Somewhere during tenth and eleventh grade, real life begins to creep up on most teens. College? Trade school? A year off to travel? A full-time job? Their overall school experiences will color the decisions they make.

Traditionally, the higher up in school students go, the less likely they are to have teachers who differentiate. Further, all kinds of forces gather to decrease the teenager's self-confidence:

- They take college entrance examinations.
- They may see their class rank on every report card.
- Tryouts for sports, band, choir, the school play, all let them know how they measure up in other ways.

With all of these factors flying at high schoolers, the overarching objective of teaching type becomes helping students establish self-awareness, self-identity, and self-confidence for schooling, careers, and social interaction.

## Preference Clarity

By high school, most students will be quite clear about three of their preferences, if not all four. Although peer pressure is still strong, more high schoolers take delight in standing out from the crowd.

- Students still tend to prefer Extraversion. Introverted Feeling students may confuse their desire to be with friends with Extraversion.
- Both Sensing and Intuitive students have more ways to find their niche with the many extracurricular activities and class choices available.
- Thinking students begin to embrace their natural bent—they want to categorize the world and explore issues of right and wrong.
- As the brain develops and more synapses form in the frontal cortex, the center of planning and reasoning, more Judging students learn to balance homework with other activities.

So, even if the high-school culture is still, as was middle school, Extraversion, Sensing, and Perceiving, students with all preferences usually begin to feel more comfortable with who they are. If they still lack clarity, it is often because their home environments don't match their natural preferences.

### Type and Careers: Going beyond Learning Styles

Most 17-year-olds are familiar with only a handful of careers—teaching, medicine, law enforcement, and whatever careers their parents, relatives, and family friends have. Understandably, parents often focus on pragmatic choices for their teenagers: affordable schooling, realistic careers, financial security.

When used correctly, type can help teens explore the 14,000 jobs listed by the government without being overwhelmed. Type should never be the *only* criteria for choosing a career. However, volumes of information exist on

- Type patterns in who chooses different professions
- How to effectively use one's preferences for the job search process
- College majors chosen by people with different preferences.

Students gain access to rich resources—on the Internet, in libraries, and through seminars presented all over the country. Further, a high percentage of college career centers use personality type in counseling students. Excellent resources include the following:

- *What's Your Type of Career* by Donna Dunning
- *Do What You Are* by Paul Tieger and Barbara Barron-Tieger
- Several Web sites, including http://www.typecan.com, http://www.typelogic.com, and http://www.personalitytype.com.

This information can help teens identify the *characteristics* of careers that might appeal to them, based on their personality, rather than specific careers. Here are some sample questions for discussion:

- There are doctors [teachers, attorneys] of every personality type. What specialties might Feeling doctors chose? Thinking doctors? *Many pediatricians and psychiatrists prefer Feeling. Thinking doctors are overrepresented in oncology and brain surgery.*
- What personality types might choose architecture? Why? *Approximately 80 percent of architects prefer Intuition; the work is conceptual rather than hands-on. And, 70 percent prefer Introversion; they often work alone.*

## THE TYPE LESSONS

As with any helpful classroom tool, type can be misused. *Don't* use type in the classroom unless you believe the following:

- All eight preferences are desirable.
- Students of every type can achieve academic excellence.

- Students have the last say as to what their preferences are. One of the basic ethics of using type is that the individual is the expert. Further, teachers do not accurately identify student learning styles, even after a full semester (Holt, Denny, Capps, & De Vore, 2005).
- You can adjust your classroom so the needs of each of the eight preferences are met at least part of the time.

## Why *Not* Teach Type to Students?

Teachers generally have three main concerns about introducing type to students.

*Will "typing" students result in labeling?* Type is about *preferences,* not static labels. Further, our students *are* labeled: Attention Deficit Disorder, Oppositional Defiance Disorder, Special Education, quiet, difficult, and so on. When type is well-used, it can decrease labels or substitute the positive language of the preferences, as the information on ADHD and Perceiving students in Chapter 3 illustrates.

*Will teaching type take time away from curriculum?* The activities in this chapter are carefully designed to help students appreciate how they and others learn, thereby reducing time spent on classroom management. Time on-task increases.

*Will students understand the concepts?* They do. Type is a *mental model* that puts patterns to behaviors, ideas, and struggles they've had.

### How Much Do You Need to Know About Type?

Educators often ask about having students take surveys or assessments to identify their personality types. Excellent instruments exist, *but they are designed to be used as part of a self-discovery process.* Interpretation is needed to help people determine their own "best fit" type. Here are the two best-known:

- The MBTI tool, normed for age 16 and up (http://www.cpp.com).
- The MMTIC, for third through eighth grade (http://www.capt.org).

Both are *self-reporting,* not *diagnostic* tools, but have excellent reliability. Students enjoy taking the instruments because they get to "argue back with the test."
Anyone can become qualified to administer these tools by completing a college course in tests and measurements or a qualifying program. Information on these programs is available at the publisher Web sites, listed above. Although the Internet is full of free type inventories, these are not researched. Instead, guide students through the self-discovery process the following type lessons provide.

## Options for Introducing Type

If you haven't used type with students before, explaining all the preferences may seem overwhelming. Here are some options.

*Teach one preference pair.* Most teachers begin with Extraversion and Introversion because of its effectiveness with classroom management.

*Teach type with a team.* Find two or three other interested teachers. Rotate students as each of you teaches one of the preference pairs.

*Designate a "type expert."* At the secondary level, one teacher might introduce the concepts to all students on a team. Or, teachers in one subject area may do so, while others use activities from Chapter 6 to reinforce type concepts.

Below are two sets of lessons, quadrant activities for the early grades and preference pair lessons for grades three and up. If you are teaching grades three through five, you can use the quadrant activities *or* the preference pair lessons, depending on your goals for teaching type.

## QUADRANT ACTIVITIES: POSITIVE EXPERIENCES IN EVERY LEARNING STYLE

Instead of teaching abstract concepts such as Extraversion and Introversion, primary teachers can introduce the four learning styles with engaging activities and concrete examples from familiar stories and movies. Four key practices help students tolerate *and* value activities that are outside their style:

*Positive images of each style.* When choosing examples of the preferences, follow two important rules:

- Avoid guessing preferences of real people without their permission. Fictional characters from books, movies, or cartoons provide a wealth of rich examples.
- Avoid "stereotyping" by ensuring that your examples (a) are a positive image of the preference you are trying to illustrate and (b) don't make students with other preferences feel as if they're missing something. For example, using Spider-man for Introversion and Intuition might make the Extraverted Sensing students feel left out *unless* you immediately add that Han Solo probably prefers Extraversion and Sensing.

*Explicit instruction that mastering different content requires different learning styles.* Emphasize, "When do we need to learn this way?" As students grasp the four styles, teachers can later describe activities, "We'll all need to be Shrek for a few minutes as we read directions. Then, we'll turn to Magic School Bus time to conduct the experiment." Students then begin to grasp the strengths of the different styles.

*Emphasis that a classroom honors all styles, but not always all at once.* Students respond to fairness. Even young students can grasp that if all activities were in their own style, other children would never get to learn in *their* preferred style.

Chart 11.1 shows sample characters and descriptions of "rules" or expectations for the four learning styles.

Introduce the learning styles in the order given in the chart because the majority of your students have these styles (65–70 percent of the population has a preference for Sensing). Use the following general lesson plan.

**Chart 11.1** Learning Style Characters and Expectations

| Type preferences | Characters and why | Expectations | Possible classroom activities[1] |
|---|---|---|---|
| *Introversion and Sensing* | **Shrek**<br>Prefers to be alone (I)<br>Routine and structure (S)<br>Dislikes interruptions (I)<br><br>**Nate the Great**<br>"I'm a detective. I work alone." (I)<br>Systematic in examining details (S)<br>Doing real, adult work (S) | Quiet, little noise<br>Following directions<br>Listening time<br>Independent work<br>Sticking to a schedule | Read-aloud time<br>Structured worksheets<br>Puzzles<br>Coloring, labeling<br>Watching demonstrations<br>Computer-assisted instruction<br>Films |
| *Extraversion and Sensing* | **Magic School Bus**<br>Learning by doing (S)<br>Using five senses (S)<br>Real life connections (S)<br>Group activities (E)<br>Large motor skills (E)<br>Exploring real places (E) | Hands-on<br>Group activities<br>Thinking out loud<br>Movement<br>Following procedures<br>Setting goals | Experiments<br>Oral reports<br>Giving demonstrations<br>Group stories<br>Field trips |
| *Introversion and Intuition* | **Charlotte**<br>**(of *Charlotte's Web*)**<br>Does her thinking alone (I)<br>Ideas from inside (I)<br>New solutions (N)<br><br>**Brian (of *The Salamander Room*)**<br>Plays alone (I)<br>Dreams of an imaginative room (N)<br>Solves new problems (N) | Quiet<br>Individual work<br>Students each produce different results<br>Choices<br>Creating new things | Writing stories, opinions, critiques<br>Inventing<br>Independent study, self-selected topics<br>Silent reading<br>Imaginative tasks and play |
| *Extraversion and Intuition* | **Morris McGurk**<br>**(*If I Ran the Circus*)**<br>Big, big ideas (EN)<br>Thinking out loud (E)<br>Creating something new out of nothing (N)<br><br>**Pippi Longstocking**<br>Creates games for others (EN)<br>Tells stories (E)<br>Elaborates, makes connections (N) | Group work<br>Creative efforts<br>Problem-solving, inventiveness<br>Performance or leadership aspects<br>Cooperative competition | Creating learning games<br>Drama<br>Student-led activities<br>Competitions<br>Leadership opportunities |

[1]Note that some of these activities are enjoyed by almost all students: field trips, reading aloud, computer time, or certain games. These become key activities for periods when content requires extended periods of learning in just one style (test days, for example!)

- Read a story or show part of a movie that introduces the exemplary character to the students.
- Discuss with the class how that student might like to learn. Post expectations. By second grade, after seeing one list, students might brainstorm ideas for the next learning style from a prompt such as, "Which expectations might be the same or different for this character?"
- Follow with an activity for that learning style, with an introduction such as, "To do this well, we'll all need to be like Nate the Great—follow directions, work alone, and look at details. We'll work quietly for about five minutes. Then you can compare work with someone else."
- As a wrap-up, encourage reflection. For Nate the Great, a teacher might ask who enjoyed the quiet so they could think. Who found it hard to be quiet?
- For subsequent quadrants, review the ones you've already talked about and compare the styles.

Below are two sample activities for each of the quadrants. Variations of these can be used at *any* grade level to introduce the four learning styles.

## Introducing Introverted Sensing

*Be a detective.* Have students "search pictures"—hidden pictures such as those found in *Highlights Magazine* or books like *Where's Waldo*. Crossword puzzles, word searches, jigsaw puzzles, and some math puzzles also fit this style. If trial and error or nonlinear thinking are needed for puzzles, they fit into Introversion/Intuition.

*Timelines, matching exercises, and other structured worksheets.* Use engaging exercises, perhaps with a touch of humor, instead of familiar practice sheets.

## Extraverted Sensing

*Color wheels.* Have students make different color wheel spinners. In groups, one would make red-yellow, another red-blue, another blue-yellow. Second graders might split their circles into six parts and experiment with making 2/3 yellow, 1/3 red and so on. Students then work together to make a color chart, based on their experiments.

*Action songs or chants.* For example, teach students to count by twos by saying one softly when their weight is on their left foot, saying two loudly when their weight is on their right foot, and so on, gradually silencing every other number.

## Introverted Intuition

*Part of the whole.* Clip and mount a small part of a picture. Ask students to guess what the entire picture might be. Examples include the stitches on a baseball, part of a well-known advertising emblem, or a dog's nose. Ask students to keep their answers to themselves until everyone has had a chance to guess.

*"Wuzzles," puns, and other independent word games.* Introverted Intuitives often love to play with words and secret codes. Or, students might solve a riddle to discover their next assignment or physical education activity.

### Extraverted Intuition

*Problem solving.* Have students work in small groups to solve *Encyclopedia Brown, Two-Minute Mysteries,* or other puzzles that involve logic or deductive reasoning.

*Group challenges.* Students can work in pairs or small groups on all kinds of creative activities, such as acting out a short scene from a story, creating an art project out of "found" objects from parents' kitchen drawers or discarded office supplies, or silly relays that groups tackle creatively. The group might have to jointly carry an orange without dropping it using supplies you provide to build a "stretcher" for it.

Use these suggestions and Chart 11.1 to generate your own ideas for quadrant activities. Throughout the year, *tell* children what kind of an activity they'll be engaging in. Occasionally, ask them which ones help them learn the most. As you read new stories, have the students discuss which style best fits the characters.

## TYPE LESSONS FOR GRADE 3 THROUGH ADULT

For Grade 3 through adult learners, a basic introduction to type has several elements.

**First**, introduce the concept of preferences by talking about handedness. Refer back to page 10. Join with your students by writing with your nonpreferred hand, then preferred hand, on the whiteboard or overhead. List the adjectives they use to describe the processes below your signatures. Emphasize that all of them could *use* both hands. Probably, many of them wrote quite legibly with their nonpreferred hand—you can develop *skills*. But, it's easier to write with their preferred hand.

Tell them that just like they have this physical preference, each person has four mental preferences.

**Second**, make sure they understand why they are learning about type. Refer back to your reflections at the start of this chapter.

**Third**, provide a 20-second history of personality type:

- Around 1920, Carl Jung, a Swiss psychologist, student of Sigmund Freud, developed his concept of types, based on observing the people he counseled.
- At the same time, in the U.S., Katherine Briggs and her daughter Isabel Myers came up with a similar way of classifying people.
- Briggs and Myers hoped that type would help people make constructive use of their differences and lead more fulfilling lives.
- Type concepts have been used for over 80 years to help people understand how they are energized, gather information, make decisions, and approach life. Organizations worldwide use type.

**Fourth,** note the following general principles about type. Teachers often make posters for each of these principles (given below in italics) and display them in their classrooms to remind students of what type is and isn't, adding clip art for visual effect.

- *Type is not a box.* Although people of the same type have some things in common, every person is still unique. Type doesn't explain everything about you.
- *Type is not a sorting system.* No one type is better than another. The best type to be is the type you are.
- *Type is not a guise that changes.* You were born a certain type. However, if everyone around you was a different type (say, you were the only Introvert in a houseful of Extraverts) it may take more time for you to find your natural fit.
- *Type is not an excuse for bad behavior.* Some types find it easier to empathize with others. Or organize their days. Or get arithmetic problems right. But if those aren't your strengths, type isn't an excuse. You can develop skills.

Then, continue the lesson, repeating the following elements for each preference pair.

- Display the definition of the preference pair and the key word. The **key word or phrase** helps students grasp the concept and avoid stereotyping. Frequently, give prompts such as "Extraversion and Introversion are about . . ." and wait for students to respond "Energy."
- Work through checklists for each preference, giving examples. Chart 11.2 contains sample checklist worksheets that students can refer to during different type activities.
- Engage all students in a hands-on type activity for each preference pair.
- Ask for a show of hands of how many students believe they hold each preference or are still unsure. Let them guess your preference. If they're right, point out that these are observable differences.
- Share the general percentages for each preference in the United States:
  o Extraversion and Introversion: a little over half prefer Extraversion
  o Sensing and Intuition: 65–70 percent Sensing
  o Thinking and Feeling: just about equal, but about 60 percent of men prefer Thinking and 60 percent of women prefer Feeling
  o Judging and Perceiving: 55–60 percent prefer Judging.
- Have students journal about which preference best describes them. Page 84 explains a modeling technique to help students produce good journal entries.
- Within the week, reinforce the concepts by using a classroom management strategy from Chapter 6 or a differentiated lesson strategy.

## Extraversion/Introversion Exercises

### Key Word: Energy

**Examples of Extraversion:** the genie in Aladdin, Pippi Longstocking, Raymond of "Everybody Loves Raymond"

**Examples of Introversion:** Harry Potter (concentrating on just two friends), Captain Picard on Star Trek, Spider-man

### Classroom Design Exercise

Use this exercise after students have made a preliminary choice of Extraversion or Introversion. You might have undecided students form a group of their own. When they see the "pure" Extravert and Introvert designs, they often decide which preference describes them best.

#### Directions

Form groups of Extraverts and Introverts, five to six students per group. Provide markers or colored pencils and large sheets of paper. Have them design a floor plan for how they would like a classroom to look. What would make for a perfect learning environment? What kind of furniture? Materials? Other things?

Most groups take at least 15 minutes to design their rooms. Have the groups quickly describe their designs to the other groups. For contrast, alternate between Extraverted and Introverted posters.

See page 12 for descriptions of common elements that Extraverted and Introverted students add to their designs.

### Tie Breakers

Use these to help students who are undecided:

- Where do you do your homework? At the kitchen table or on the phone with friends (E), or in your room away from distractions (I)?
- After school, are you ready to be with friends right away (E) or do you enjoy more time alone, listening to music or reading, before getting together with friends (I)?

## Sensing/Intuition Exercises

### Key Word: Information

**Examples of Sensing:** Thomas Edison, Winnie-the-Pooh, Han Solo

**Examples of Intuitive:** Albert Einstein, Luke Skywalker, Kenny in *The Watsons Go to Birmingham—1963*

## Object Lesson

Display a simple object (apple, two-liter pop bottle, cup, eraser) and ask students to write about the object. Don't say "Describe" or you'll get all Sensing responses.

Display a definition of Sensing and Intuition, using the language from page 14. Have student volunteers read their examples. Ask the class decide whether each one is Sensing or Intuitive in style. In describing an apple, Sensing types might say "red, shiny, black stem, wider at top, crunchy . . ." Intuitive examples might read, "red, cooks up for sauce or pies, Johnny Appleseed, pioneers, trees for climbing, etc."

Emphasize that all students can do a good job at writing either a Sensing or an Intuitive response, but usually one is easier or comes more naturally.

As an extension, break students into pairs. Have them list 20 Sensing responses (facts about the object) and 20 Intuitive responses (what the object reminds them of, other uses for the object). As they prepare their lists, ask them to think about which list is hardest to complete. Most students discover that they *prefer* working on one list more than the other. This works particularly well with two-liter pop bottles.

**Note:** An alternative writing prompt is "Write about a snowman" (described on page 23)

## Tie Breakers

Use these to help students who are undecided:

- Think about how you handle details. Sensing types (S) can often put things back exactly where they found them (the cookies were on the second shelf, right-hand side of the cupboard) while Intuitive types (N) may have only a vague notion of where they got something (the cookies were in the cupboard).
- How do you tell about your weekend? Do you tend to give highlights from Friday, Saturday, and Sunday in order (S)? Or, do you skip all over the place, perhaps even talking about ideas instead of events (N)?

## Thinking/Feeling Exercises

### Key Word: Decisions

**Examples of Thinking**: James Bond, Wolverine in *X-Men*, Mary Poppins, Hermione Granger

**Examples of Feeling**: Charlie Brown, Xavier in *X-Men*, Maria in *The Sound of Music*, Ron Weasley

### Ticket Dilemma Exercise

Divide students into type-alike groups of Thinkers and Feelers, five to six students to a group. Ask the undecided students to form their own group.

Tell students, "You have ___ tickets to the hottest event in town [set the number so several won't be able to go]. How will you decide who gets to go? What would be the fairest method?"

Give them the specifics: a major rock concert, sporting event, or theatrical production that would be of interest to almost everyone. How will they decide who will go? Let them know that the groups who are sure of their preference for T or F will report to the larger group on how they decided.

Thinkers usually come up with a method that is objective and fair because everyone gets an equal chance (drawing straws, highest grades, etc.).

Feelers usually come up with a method that lets those who are most deserving go (who likes the event the most, who just went through some terrible life event, etc.). Or, Feelers will fund-raise so that everyone can go.

### Tie Breakers

Use these to help students who are undecided:

- A friend has a new shirt and asks you whether you like it. You think it's ugly. Would you say, "It isn't my favorite" (T), or would you say, "That's really different" or lie completely and say you love it (F)?
- Do you like studying about math, science, or computer programming (more T), or people, cultures, and values (more F)?

## Judging/Perceiving Exercises

### Key Words: Approach to Life

**Examples of Judging**: Princess Leia from *Star Wars,* the old dog in *Homeward Bound,* the mother in *The Watsons Go to Birmingham—1963*

**Examples of Perceiving**: Calvin (& Hobbes), Sodapop in *The Outsiders* , everyone in *Surviving the Applewhites* except E.D.

### Homework Exercise

Post the following signs along a wall.

| For grades 3–9 | For grade 10 through adult |
|---|---|
| Do it right away | Done before midterm break |
| Do it the second night before playing | Choose topic before midterm break |
| Up late to finish the project | Up late to finish the project |

The signs for younger grades assume that they have three days to finish an assignment. Ask students to think about how they approach big homework assignments and then choose a place along the continuum formed by the signs.

Explain that people at the Judging end do their best work when they're in control. At the other end, Perceiving types often do their best work at the last minute. They may not feel inspired until the pressure is on. Emphasize that both are legitimate approaches.

Ask students at either end to comment on what it feels like when they have to operate out of their preferences, when a Judging type faces a tight deadline or a Perceiver tries to start a project too early. Judging types will talk about stress and may even say their accuracy or inspiration suffered. Perceivers will often say they can't even think until the last minute.

### Tie Breakers

Use these to help students who are undecided:

- How long does it take you to order at a restaurant? Do you kind of know what you want (J), or do you read the whole menu, check what friends are having, see what's being brought to other tables, etc. (P)?
- Do you usually choose a topic for a report or project and stick with it (J), or do you often change topics (P)?

**Chart 11.2    Student Type Checklist**

---

## Extraversion or Introversion

Where do you get your **Energy?**

| *E*XTRAVERSION | *I*NTROVERSION |
|---|---|
| *Your energy comes from being with others or from activities.* | *Your energy comes from time away from others or a few in-depth activities.* |
| ☐ Thinks out loud (talks!) | ☐ Thinks inside (quiet!) |
| ☐ Likes to work in groups | ☐ Likes to work alone or with close friend |
| ☐ Likes noise | ☐ Dislikes noise |
| ☐ Prefers to speak | ☐ Prefers to read or write |
| ☐ Lots going on | ☐ One activity at a time |
| ☐ Says what they're thinking | ☐ Keeps thoughts inside |

Remember: Extraverts need some time alone. Introverts need time with people. The question is how much and for how long?

Circle which describes you best:

**E**(Extraversion)                    **I**(Introversion)                    **U**(Not Sure)

## Sensing or Intuition

What **Information** gets your attention?

| *S*ENSING | I*N*TUITION |
|---|---|
| *Perceiving what is, the information the five senses can gather.* | *Perceiving what could be, through hunches, connections, analogies* |
| ☐ Likes facts and concrete things | ☐ Likes ideas and imagination |
| ☐ Experience first | ☐ Explanation first |
| ☐ Sees the trees—details | ☐ Sees the forest—big ideas |
| ☐ Wants clear expectations | ☐ Wants room to roam |
| ☐ Step-by-step learning | ☐ Random learning |
| ☐ Practical, common sense | ☐ New insights |

Remember: Sensing types use facts to build to the big picture. Intuitive types start with the big picture and use facts to support it.

Circle which describes you best:

**S**(Sensing)                    **N**(INtuition)                    **U**(Not Sure)

## Thinking or Feeling

How do you make **Decisions?**

*T*HINKING

*Making decisions based on logic, impartial standards.*

☐ Decide with head

☐ Principles important

☐ Work first

☐ Quick to give advice

☐ Find the flaw

☐ Reasons—objective truth

*F*EELING

*Making decisions by stepping into the shoes of those involved.*

☐ Decide with heart

☐ Feelings important

☐ Friendship first

☐ Quick to give comfort

☐ Find the positive

☐ Values—personal choice

Remember: Thinkers have feelings. Feelers have thinking skills.

Circle which describes you best:

**T**(Thinking)  **F**(Feeling)  **U**(Not Sure)

## Judging or Perceiving

How do you **Approach Life?**

*J*UDGING

*Approaching life by planning your work and working your plan.*

☐ You plan your work—stick to it

☐ Organized

☐ Work before play

☐ Steady effort

☐ Schedules and lists

☐ Enjoy finishing

*P*ERCEIVING

*Approaching life by taking advantage of the moment.*

☐ You go with the flow—keep options open

☐ Flexible

☐ Play and work together

☐ Last-minute effort

☐ Spur of the moment

☐ Enjoy starting

Remember: Judging types ARE NOT JUDGMENTAL. They like to come to "judgments." Perceivers ARE NOT more PERCEPTIVE. They like to get more "perceptions" or information.

Circle which describes you best:

**J**(Judging)  **P**(Perceiving)  **U**(Not Sure)

**My Type is** ___ ___ ___ ___
    (E or I)  (S or N)  (T or F)  (J or P)

# Resource: Type Terms Bookmark

## Type Terms Bookmark

| | |
|---|---|
| Extraversion (**E**) | Gaining energy through action and interaction, the outside world |
| Introversion (**I**) | Gaining energy through reflection and solitude, the inner world |

Keyword: **Energy**

| | |
|---|---|
| Sensing **(S)** | *First* paying attention to *what is,* to information you can gather through your five senses—the facts |
| INtuition **(N)**\* | *First* paying attention to what *could be,* to hunches, connections or imagination—a sixth sense |

Keyword: **Information**

| | |
|---|---|
| Thinking **(T)** | Making decisions through objective, logical principles |
| Feeling **(F)** | Making decisions by considering the impact of each alternative on the people involved |

Keyword: **Decisions**

| | |
|---|---|
| Judging (**J**): | A preference for planning their work and working their plan |
| Perceiving (**P**): | A preference for staying open to the moment |

Keyword: **Approach to Life**

---

\*Note that the *I* was used for Introversion, so the *N* stands for INtuition.

# References

Armstrong, T. (1995). *The myth of the ADD child.* New York: Dutton/Penguin.

Beers, K. (2003). *When kids can't read.* Portsmouth, NH: Heinemann.

Bliatout, B. T., Downing, B. T., Lewis, J., & Yang, D. (1988). *Handbook for teaching Hmong-speaking students.* California: Folsom Cordova Unified School District.

Centers for Disease Control and Prevention. (2005). Attention-Deficit/Hyperactivity Disorder (ADHD)—Symptoms of ADHD. Retrieved on May 27, 2005 from http://www.cdc.gov/ncbddd/adhd/symptom.htm

Chapman, C., & King, R. (2005). *Differentiated assessment strategies: One tool doesn't fit all.* Thousand Oaks, CA: Corwin Press.

Chittenden, E., & Salinger, T., with Bussis, A. M. (2001). *Inquiry into meaning: An investigation of learning to read.* New York: Teachers College Press.

Cleary, B. (1953). *Otis Spofford.* New York: Dell. (1980 Yearling edition.)

Csikszentmihalyi, M. (1997). *Finding flow: The psychology of engagement with everyday life.* New York: Basic Books.

Delpit, L. (1995). *Other people's children: Cultural conflict in the classroom.* New York: New Press.

Elley, W. B. (2000). The potential of book floods for raising literacy levels. *International Review of Education, 46,* 233–255.

Fiske, E. B. (1991). *Smart schools, smart kids.* New York: Simon & Schuster.

Fosnot, C. T., & Dolk, M. (2001). *Young mathematicians at work: Constructing multiplication and division.* Portsmouth, NH: Heinemann.

Fosnot, C. T., & Dolk, M. (2002). *Young mathematicians at work: Constructing fractions, decimals, and percents.* Portsmouth, NH: Heinemann.

Fractor, J. S., Woodruff, M. C., Martinez, M. G., & Teale, W. H. (1993). Let's not miss opportunities to promote voluntary reading: Classroom libraries in the elementary school. *The Reading Teacher, 46,* 476–484.

Gay, G. (2000). *Culturally responsive teaching: Theory, research and practice.* New York: Teachers College Press.

Giger, K. (1996). Type goes to school: Reducing school "drop-outs" through the use of type and temperament. *CAPT Educational Conference Proceedings,* 387–394.

Gregory, G. H., & Chapman, C. (2002). *Differentiated instructional strategies: One size doesn't fit all.* Thousand Oaks, CA: Corwin.

Hale, J. E. (1994). *Unbank the fire: Visions for the education of African American children.* Baltimore: Johns Hopkins Press.

Hale-Benson, Janice E. (1982). *Black children: Their roots, culture, and learning styles.* Baltimore: The Johns Hopkins University Press.

Hammer, A. E. (Ed.). (1996). *MBTI applications: A decade of research on the Myers-Briggs Type Indicator.* Mountain View, CA: Consulting Psychologists Press, Inc.

Heacox, D. (2002). *Differentiating instruction in the regular classroom: How to reach and teach all learners, grades 3–12.* Minneapolis: Free Spirit Publishing.

Holt, C. R., Denny, G., Capps, M., & De Vore, J. B. (2005). Teachers' ability to perceive student learning preferences: "I'm sorry, but I don't teach like that." *Teachers College Record,* February 25, 2005. Retrieved May 27, 2005 from http://www.tcrecord.org/Content.asp?ContentId=11767

Huelsman, C. B., III. (2002). *Mathematics anxiety: An interdisciplinary approach.* Master's thesis, Marylhurst University.

Hyerle, D. (Ed.). (2004). *Student success with Thinking Maps* . Thousand Oaks, CA: Corwin.

Jensen, E. (1998). *Teaching with the brain in mind.* Alexandria, VA: Association for Supervision and Curriculum Development.

Kamii, C., & Dominick, A. (1998). The harmful effects of algorithms in grades 1–4. In L. Morrow & M. Kenney (eds.), *The teaching and learning of algorithms in school mathematics.* Reston, VA: National Council of Teachers of Mathematics.

Kaulback, B. (1984). Styles of learning among Native children: A review of the research. *Canadian Journal of Native Education, 11,* 27–37.

Korman, G. (2002). *No more dead dogs.* New York: Hyperion.

Ladson-Billings, G. (1994). *The dreamkeepers: Successful teachers of African American children.* San Francisco: Jossey-Bass.

Lawrence, G. (1993). *People types and tiger stripes* (3rd ed.). Gainesville, FL: Center for Applications of Psychological Type.

Lee, S. J. (2002) Learning "America": Hmong American high school students. *Education and Urban Society, 34*(2), 233–246.

Loomis, A. (1999). *Write from the start.* Gainesville, FL: Center for Applications of Psychological Type.

Ma, L. (1999*). Knowing and teaching elementary mathematics: Teachers' understanding of fundamental mathematics in China and the United States.* Mahwah, New Jersey: Lawrence Erlbaum Associates.

MacKenzie, G. (1996). *Orbiting the giant hairball: A corporate fool's guide to surviving with grace.* New York: Viking.

Marzano, R. J., Pickering, D. J., & Pollack, J. E. (2001). *Classroom instruction that works: Research-based strategies for increasing student achievement.* Alexandria, VA: Association for Supervision and Curriculum Development.

McCarthy, B., & McCarthy, D. (2006). *Teaching around the 4MAT cycle: Designing instruction for diverse learners with diverse learning styles.* Thousand Oaks, CA: Corwin.

Melear, C. T., & Alcock, M. W. (1998). Learning styles and personality types of African American children: Implications for science education. Paper presented at the 71st annual meeting of the National Association for Research in Science Teaching, San Diego, CA, April 19–22, 1998.

Mueller, P. N. (2001). *Lifers: When readers struggle from the start.* Portsmouth, NH: Heinemann.

Murphy, E. (1992). *The developing child: Using Jungian type to understand children.* Palo Alto, CA: Consulting Psychologists Press.

Murphy, E., & Meisgeier, C. (1987). *Murphy-Meisgeier Type Indicator for Children manual.* Gainesville, FL: Center for Applications of Psychological Type.

Myers, I. B., with Myers, P. B. (1993). *Gifts differing: Understanding personality type.* Palo Alto, CA: Consulting Psychologists Press.

Myers, I. B., McCaulley, M., Quenk, N., & Hammer, A. (1998). *MBTI manual: A guide to the development and use of the Myers-Briggs Type Indicator* (3rd ed.). Palo Alto, CA: Consulting Psychologists Press.

National Reading Panel. (2004). Report of the National Reading Panel: Teaching children to read. Findings and determinations of the National Reading Panel by topic areas. Retrieved on October 3, 2005 from http://www.nichd.nih.gov/publications/nrp/findings.htm

National Urban Alliance. (2005). *Most essential strategies.* Workshop materials. New York: National Urban Alliance.

Naylor, P. R. (2000). *Jade green.* New York: Athenium.

Nieto, S. (1999). *The light in their eyes: Creating multicultural learning communities.* New York: Teachers College Press.

Nuby, J. F., & Oxford, R. L. (1998). Learning style preferences of Native American and African American secondary students. *Journal of Psychological Type, 44,* 5–19.

Nunley, K. F. (2006). *Differentiating the high school classroom: Solution strategies for 18 common obstacles.* Thousand Oaks, CA: Corwin.

Oberkircher, C. (2006). Use of type by school professionals: Diagnosticians, counselors and school psychologists. Presentation given April 1, 2006, at the Lighthouse Schools Conference, Center for Applications of Psychological Type, Gainesville, Florida.

Ogle, D. (1986). K-W-L: A teaching model that develops active reading of expository text. *The Reading Teacher, 39,* 564–570.

O'Neil, B. A. (1986). An investigation of the relationship between teacher/student personality type and discipline referrals in two Massachusetts high schools (Doctoral dissertation, Boston University, 1986). *Dissertation Abstracts International, 47/04-A,* 1141.

Parker, R. E. (1993). *Mathematical power.* Portsmouth, NH: Heinemann.

Payne, R. K. (1996). *A framework for understanding poverty.* Highlands, TX: aha! Process, Inc.

Payne, R. K. (1998). *Learning structures.* Highlands, TX: aha! Process, Inc.

Resnick, L. B. (1995). From aptitude to effort: A new foundation for our schools. *Daedalus, 124*(4), 55–62.

Robinson, D. C. (1994). Use of type with the 1990 United States Academic Decathlon program. In *Proceedings: Orchestrating Educational Change in the 90's—The Role of Psychological Type,* 35–41. Gainesville, FL: Center for Applications of Psychological Type.

Robinson, D. C. (2001). Multicultural applications: Adaptive type among African Americans. *Proceedings of the Association for Psychological Type Fourteenth Biennial International Conference* (pp. 195–211). Chicago: Association for Psychological Type.

Rosin, P. L., & Boersma, F. J. (1993). A psychological type comparison of Cree (Native American) and non-native Canadian junior high students. In R. A. Moody (Ed.), *Psychological type and culture—East and west: A multicultural research symposium* (pp. 121–136). University of Hawaii, January 1993. Gainesville, FL: Center for Applications of Psychological Type.

Rowe, M. B. (1974a). Pausing phenomena: Influence on the quality of instruction. *Journal of Psycholinguistic Research, 3,* 203–224.

Rowe, M. B. (1974b). Wait-time and rewards as instructional variables, their influence on language, logic and fate control. Part 1: Wait-time. *Journal of Research in Science Teaching, 11,* 81–94.

Senge, P., Cambron-McCabe, N., Lucas, T., Smith, B., Dutton, J., & Kleiner, A. (2000). *Schools that learn.* New York: Doubleday.

Shade, B., Kelly, C., & Oberg, M. (1997). *Creating culturally responsive classrooms.* Washington, DC: American Psychological Association.

Smutny, J. F., & von Fremd, S. E. (2004). *Differentiating for the young child: Teaching strategies across the content areas (K–3).* Thousand Oaks, CA: Corwin.

Sprenger, M. (2003). *Differentiation through learning styles and memory.* Thousand Oaks, CA: Corwin.

Stead, T. (2005). Opening the door to a world of possibilities. *American Educator, 29*(3), 31–33.

Stein, M. K., & Smith, M. S. (1998). Mathematical tasks as a framework for reflection: From research to practice. *Mathematics Teaching in the Middle School, 3*(4), 268–275.

Stevens, A. (1991). *On Jung.* New York: Penguin.

Strauss, V. (2005, May 30). Curricula turn book lovers into book haters: Standardized testing and other education demands choke fun out of school reading, some experts say. *Chicago Tribune* Online Edition. Retrieved June 1, 2005 from http://www.chicagotribune.com

Tomlinson, C. A. (1999). *The differentiated classroom: Responding to the needs of all learners.* Alexandria, VA: ASCD.

Tomlinson, C. A., Kaplan, S. N., Renzulli, J. S., Purcell, J., Leppien, J., & Burns, D. (2002). *The parallel curriculum: A design to develop high potential and challenge high-ability learners.* Thousand Oaks, CA: Corwin.

Trueba, H. T., Jacobs, L., & Kirton, E. (1990). *Cultural conflict and adaptation: The case of Hmong children in American society.* New York: Falmer.

Voigt, C. (1982). *Dicey's song.* New York: Simon Pulse.

Wilkes, J. W. (2004). Why do Intuitives have an advantage on both aptitude and achievement tests? Unpublished paper presented at the International Conference of the Association for Psychological Type, Toronto, Canada, July 2004.

Wilson, B. L., & Corbett, H. D. (2001). *Listening to our urban kids: School reform and the teachers they want.* Albany, NY: State University of New York Press.

Worthy, J., & Roser, N. (2004). Flood ensurance: When children have books they can and want to read. In D. Lapp, C. C. Block, E. J. Cooper, J. Flood, N. Roser, & J. V. Tinajero (Eds.). *Teaching all the children: Strategies for developing literacy in an urban setting* (pp. 170–192). New York: Guilford.

# Index

**CORWIN PRESS**